The Life of God in the Soul

The Life of God in the Soul

The Integration of Love, Holiness and Happiness in the Thought of John Wesley

David B. McEwan

Paternoster is an imprint of Authentic Media
52 Presley Way, Crownhill, Milton Keynes, Bucks, MK8 0ES

www.authenticmedia.co.uk
Authentic Media is a division of Koorong UK, a company limited by guarantee

09 08 07 06 05 04 03   8 7 6 5 4 3 2 1

British Library Cataloguing in Publication Data
A catalogue record for this book is available from the British Library

ISBN 978–1–84227–800–8

Typeset by H.F. Griffiths
Printed and bound in Great Britain
for Paternoster

Series Preface

The Evangelical movement has been marked by its union of four emphases: on the Bible, on the cross of Christ, on conversion as the entry to the Christian life and on the responsibility of the believer to be active. The present series is designed to publish scholarly studies of any aspect of this movement in Britain or overseas. Its volumes include social analysis as well as exploration of Evangelical ideas. The books in the series consider aspects of the movement shaped by the Evangelical Revival of the eighteenth century, when the impetus to mission began to turn the popular Protestantism of the British Isles and North America into a global phenomenon. The series aims to reap some of the rich harvest of academic research about those who, over the centuries, have believed that they had a gospel to tell to the nations.

To the memory of Belinda "BJ" Allder
We were privileged to witness the life of God in her soul
"under His sky"
4-5-1978 – 15-2-2012

Contents

Acknowledgements

This book's origins go back to my PhD research into John Wesley's theological methodology in pastoral practice. In my work I came across several letters where John made the point that God can form us as much by pleasure as by pain. This seemed a far cry from the common picture of Protestant evangelical theology and its strong emphasis on the cross and suffering. I could not follow this up for my thesis but was determined to return to it at some point. The opportunity to do so arose several years ago thanks to the encouragement of Dr Mike Parsons, the Commissioning Editor of Paternoster. This book is the result.

I wish to express my thanks and gratitude to a number of people who were instrumental in helping me in my research and writing. An invitation from Dr Geordan Hammond to be a Visiting Fellow at the Manchester Wesley Research Centre in the northern summer of 2012 enabled me to make a solid start on the new work. Being able to present an early outline of the book's key themes in a paper delivered at the One-Day Manchester Theology Conference that year was particularly helpful. The faculty and staff at Nazarene Theological College-Manchester have been gracious hosts and good conversation partners over the three summers I was able to spend at the college. In particular I wish to thank Dr Deirdre Brower-Latz, Dr Kent Brower, Dr Tom Noble, Dr Peter Rae and Dr David Rainey for their support and inspiration. I had the privilege of being involved with a number of graduate classes at the college and found many of the student presentations and subsequent conversations very valuable in shaping some of my thoughts. In 2013 I was appointed as an Honorary Senior Research Fellow in the School of Religion at the University of Queensland through the good offices of Neil Pembroke, Associate Professor in Practical Theology and Director of Teaching and Learning. This provided me with office space to work and access to the University's library and excellent on-line resources. A paper presented at one of the School's theology seminar days enabled me to further refine some of my ideas. I owe a particular debt of gratitude to the Principal of Nazarene Theological College-Brisbane, Dr Bruce Allder. Apart from my regular research and writing time each week, Bruce allowed me extra study leave at a number of critical points to finish sections of the book. My fellow faculty members, Rob Fringer, Richard Giesken and Roland Hearn all shared insightful conversations and reflections, as did other members of the staff and the students I had the privilege to teach. Two years ago I took on the part-time pastoral oversight of the Logan Community Church of the Nazarene; the congregation's friendship and support is really appreciated. Very special thanks are due once again to Heather Griffiths for her diligence and hard work preparing the manuscript for submission to the publisher.

My greatest thanks go to my own wife and family; they have been my rock in often stormy seas. I don't have the words to express the debt of love I owe to my wife Chris, for without her constant help and encouragement this project would not have been finished. Once more, she has freely given her blessing as I spent many weeks away from home working on the book. I owe an equally large debt of gratitude to our children and their spouses, James and his wife Candice, Shona and her husband Aaron, for the many ways they enrich my life.

David B. McEwan
Nazarene Theological College
Brisbane
October 2014

Abbreviations

Letters (Telford)	*The Letters of the Rev. John Wesley.* 8 vols., ed. John Telford. London: Epworth Press, 1931.
Notes (NT)	John Wesley, *Explanatory Notes upon the New Testament.* London: Wesleyan Methodist Book Room, n.d.
Works (Jackson)	*The Works of John Wesley.* 14 vols., 3rd ed., ed. Thomas Jackson. London: Wesleyan Methodist Book Room, 1872. Reprint, Kansas City, MO: Beacon Hill Press of Kansas City, 1979.
Works	*The Bicentennial Edition of the Works of John Wesley.* 35 vols. Projected, ed.-in-Chief, Frank Baker. Nashville, TN: Abingdon Press, 1984-. Vols. 7, 11, 25 and 26 of this edition originally appeared as the *Oxford Edition of the Works of John Wesley.* [Oxford: Clarendon, 1975-1983].

Vols. 1-4: *Sermons I, II, III, and IV,* ed. Albert C. Outler, 1984-1987.

Vol. 7: *A Collection of Hymns for the Use of the People Called Methodists,* eds. Franz Hildebrandt & Oliver Beckerlegge, 1983.

Vol. 9: *The Methodist Societies: History, Nature, and Design*, ed. Rupert E. Davies, 1989.

Vol. 10: *The Methodist Societies: The Minutes of the Conference*, ed. Henry D. Rack, 2011.

Vol. 11: *The Appeals to Men of Reason and Religion and Certain Related Open Letters,* ed. Gerald R. Cragg, 1989.

Vol. 12: *Doctrinal and Controversial Treatises I,* ed. Randy L. Maddox, 2012.

Vol. 13: *Doctrinal and Controversial Treatises II*, eds. Paul Wesley Chilcote and Kenneth J. Collins, 2013.

Vol. 18: *Journals and Diaries I, 1735-38*, eds. W. Reginald Ward & Richard P. Heitzenrater, 1988.

Vol. 19: *Journals and Diaries II, 1738-43*, eds. W. Reginald Ward & Richard P. Heitzenrater, 1990.

Vol. 20: *Journals and Diaries III, 1743-54*, eds. W. Reginald Ward & Richard P. Heitzenrater, 1991.

Vol. 21: *Journals and Diaries IV, 1755-65*, eds. W. Reginald Ward & Richard P. Heitzenrater, 1992.

Vol. 22: *Journals and Diaries V, 1765-75*, eds. W. Reginald Ward & Richard P. Heitzenrater, 1993.

Vol. 23: *Journals and Diaries VI, 1776-86*, eds. W. Reginald Ward & Richard P. Heitzenrater, 1995.

Vol. 24: *Journals and Diaries VII, 1787-91*, eds. W. Reginald Ward & Richard P. Heitzenrater, 2003.

Vol. 25: *Letters I, 1729-39*, ed. Frank Baker, 1980.

Vol. 26: *Letters II, 1740-55*, ed. Frank Baker, 1982.

Chapter 1

Introduction

In Mark 12:28 a teacher of the law asked Jesus a critical question: "Of all the commandments, which is the most important?"[1] This is a question that goes to the very heart of our Christian faith – what is its core, its essence? The Westminster Shorter Catechism answered: "Man's chief end is to glorify God, and to enjoy him for ever."[2] We then have to ask, how do we glorify God, let alone enjoy him forever? This, in turn, must relate to the nature of the God whom we are called to glorify, and the type of relationship we can have with him? The impression is often created that the goal of human life is to be holy, because it is a life of holiness that will most glorify God and Jesus could have quoted such verses as Leviticus 11:44, 45; 19:2; 20:7, 26 to that end. If we see God primarily as holy and ourselves as sinful and unholy, then in order to glorify God the gulf between us must be overcome. Some Christians feel that we are required to actively work at minimising those elements of our life that create a barrier between ourselves and God. This is best done by obeying the rules and regulations given to us in Scripture so that our behaviour conforms to God's requirements. For some Christians it is a matter of holding correct doctrines, since the essence of Christianity is about assent to rational beliefs. For others is it primarily about correct worship centred in the sacramental life of the church, or its preaching, or some other liturgical practice. In all cases, it is important that we know what it is that God requires of us, so that we can put it into practice. This places an emphasis on the role of education. For others, it is about the way we show compassion and mercy to others, seeking to supply their needs. Some have felt that there is nothing we can do to overcome this gap and we must wait for God to act on our behalf and the best way to do that is through a life of self-denial, relinquishing everything that would hinder God's working in us.

There is, of course, truth in all of these assertions and biblical support can be found for each one of them. We tend to hold to one of them as our primary understanding and then make use of some elements from the others as the need arises. Donald Alexander notes that some of these approaches are more fruitful than others in seeking to live a life that will glorify God. The tension lies at the

---

[1] Mk. 12: 28. (NIV). *The Holy Bible, New International Version*®, NIV® Copyright © 1973, 1978, 1984, 2011 by Biblica, Inc.® Used by permission. All rights reserved worldwide.

[2] *Works*, 12: "An Extract from the *Shorter Catechism* of the Westminster Assembly," 93.

point between God's role and our responsibility. If being holy is primarily about careful observance of rules and regulations then the focus tends to be on our performance of them. It binds spirituality to secondary concerns, making holiness synonymous with defined patters of social correctness, elevating principles over relationships, with duty being more important than people. If we focus on correct doctrinal belief we can be isolated from the demands of a hurting world and it raises problems of what to do with other Christians who do not believe as we do. Furthermore, as long as our theology is 'correct' we can be isolated from the demands of a hurting world. A similar outcome arises if we swap correct doctrine for correct worship. On the other hand, an emphasis on self-denial and asceticism leads us to value the spiritual over the physical, leading to an unhealthy dualism in which the inner life is regarded as more important than my neighbour's physical needs.[3] In Western nations there is a strong note of individualism, making religious faith primarily a private experience and therefore spiritual development is largely a solitary endeavour. In terms of spiritual practices, the emphasis lies upon private Bible study and private prayer – the 'personal devotions' or 'quiet time.' We are encouraged to read devotional books and to cultivate devotional practices to improve its quality. Even group activities like Bible studies are often about sharing knowledge to make us better informed, and prayer meetings in some Protestant evangelical churches are simply a collection of individuals praying. Many of the current worship practices in these churches are also very individualistic. The question, it seems to me, is not really whether all this is wrong, but whether it is adequate?

To return to the question posed by the teacher of the law: it gave Jesus the widest possible range of options for his answer, drawing from the whole range of Hebrew Scripture texts and religious commentaries. It would be important for Jesus to pick carefully and he could have selected one of the Ten Commandments, or emphasised something about correct belief, correct worship or correct practice. Surprisingly, he focuses on love and relationship with the one, true God, and then equally with other people.

> "The most important one," answered Jesus, "is this: 'Hear, O Israel: The Lord our God, the Lord is one. Love the Lord your God with all your heart and with all your soul and with all your mind and with all your strength.' The second is this: 'Love your neighbor as yourself.' There is no commandment greater than these."[4]

The first part of the answer is the *Shema* (from Deut. 6:4-5) and the second part about loving the neighbour came from the Levitical code (Lev. 19:18). The two verses were very well-known, but Jesus links them interdependently and

---

[3] Donald L. Alexander, *The Pursuit of Godliness: Sanctification in Christological Perspective*. Lanham: University Press of America, 1999.
[4] Mk. 12:29-31. (NIV).

together they clearly place the primary emphasis on loving relationships rather than beliefs, rituals or practices. This is further underscored in the conversation Jesus has with his disciples just before his crucifixion: "A new command I give you: Love one another. As I have loved you, so you must love one another. By this everyone will know that you are my disciples, if you love one another."[5] It is not that beliefs, rituals and practices are unimportant, but that they are clearly subordinate to the primacy of love and relationships.[6] Jesus seems to indicate that belief, worship, behaviour must flow from this and that being a Christian is not primarily a private, individualistic experience, but it is to be in a network of relationships with God and the neighbours. Spiritual formation cannot *primarily* be about knowing, doing or even 'being' as a static conception in an atomistic and individualistic way; it is essentially about forming loving connections. This means that the deepening our relationship with God finds concrete expression in the quality of our relationship with the neighbour, and it requires the inclusion of the neighbour as an *essential* condition of our fellowship with God.

The danger here is to think of 'love' and 'relationship' as empty terms that we can then fill with our own understanding, and often we simply reduce them to a set of emotions. This is why it is important to allow God's voice to be heard and not simply Hollywood's (or any other media or social group). The beginning point in understanding the true nature of love and relationship is the Triune God revealed to us in Christ and in Scripture. Yet even here, we all have our theological frameworks for reading, understanding and applying the evidence of the biblical text and its interpretation over the past two thousand years. This book takes an intentional Wesleyan perspective and seeks to apply this to the Christian life and spiritual formation today.[7]

At the heart of John Wesley's theological understanding was the claim that the essential nature of God is love and this is expressed relationally within the Triune Godhead and then with the creatures that God made – especially human

---

[5] Jn. 13:34-35. (NIV).

[6] See the end of the conversation between the teacher of the law and Jesus in Mk. 12:32-34.

[7] John Wesley (1703-91) was the major founder and leader of the Methodist United Societies in Britain, guiding the movement theologically, spiritually and organisationally. Following his death, it became a major Protestant denomination, establishing itself in many parts of the world. It has also influenced many other denominations that trace their origins back to Wesleyan roots. For books on Wesley's life and the formation of Methodism, see Kenneth J. Collins, *A Real Christian: The Life of John Wesley* (Nashville: Abingdon Press, 1999); Richard P. Heitzenrater, *The Elusive Mr. Wesley*, 2nd ed. (Nashville: Abingdon Press, 2003); Richard P. Heitzenrater, *Wesley and the People Called Methodists*, 2nd ed. (Nashville: Abingdon Press, 2013); Henry D. Rack, *Reasonable Enthusiast: John Wesley and the Rise of Methodism*, 3rd ed. (London: Epworth Press, 2002); John Munsey Turner, *John Wesley: The Evangelical Revival and the Rise of Methodism in England* (London: Epworth Press, 2002).

beings. The content of this love is defined by God's nature and activities, particularly as they are revealed to us in the person and work of Jesus Christ. Of vital importance are the relationships God establishes with human beings, described in the Creation account in Genesis through to the coming of Christ and the ongoing work of the Spirit in the Church and the world. If Wesley's reading of Scripture is valid, then it is a network of loving friendships between God and each person that lies at the heart of Creation itself, and we are created to love God supremely and to love each other; everything else is then a means to this end. Loving relationships in this context are inherently transformational; you cannot remain the same if you are in genuine, loving connection with another because of an authentic desire to please them through shared conversations and interests. Loving another with integrity means you cannot do, say or think things that would damage or diminish the other and still claim to truly love. This is where the biblical concern for holiness is seen – not as some abstract quality or standard, but with reference to the quality of the divine love that shaped us in creation and is shared with us as an intrinsic element of our original nature. To love as God loves is to be holy as God is holy because divine love and selfishness, self-centredness and self-will are absolutely incompatible. To love the Lord is to be formed by that bond – which is where ethics, morality, obedience, and duty fits – they all flow from a right relationship.

If we love as God loves, and share the essential quality of his nature, then we must be living as God always intended for us to live. Such a life must surely then be described as a life of happiness. If we have problems trying to clearly define and understand love from a biblical perspective, how much more do we wrestle with the notion of happiness? This is one of the major human aspirations and there are so many ways in which it is defined and pursued. Even though we may struggle to define and pursue it, we know that we don't want to spend our lives in misery and pain. Once more, the goal in Christianity must be to grasp what the Bible teaches and demonstrates. Wesley, perhaps surprisingly, had a great deal to say on this topic and was deeply convinced that God desired the happiness of all his creatures. He took some effort to describe what he understood the Bible to teach about happiness. The question is: to what degree is this available to human beings now in the light of human sinfulness and the reality of suffering and pain? Apart from dealing with the topics of love, holiness and happiness in his more formal writings (sermons, journals, occasional pieces), he also covered them extensively in his letters that were written to a wide range of people seeking his spiritual advice, with many of whom he maintained a lengthy personal correspondence. In particular, the questions of pain and suffering arose frequently and the part they played in spiritual formation.

Wesley wrote a letter to his mother Susanna (May 28, 1725) in which he comments on his reading of Thomas à Kempis' *Imitatio Christi*. He thought à

Kempis was a person of great piety and devotion, but disagreed with some of his main points:

> I can't think that when God sent us into the world he had irreversibly decreed that we should be perpetually miserable in it. If it be so, the very endeavour after happiness in this life is a sin, as it is acting in direct contradiction to the very design of our creation. What are become of all the innocent comforts and pleasures of life, if it [is] the intent of our creator that we should never taste them? If our taking up the cross implies our bidding adieu to all joy and satisfaction, how is it reconcilable with what Solomon so expressly affirms of religion that her ways are ways of pleasantness, and all her paths peace? A fair patrimony indeed which Adam has left his sons, if they are destined to be continuously wretched! *And though heaven is undoubtedly a sufficient recompense for all the afflictions we may or can suffer here, yet I am afraid that argument would make few converts to Christianity if the yoke were not easy, even in this life, and such a one as gives rest, at least as much as trouble* [emphasis mine].[8]

Many Christians in every age have believed that real spiritual progress can only be made through pain and suffering, as these are essential to purge us from our sinful attachment to the things of this world. Happiness on earth would be at best fleeting, with true, lasting happiness only possible in heaven. Wesley acknowledges the common defence given by some Christians that the benefits of eternity in heaven will put the sufferings we experience during our time on earth into perspective, since we will gain far more than we lose. This is how many would read Paul's words in 2 Corinthians 4:17 which says that "our light and momentary troubles are achieving for us an eternal glory that far outweighs them all." (NIV) Wesley is not convinced by this argument and he also rejects the understanding that nothing is an affliction to a good person and we ought to thank God for sending us misery! He thinks this is contrary to God's design.[9] In the same letter he rejects the notion that "all mirth is vain and useless, if not sinful" for the Psalmist clearly emphasises rejoicing in the Lord and being joyful.[10] Yet in his first extant sermon a few months later (October 1725) we have this rather grim evaluation of our present life on earth:

> The miseries of life have been so copiously described and the inconsistency of perfect happiness with this state of probation so clearly evinced by many writers that reason alone would easily induce us to give sentence on their side. This is confirmed by the testimony of daily experience, too great an assurance of so melancholy a truth. The words of Jacob, 'Few and evil have been the days of the years of thy servant,' [Gen. 47:9] may be justly applied to the whole race of mankind. Such is the inheritance which the sin of our first father has entailed on his whole posterity. We meet with a far greater multitude of objects that excite a

---

[8] *Works* 25: 162-63.
[9] *Works* 25: 163.
[10] *Works* 25: 163.

painful than which raise in us pleasing reflection; and the number of our faculties is in this respect a great inconvenience, since they afford us so many more capacities of suffering: every sense being an inlet to bodily pain, and every power of the mind [an inlet] to vexation of spirit.

Nor shall we wonder that so small a part of our life can lay any claim to real happiness, if we consider how many circumstances must concur to compose it. The disorder of any one part of the body is sufficient indeed to give us pain; but till the whole is in such a particular state as rightly to perform all its offices we are not capable of any degree of pleasure. And so likewise in the mind: a single desire is able to make us effectually miserable, while happiness is not to be obtained without the concurrence of all.[11]

This unhappiness cannot be overturned by gaining more wisdom; rather it will make the person even more aware of their misfortune.[12] He is sure that only the prospect of life after death enables us to bear with the suffering we experience in this life.[13] However, he is clear that "The desire of happiness is inseparably [bound] to our nature, and is the spring which sets all our faculties a-moving."[14] Real happiness is only possible after death when we are delivered from all care, affliction, danger, anguish and anxiety. In particular, it is only after death that we can be free from all sin and its corrupting impact on bodily life.[15]

These two contrasting views, shared so closely together, highlight the problem for many Christians – the gulf between our understanding of God's original intentions and our present human reality. To what degree is genuine and lasting happiness possible here and now? Is it only for a very few who live without personally experiencing want, pain or suffering? Wesley wrestled with this question as we all do. Over the course of his ministry he worked towards an answer based upon his understanding that the essential nature of God is love; that we were created in love to live in love with God and neighbour; such a life reflects God's character and nature and in living this way we can be genuinely happy. In a letter to James Knox (May 30, 1765), he commented on how he had moved away from his earlier understanding of the gospel: "Do you now see that true religion is not a negative or an external thing, but *the life of God in the soul of man* [emphasis mine], the image of God stamped upon the heart?"[16] It was unthinkable to Wesley that God's life would be miserable and unhappy! This "life of God" is succinctly described by Wesley in a letter to Lawrence Coughlan: "I told you it was love; the love of God and our neighbour; the image of God stamped on the heart; the life of God in the soul of man; the mind

---

[11] *Works* 4: "Death and Deliverance," 206.
[12] *Works* 4: "Death and Deliverance," 207.
[13] *Works* 4: "Death and Deliverance," 206.
[14] *Works* 4: "Death and Deliverance," 209.
[15] *Works* 4: "Death and Deliverance," 212.
[16] *Letters* (Telford) IV: 302.

that was in Christ, enabling us to walk as Christ also walked.[17] Many had objected to Wesley identifying this as Christian perfection,[18] and so he told Coughlan to call it whatever he wanted because it was unimportant to those who have received "that deep communion with the Father and the Son, whereby they are enabled to give Him their whole heart, to love every man as their own soul, and to walk as Christ also walked."[19]

This book explores how Wesley was able to confidently link love with holiness with happiness as a life to be lived here and now, and it is based on his own extensive material (particularly his correspondence). The book will not be an examination of his theology as such, as this has been covered in many other publications.[20] Nor will it attempt to examine the origins and essential nature of love, holiness or happiness philosophically.[21] As a pastoral theologian, he was much more interested in the biblical material and how love, holiness and happiness inter-relate in terms of personal and community spiritual formation. This is not to say Wesley's is the only way to view these, nor is it my intention to argue that his perspective is the best. Rather, given his views and applications, how does this help us today in becoming more like Christ? In looking at the spiritual advice offered by Wesley it is easy to dismiss it because he lived in a different century with different customs and life setting to our own. There are doubtless areas in which his advice is shaped by his context and it may not be particularly applicable to our situation. However, we need to look beyond the historical and cultural differences and focus on what is shared because we are also people who live in relationships. I should mention at this point that Wesley predominantly uses male-gendered language in his writings and I have left this in place in direct quotations while using gender-inclusive language elsewhere. The goal of this book is to help us see how his rich pastoral understanding of the life of God manifested in the soul might enable us to discover how we can experience that same quality of relationship with both God and neighbour characterised by a life of love, holiness and happiness. The goal is not, therefore, to look at Wesley's spiritual direction for concrete practices that we can simply implement without change, but to see how his insights might help us to live today in ways that are personally and communally reflective of the character of God revealed to us in the Lord Jesus Christ.

---

[17] *Letters* (Telford) V: 101-02.

[18] *Letters* (Telford) V: 102.

[19] *Letters* (Telford) V: 103.

[20] See, for example, Kenneth J. Collins, *The Theology of John Wesley: Holy Love and the Shape of Grace* (Nashville: Abingdon Press, 2007); Randy L. Maddox, *Responsible Grace: John Wesley's Practical Theology* (Nashville: Kingswood Books, 1994); Herbert B. McGonigle, *Sufficient Saving Grace: John Wesley's Evangelical Arminianism* (Carlisle: Paternoster Press, 2001);

[21] Suggested readings will be offered at appropriate points in the text for those wishing to explore these areas in more depth.

In chapter 2 we begin with an exploration of Wesley's understanding of the original state of humanity as created by God, examining in particular the quality of relationship between the first humans and God. It seeks to show how the qualities of love, holiness and happiness were intimately intertwined as essential elements of the image of God. A relationship of love requires the ability to freely choose and remain with the other. For this freedom to be real we must have the option of saying 'no' as well as saying 'yes' to a real choice to maintain, modify or reject the relationship. The chapter then explores what happened when the original humans said 'no' to God and the consequences that flowed from their choice. It concludes by examining God's provision of salvation that sought to re-establish a right relationship through the atoning death of Christ, and how this impacts our love, holiness and happiness. In chapter 3 we look at Wesley's understanding of the nature of the life of God in the soul – what it appears like in daily life and practice. Wesley uses the Sermon on the Mount to illustrate the authentic Christian life that can be lived now by God's grace. The emphasis remains on love, holiness and happiness as these are experienced and demonstrated in our relationship with God and with other people. In chapters 4 and 5 we turn our attention to the practical pastoral advice that Wesley shared through his extensive correspondence. In chapter 4 the focus is on the elements of our nature and character that have a negative impact on our spiritual life. These are the places where temptation readily provokes a selfish and self-willed response. In chapter 5 the focus is on the positive helps that need to be cultivated if we are to experience the fullness of the life of God in the soul. This is then illustrated in chapter 6 by Wesley's personal letters to five people (Mary Bishop, Ann Bolton, Philothea Briggs, Alexander Knox, Miss J. C. March) with whom he corresponded over a lengthy period of time. They cover a range of issues that were troubling them and for which they sought Wesley's advice. Whilst a number of other people had equally long correspondence with him, these five illustrate his pastoral approach to a range of very practical questions that remain of great concern today. Finally, in chapter 7 the material is drawn together and some of the practical implications for our spiritual life and relationships are offered, so that we too may experience the life of God in our soul in all its fullness.

Chapter 2:

The God-Human Relationship:
as Created, Damaged, and Renewed

While John Wesley is not a major systematic theologian,[1] his theological framework is soundly based on the Catholic and Anglican consensus from the time of the Fathers in the first few centuries of the Christian era. His interest does not lie with philosophical and speculative questions about the nature of God; rather it is with the practical concerns of what it means when the Bible says we were created in God's image and what then happens to this image as a result of sin and subsequent salvation in Christ. This chapter seeks to lay out Wesley's theological understanding of our relationship with God and with each other in terms of salvation history, beginning with the creation account, the impact of sin, salvation in Christ, and then the new creation.

God and Humanity: The Creation

In a letter Wesley wrote to Samuel Sparrow on the doctrine of Original Sin, he makes the comment that "I know not what honour we can pay to God if we think man came out of His hands in the condition wherein he is now."[2] We so often begin our exploration of the God-human relationship by reflecting on our present existence and this leads to a distorted picture due to the reality of human sinfulness. Wesley's theology is firmly based on his understanding of the nature of the God-human relationship as it was originally intended to be and can be again through the work of Christ. Living outside of a right relationship with God, we are "ignorant, wretched, guilty," and this does not reflect our "wise, happy, and holy Creator."[3] It is in sharp contrast to our original state in which God made humans "perfectly holy and perfectly happy."[4]

---

[1] He is best classified as a 'pastoral theologian'; see Frank Baker, "Practical Divinity-John Wesley's Doctrinal Agenda for Methodism," *WTJ* 22, no. 1 (Spring, 1987): 7-15; Robert E. Cushman, *John Wesley's Experimental Divinity: Studies in Methodist Doctrinal Standards* (Nashville: Abingdon Press, 1989); Randy L. Maddox, "John Wesley: Practical Theologian?" *WTJ* 23, no. 1-2 (Spring-Fall, 1998): 122-47; David B. McEwan, *Wesley as a Pastoral Theologian: Theological Methodology in John Wesley's Doctrine of Christian Perfection* (Milton Keynes: Paternoster, 2011);

[2] *Letters* (Telford) V: 327.

[3] *Works 4*, "The Image of God," 292.

[4] *Works 2*, "The Mystery of Iniquity," 452.

Love, Holiness, Happiness and the Image of God

In considering the creation account in Scripture (primarily Genesis 1-2), Wesley believed that human beings as creatures were "a compound of matter and spirit; and that it was ordained by the original law that during this vital union neither part of the compound should act at all but together with its companion; that the dependence of each upon the other shall be inviolably maintained; that even the operations of the soul should so far depend upon the body as to be exerted in a more or less perfect manner, as this was more or less aptly disposed."[5] Even if we disagree with this dualist understanding of the human person, it is important to note that Wesley sees the two components as being interdependent, so that anything that impacts the one also impacts the other. There is a strong appreciation of the beauty and harmony of the whole of God's original creation, and this was not interrupted by evil of any kind: no sorrow, no pain, no suffering. However, only humans were created in the image of God, and this is seen essentially in relational terms:

> Above all (which was his highest excellence, far more valuable than all the rest put together) he was a creature capable of God, capable of knowing, loving, and obeying his Creator. And in fact he did know God, did unfeignedly love and uniformly obey him. This was the supreme perfection of man, as it is of all intelligent beings—the continually seeing and loving and obeying the Father of the spirits of all flesh. *From this right state, and right use of all his faculties, his happiness naturally flowed.* [emphasis mine] In this the essence of his happiness consisted; but it was increased by all the things that were round about him.[6]

Note that this ties human happiness to our relationship with God and fulfilling his creative purposes for us. It is intimately linked to the quality of these relationships and not to the enjoyment of any other aspect of the creation, nor is it linked with our emotions and feelings as such. The second chapter of Genesis seems to indicate that the original 'human creature' by itself was incomplete and God carried out a further creative act to make both male and female. Only then was humanity complete, signifying that the isolated human in relationship with God alone was not sufficient for human flourishing.[7] This is a point that will be explored in more depth in later chapters.

---

[5] *Works 4*, "The Image of God," 296.

[6] *Works 2*, "The General Deliverance," 439. H. Ray Dunning points out that this is as close to a "connotative definition" of happiness as Wesley gives; see H. Ray Dunning, *Reflecting the Divine Image: Christian Ethics in Wesleyan Perspective* (Downers Grove: InterVarsity Press, 2003), 37. For a more thorough analysis of Wesley's understanding of happiness, see Sarah Heaner Lancaster, *The Pursuit of Happiness: Blessing and Fulfillment in Christian Faith* (Eugene: Wipf & Stock, 2011).

[7] See Joseph Coleson, *'Ezer Cenegdo: A Power like Him, Facing Him as Equal*, 3rd ed. (Grantham: Wesleyan/Holiness Women Clergy, 1996).

Wesley understands the nature of the image of God in a number of ways. The "natural" image indicates that we are a spirit endued with "understanding … a will, with various affections (which are only the will exerting itself in various ways) that he might love, desire, and delight in that which is good; otherwise his understanding had been to no purpose."[8] Humans were also created in the moral image of God, "in righteousness and true holiness," so that our understanding and all our affections were without blemish and perfect; set right and properly exercised on their proper objects.[9] He notes that all our affections were equally rational, even and regular,

> if we may be allowed to say 'affections', for properly speaking he had but one: *man was what God is, Love*. [emphasis mine] Love filled the whole expansion of his soul; it possessed him without a rival. Every movement of his heart was love: it knew no other fervour.[10]

The focus of the creation narrative is the relationship between the Creator and the human creature, and this relationship is essentially defined by love.[11] This was no isolated reference, but lies at the heart of his whole theological framework:

> For to this end was man created, to love God; and to this end alone, even to love the Lord his God with all his heart, and soul, and mind, and strength. But love is the very image of God: it is the brightness of his glory. By love, man is not only made like God, but in some sense one with him. He 'dwelleth in God, and God in him'; and 'he that is thus joined to the Lord is one spirit.'[12]

For Wesley, it is love that is the essence of the life of the Triune God and it is this same quality that lies at the heart of being human—both in terms of relationship with God and with the neighbour.[13] Furthermore, "By the free,

---

[8] *Works 2*, "The End Of Christ's Coming," 474. See also: *Works 2*, "The General Deliverance," 438-39.

[9] *Works 2*, "The End Of Christ's Coming," 475.

[10] *Works 4*, "The Image of God," 294-95. See also: *Works 4*, "A Single Intention," 377; *Works 1*, "The Righteousness of Faith," 204-205; *Works 2*, "The New Birth," 188.

[11] See *Works 1*, 225-35, 348-50.

[12] *Works 4*, "The One Thing Needful," 355. See also: *Works 1*, "Justification by Faith," 184; *Works 1*, "Upon our Lord's Sermon on the Mount, VI," 581.

[13] The focus on the essential nature of God as love is not unique to Wesley and several recent books emphasise its rich heritage in the theology of the church, especially the contributions of Augustine and Thomas Aquinas. See for example: Gary Chartier, *The Analogy of Love: Divine and Human Love at the Center of Christian Theology* (Exeter: Imprint Academic, 2007); Werner G. Jeanrond, *A Theology of Love* (London: T & T Clark, 2010); Kenneth M. Loyer, *God's Love through the Spirit: The Holy Spirit in Thomas Aquinas and John Wesley* (Washington: Catholic University Press of America, 2014); Thomas Jay Oord, *The Nature of Love: A Theology* (St. Louis: Chalice Press,

unmerited love of God he was holy and happy; he knew, loved, enjoyed God, which is (in substance) life everlasting. And in this life of love he was to continue for ever *if* [emphasis mine] he continued to obey God in all things."[14] It is important to note here that Wesley sees both love and happiness in dynamic terms. The quality of the relationship with God and the neighbour is not static but can either become deeper and richer, or shallower and poorer. Since the original creation was free of sin, pain and suffering, it reminds us that these are not necessary elements for deepening our relationship with God, forming our character and increasing our happiness.

Liberty and the Image of God

Wesley believed that God could have created us in such a way that we had no real power of choice and this would remove any possibility of misery or death. Because God freely made us in love and for love, human beings had to be capable of freely returning the love they received, and that requires the ability to exercise genuine choice. A love that is compelled through original design, or by simple coercion from a greater power, would not be love at all—it would reduce us to robots or to puppets. "Love is perfect freedom. As there is no fear, or pain, so there is no constraint in love. Whoever acts from this principle alone, he doth whatsoever he will."[15] People were given liberty and freedom to keep or change this first estate, with no compulsion from God or any other being, making the human person the "sole lord and sovereign judge of his own actions."[16] Wesley is adamant that without the power to choose the good and refuse what was not, a genuinely loving relationship was impossible. "Without this both the will and the understanding would have been utterly useless. Indeed without liberty man had been so far from being a *free agent* that he could have been no *agent* at all. For every *unfree being* is purely passive, not active in any degree... He that is not free is not an agent, but a patient [that is, one acted upon]."[17] He goes on to say that "where there is no liberty there can

---

2010). A recent systematic theology by Gerald Bray is organised around the declaration that God is love; see Gerald Bray, *God is Love: A Biblical and Systematic Theology* (Wheaton: Crossway, 2012).

[14] *Works 1*, "Justification by Faith," 184-85. Albert Outler points out in n. 18 on p. 185 that holiness and happiness have long been linked in the Anglican (catholic) tradition. Wesley also links the integrity of God's design for humanity (happiness) and his demand upon it (holiness) and this is consistent throughout his life and ministry, but with important nuances. Outler says that "if holiness is active love toward God and neighbour, then happiness is one's enjoyment and security in such love." In *Works* 1, "Introduction," 35, Outler says in n. 28 that the correlation is found in no less than 30 sermons. See also *Works 4*, "The Love of God," 331.

[15] *Works 4*, "The One Thing Needful," 355.

[16] *Works 4*, "The Image of God," 295.

[17] *Works 2*, "The End Of Christ's Coming," 475.

be no moral good or evil, no virtue or vice. There is no virtue but where an intelligent being knows, loves, and chooses what is good; nor is there any vice but where such a being knows, loves, and chooses what is evil."[18] This had to be a genuinely free choice because "'liberty necessitated', or overruled, is really no liberty at all. It is a contradiction in terms. It is the same as 'unfree freedom', that is, downright nonsense."[19] The human "as a free agent...steadily chose whatever was good, according to the direction of his understanding. In so doing he was unspeakably happy, dwelling in God and God in him having an uninterrupted fellowship with the Father and the Son through the eternal Spirit; and the continual testimony of his conscience that all his ways were good and acceptable to God."[20] God freely gave "his creatures [the] liberty of embracing either good or evil, to put happiness and misery in their own hands, to leave them the choice of life and death."[21] Humanity, as created, was already holy and happy, enjoying the favour of God and could continue in this by a perfect, uninterrupted obedience to the whole law.[22] Human beings were created with the ability to render the required perfect obedience in everything.[23] Furthermore, this was to be done perfectly in degree: "Nor did it answer the demand of this covenant to love God with every power and faculty, unless he were loved with the full capacity of each, with the whole possibility of the soul."[24]

For human freedom to be real it had to have some form of clear test, an alternate choice; otherwise it was not real liberty (which is the power of contrary choice).[25] Wesley believed that God gave to humanity a "perfect law" requiring full and perfect obedience, which Adam was able to give. The demand of the law's righteousness was "Thou O man of God, stand fast in love, in the image of God wherein thou art made. If thou wilt remain in life, keep the commandments which are now written in thy heart. Love the Lord thy

---

[18] *Works 2*, "The End Of Christ's Coming," 475. See also *Works 2*, "On Predestination," 417; *Works 2*, "On the Trinity," 376; *Works 4*, "The One Thing Needful," 356; *Works 4*, "On Guardian Angels," 225-35; *Works 2*, "On the Fall of Man," 401.

[19] *Works 2*, "The End Of Christ's Coming," 475.

[20] *Works 2*, "The End Of Christ's Coming," 475-76. Wesley defines conscience as "a faculty or power, implanted by God in every soul that comes into the world, of perceiving what is right or wrong in his own heart or life, in his tempers, thoughts, words, and actions." See *Works 1*, "The Witness of our own Spirit," 302.

[21] *Works 4*, "The Promise of Understanding," 285. See n.19 and how he follows Augustine here. He believes that evil can be classified as either natural, moral or penal, with only moral and penal evil resulting from our own choices, because God is just and good and therefore cannot be the author or source of evil.

[22] *Works 1*, "The Righteousness of Faith," 208-209.

[23] *Works 1*, "The Righteousness of Faith," 204-205. Wesley identifies this as the "covenant of works."

[24] *Works 1*, "The Righteousness of Faith," 205.

[25] *Works 4*, "The Image of God," 295-96.

God with all thy heart. Love as thyself every soul that he hath made. Desire nothing but God!"[26] Wesley goes on to say that it may be doubted if we would choose evil knowing it to be such, "But it cannot be doubted he might mistake evil for good. He was not infallible; therefore not impeccable."[27] Humanity was not created knowing all things (that would make us divine), so ignorance is not in itself evil, though it may lead to evil if wrong choices are made. In reflecting upon Genesis 2:17 and the command not to eat the fruit from the tree of the knowledge of good and evil, Wesley comments, "To the entire law of love which was written in his heart (against which, perhaps, he could not sin directly) it seemed good to the sovereign wisdom of God to superadd one positive law."[28] He saw this as God providing a clear test of the quality of the relationship that was unambiguous: continue to trust me and don't eat this fruit and live; don't trust me, eat this fruit and die. This perfect existence came to an end when Adam and Eve succumbed to the temptation to doubt God's love and goodness, ceased to trust him and ate the forbidden fruit.[29] The critical issue is not, therefore, the extent of human knowledge, but the depth of human trust. Lacking omniscience, humanity either had to trust God for those areas of life that were not understood and obey on the basis of trust alone, or refuse to trust and try and find answers for themselves. The creature will never be equal to the Creator, but the temptation lies at the point of the possibility of knowing, doing, being more than we are now on our own terms rather than God's. If we doubt God's love and goodness, then we may be persuaded that our best option is to take matters into our own hands and cross the boundary the Creator put in place for our well-being and safety, believing that the boundary is in fact a restriction on our freedom rather than its guarantee.

God and Humanity: The Fall and its Consequences

In the sermon "The New Birth" Wesley re-emphasises that the image of God in humans is chiefly the "moral image" of righteousness and true holiness, and

---

[26] *Works 1*, "The Righteousness of Faith," 205. See also *Works 4*, "The Love of God," 331.

[27] *Works 2*, "The End Of Christ's Coming," 476.

[28] *Works 1*, "Justification by Faith," 184. In n. 17 Outler compares this sermon with *Works 4*, "The Image of God," 290-303; he notes that both assume this paradisiacal state as 'normal' and 'normative' for human existence; so salvation is to restore this image. See also *Works 1*, "Salvation by Faith," 117-30 and *Works 2*, "Original Sin," 170-85.

[29] Wesley at one point speculated that Lucifer, the devil "the first being who by the abuse of his liberty introduced evil into the creation... [by being] self-tempted to think too highly of himself. He freely yielded to the temptation, and gave way first to pride, then to self-will." Other angels fell with him, losing their glory and happiness; driven from heaven the devil sought to deprive humans of the happiness they had. He used the serpent to deceive Eve and "persuaded her to disbelieve God." See *Works 2*, "The End Of Christ's Coming," 476-77. He draws his understanding largely from Isa. 14:13-14.

both of these qualities are tied to love and relationship: "Righteousness is the fruit of God's reigning in the heart. And what is righteousness but love? The love of God and of all mankind, flowing from faith in Jesus Christ, and producing...every right disposition of heart toward God and toward man."[30] This implies that righteousness is primarily a right relationship rather than meeting some standard of law or rule. He is certain that "Love is the health of the soul, the full exertion of all its powers, the perfection of all its faculties."[31] Furthermore, "if we suppose an intelligent creature not to love God, not to be righteous and holy, we necessarily suppose him not to be good at all; much less to be 'very good'."[32] Yet, as we have seen, humanity was not created immutable but placed in a state of probation with a range of outcomes dependent on our own choice. In his reading of Genesis 3:1-13, Wesley believed that in the conversation with the serpent "sin began" at the point of Eve's "unbelief," when she trusted the serpent rather than God.[33] This unbelief led to pride when she thought she was "Capable of finding a better way to happiness than God had taught her. It begot self-will:... It begot foolish desires, and completed all by outward sin."[34] As a result of their free choice, seeking to be governed by their own will and to seek happiness in the creation rather than the Creator,[35] they "lost both the knowledge and the love of God, without which the image of God will not subsist."[36] Furthermore, "When he lost his innocence he lost his happiness. He painfully feared that God in the love of whom his supreme happiness before consisted... He fled from him who was till then his desire, and glory, and joy."[37] The critical problem was not a lack of knowledge or information, for God had made plain what the requirement was and the consequences of disregarding it. A relationship of love cannot flourish without trust and when it came to the choice of continuing to trust God and his word, or trusting the serpent and its word, they chose the latter. Wesley pictured Adam joining Eve in the betrayal of love and trust, as they both ate the fruit and God's life in the soul was extinguished, losing "the whole moral image of God," rendering them unholy, unhappy, and full of guilt and fear.[38]

Whatever we may think of the details of Wesley's explanation, the crucial point being made is the loss of relationship caused by a refusal to continue to trust. In failing to continue to trust the God who had created and loved them,

---

[30] *Works* 1, "Upon our Lord's Sermon on the Mount, IX," 642. See also *Works* 2, "The New Birth," 188.

[31] *Works* 4, "The One Thing Needful," 356.

[32] *Works* 2, "The New Birth," 188-89.

[33] *Works* 2, "On the Fall of Man," 403.

[34] *Works* 2, "The End Of Christ's Coming," 477.

[35] *Works* 2, "On the Fall of Man," 403.

[36] *Works* 2, "The New Birth," 189.

[37] *Works* 2, "On the Fall of Man," 403.

[38] *Works* 2, "The End Of Christ's Coming," 477. See also *Works* 4, "The Image of God," 295-99.

they effectively turned away from the relationship and sought for love and happiness in each other and in the gifts of the creation. This distorted their relationships and has impacted every relationship since. The consequences are clear and Wesley specifically mentions the sentence on the woman about desiring her husband and him ruling over her: "Was there till now any other inferiority of the woman to the man than that which may conceive in one angel to another?"[39] This is a vital point in Wesleyan thought—the 'submission' of the woman to the man is a consequence of sin, and not by original creation. As we saw earlier, Wesley believed body and soul are intimately interlinked and cannot be separated; what impacts the one also impacts the other. The consequences of their choice also impacted the physical body as it experienced weakness, sickness, pain and finally death.[40] "And by sad experience we find that this 'corruptible body presses down the soul'. It very frequently hinders the soul in its operations, and at best serves it very imperfectly." [41] He notes that the other creatures God had created were not directly "capable of God" and they relate to humans as channels of blessing, and so we get the present state of cruelty and savagery, in which humanity fully participates. If people are distinguished from beasts by being "capable of God, capable of knowing, and loving, and enjoying him; then whoever is 'without God in the world'— whoever does not know, or love, or enjoy God, and is not careful about the matter—does in effect disclaim the nature of man, and degrade himself into a beast."[42]

In his sermon "Original Sin" Wesley states that the Bible affirms that Adam and Eve "lost the life and the image of God" and so did all their progeny. Due to this sin we have no knowledge of God,[43] and

> Having no knowledge, we can have no love of God: we cannot love him we know not... No man loves God by nature... What we love, we delight in: but no man has naturally any delight in him. We take no pleasure in him at all; he is utterly tasteless to us. To love God! . . . We cannot naturally attain to it.[44]

The consequence is pride, idolatry, self-will, and the love of the world: "What is more natural to us than to seek happiness in the creature instead of the Creator. To seek that satisfaction in the work of his hands which can be found in God only?"[45] Humanity had now placed itself in a situation where an

---

[39] *Works* 2, "On the Fall of Man," 404.

[40] *Works* 2, "The End Of Christ's Coming," 477.

[41] *Works* 2, "On the Fall of Man," 405.

[42] *Works* 2, "The General Deliverance," 449-50.

[43] *Works* 2, "Original Sin," 173-78.

[44] *Works* 2, "Original Sin," 178.

[45] *Works* 2, "Original Sin," 179-80. See also *Works* 4, "The Love of God," 338. See n. 37 where the essence of sin is clearly characterised as a disease that infects every part of human life.

intimate, loving relationship with God was no longer the norm and was not even attractive. "But when he [man] had wilfully degraded himself from that state of happiness and perfection, by transgressing the single prohibition which was appointed for the test of his love, a more particular law became needful for him, for a remedy of those many inventions he had found out, whereby, being alienated from the love of God, he was enslaved to the love of his creatures and consequently to error and vice, to shame and misery."[46] It is from this misdirected love that all other negative motives, desires and behaviours arose. In a very real sense, loving God was no longer natural and, without any divine action, would remain our life-long orientation. God therefore gave a series of laws as a means to make us aware of our present state. Wesley saw these are temporary because "till his nature was renewed after the image of him that created him, it pointed out all those thoughts, and words, and works, by so many express injunctions, which the love of God, when that was the spring of his soul, produced without any injunction."[47] In other words, the laws were given to demonstrate the fault, not to be its solution: "The negative commands, what are they but so many cautions against what estranges us from the love of God? And the positive either enjoin the use of the means of grace, which are only so many means of love, or the practice of those particular virtues which are the genuine fruits of love, and the steps whereby we ascend from strength to strength, towards a perfect obedience of the first and great commandment."[48] The goal is clearly a restoration of the loving relationship between God and humanity, as well as between human beings, but rules and regulations are impotent to achieve it. The real tragedy was not the death of the body as such, but the 'spiritual death'—the loss of the life and image of God—that has resulted from the broken relationship.[49] Jesus Christ is the great Physician to heal our diseased souls: "Know your disease! Know your cure! ... By nature ye are wholly corrupted; by grace ye shall be wholly renewed."[50]

God and Humanity: Salvation in Christ

Given the perfection of the world as created, and the perfect love that existed between God and humanity, why then did God not prevent the conditions that led to the wrong choice in the garden or simply overrule its consequences, eliminating all the pain and suffering that followed it? The question is one that we all wrestle with as we look at the evil in our world, and the immense pain and suffering experienced by individuals, communities, nations and other creatures that results from it directly or indirectly. Wesley, like all Christian

---

[46] *Works* 4, "The Love of God," 331.
[47] *Works* 4, "The Love of God," 331.
[48] *Works* 4, "The Love of God," 332.
[49] *Works* 2, "The New Birth," 189-94.
[50] *Works* 2, "Original Sin," 185.

thinkers, has to wrestle with this and it is made all the more difficult by his conviction that God is love, God is good and God is all-powerful. As we shall see in a moment, the answer that he gives may not be acceptable to many of us (though it has a strong pedigree in the Christian tradition), but I do think the foundation for his answer is compelling. In the sermon "On Divine Providence" Wesley affirms that God is the Creator, infinite in wisdom, power and goodness. As such, he could easily remove all sin "with its attendant pain" in a moment, but to do so would be to counteract himself and all he has been doing since creating us. We are made like him, a spirit with understanding, will (or affections) and liberty. To remove sin and pain by God's own unilateral action is simply "omnipotence" and not wisdom.[51] Wesley is deeply convinced that love and liberty go together as a creational given. God was free to make or not make the creation we inhabit; he was free to make or not make the structures of our universe in the way that he did, with the 'laws' that govern its operations; he was free to make or not make a creature like us, capable of a loving relationship with him and reflecting his image. Wesley rejected the notion that God, having made the choices that he did, would then arbitrarily overturn it all. Nowhere was this more critical than his creational endowment of humanity with the capability of knowing, loving and relating to him—which required "liberty." What was true of our life originally, must be true of our life now, or else we are no longer human in the way that God intended.

In the sermon "On Predestination" he deals with the way that our relationship with God is restored, but the point he makes applies equally well to the original creation. God forces no one to believe—either in the original creation or at any point since: "this he could not do without destroying the nature which he had given you. For he made you free agents; having an inward power of self-determination, which is essential to your nature. And he deals with you as free agents from first to last."[52] Wesley upholds the notion that God "knows" all who will believe, but does not "cause" them to do so, for we are "free in believing, or not believing... Indeed if man were not free he could not be accountable either for his thoughts, words, or actions. If he were not free he would not be capable either of reward or punishment... Virtue or vice, of being either morally good or bad."[53] This applies equally to our eternal destiny and Wesley makes the point that all those spend eternity apart from God do so because of their own choice, astounding as it may seem "that a man, that a creature endued with reason, should voluntarily choose (I say choose; for God forces no man into inevitable damnation:...) shall choose thus to lose his own

---

[51] *Works* 2, "On Divine Providence," 540-41.

[52] *Works* 2, "The Signs of the Times," 531.

[53] *Works* 2, "On Predestination," 417. See also *Works* 2, "On the Trinity," 376; *Works* 2, "The General Spread of the Gospel," 488-89. For a full treatment of predestination by Wesley see "Predestination Calmly Considered" in *Works* 13, 258-320; *Works* 13, "A Dialogue Between a Predestinarian and His Friend," 227-38.

soul."[54] He notes that if our fate to be saved or damned was decreed by God, then it would be right to blame God for not preventing Adam's sin—but there is no such decree "and none ever was or can be a loser but by his own choice." For God

> Made man in his own image, a spirit endued with understanding and liberty. Man abusing that liberty produced evil, brought sin and pain into the world. This God permitted in order to a fuller manifestation of his wisdom, justice, and mercy, by bestowing on all who would receive it an infinitely greater happiness than they could possibly have attained if Adam had not fallen.[55]

Here Wesley largely follows the teaching of Augustine—that we gained more by salvation in Christ than we lost by the sin of Adam. This is where many today are uncomfortable with the flow of the argument: how can it ever be a sign of love to allow so much suffering and pain, particularly for those harrowing cases of painful and destructive illness with which we are all familiar, let alone the unimaginable suffering brought about by environmental disasters or war?

Before we go on to follow the rest of Wesley's argument, it is important to re-emphasise that sin and its consequent damage was not a necessity written into the structure of creation. It was perfectly possible for human beings to flourish without ever knowing pain or suffering and it will be so again after the return of Christ. This means that the time between the Fall and the renewal of all things is not what God intended or desired, but it had to be a real option for a creature endowed with liberty. The unspeakable tragedy is that the consequences of that first wrong choice have impacted the whole of creation and every person ever since. We are all born into a world ravaged by the consequences of loving the creature above the Creator, and the corruption, dysfunction and disorder that has brought. Given this reality, which will not change just because we wish it would, are we now ultimately worse off than if we had not sinned? This is, of course, all speculation on our part, but it is a genuine question that deserves a thoughtful answer. For Wesley, that answer has to be tied to the nature of God as love. It is inconceivable that that the power of sin, death and hell should have the last word or be able to rob humanity of the fullness of life. A God of love would not abandon humanity and leave them at the mercy of evil for ever. The very nature of love as it has been revealed to us in Christ means that in creating us with the potential to reject him, he would also seek to reconcile and restore the relationship if we made the wrong choice.[56] It is a very poor quality of love that would simply abandon the beloved because of one wrong choice—or even a series of them. If

---

[54] *Works* 3, "The Important Question," 188. See also *Works* 2, "On Eternity," 366.

[55] *Works* 2, "God's Love to Fallen Man," 434.

[56] There is endless speculation as to why there was no salvation offered to those angelic beings that rebelled, but Scripture gives us very little information about it.

we as human beings will work at restoring broken relationships between husband and wife, parent and child, sibling with sibling and friend with friend, how infinitely more will God our loving Creator. If the core of what it means to be human is to be loved and to love, and in this is our greatest happiness, then it is possible that a restored relationship can be richer and deeper than one that was not broken in the first place. It is in this light that Wesley writes: "May the Lover of men open the eyes of our understanding to perceive clearly that by the fall of Adam mankind in general have gained a capacity, ... of being more holy and happy on earth; and ... of being more happy in heaven, than otherwise they could have been."[57] Prior to the Fall, we could have loved God as Creator, Preserver, Governor but not as Saviour, or the Holy Spirit as the Revealer of God and his mercy. Wesley reminds us that we love God because he first loved us, "But the greatest instance of his love had never been given if Adam had not fallen."[58] Salvation then shows that "amazing display of the Son of God's love to mankind."[59] We cannot know in what ways God's love would have been shown to us if we had not sinned, but given that we have, then the depths of God's love for us is clearly seen in the life, death and resurrection of the Lord Jesus Christ. This display of divine love then increases our love for neighbour. I John 4:11 clearly infers that if God so loved us, then we ought to love each other; "But this motive to brotherly love had been totally wanting if Adam had not fallen. Consequently we could not then have loved one another in so high a degree as we may now. Nor could there have been that height and depth in the command of our blessed Lord, 'As I have loved you, so love one another.'"[60]

In the context of human sinfulness and our present condition, our love for God and neighbour can be displayed and exercised in ways that would not have been possible otherwise. There are some qualities that are perhaps better expressed and developed in the face of pain and suffering. Had we not sinned, they would have developed in other ways; for example, simply facing demanding challenges and tasks as part of our stewardship of the earth. Wesley never sees pain and suffering as 'good' but they may be a *means* to good: "For how much good does he continually bring out of this evil! How much holiness and happiness out of pain!"[61] In this carefully qualified sense he can see suffering and pain as "blessings," since all our "passive graces" are built on how we respond to them—endurance, resignation to God's will, and our witness in suffering to others.[62] Likewise, Wesley thinks that patience,

---

[57] *Works* 2, "God's Love to Fallen Man," 424-25. See also: *Works* 2, "God's Love to Fallen Man," 435; *Works* 2, "God's Approbation of His Works," 387-99; *Works* 2, "On the Fall of Man," 411-12.

[58] *Works* 2, "God's Love to Fallen Man," 427.

[59] *Works* 2, "God's Love to Fallen Man," 427.

[60] *Works* 2, "God's Love to Fallen Man," 428.

[61] *Works* 2, "God's Love to Fallen Man," 428.

[62] *Works* 2, "God's Love to Fallen Man," 429.

meekness, gentleness, long-suffering are most real in the face of evil.[63] Even if God had "divinely infused" these qualities into our hearts, there would have been no use or exercise for them. It is as we exercise of all these graces that "our happiness [will] increase, even in the present world." Likewise, suffering may give opportunities of doing good (benevolence, compassion, and mercy) in ways that otherwise might not be experienced.[64] "Accordingly the more good we do (other circumstances being equal) the happier we shall be."[65] This has clear implications for life in eternity, as we gain "many holy tempers which otherwise could have had no being (resignation to God, confidence in him in times of trouble and danger, patience, meekness, gentleness, long-suffering and the whole train of passive virtues)... And on account of this superior holiness they will then enjoy superior happiness" and all will be rewarded according to their works; for suffering as well as choosing the will of God (2 Cor. 4:17 and "abundant glory"). So while suffering will be no more in eternity, the blessings occasioned by it will never end.[66]

As we saw earlier, Wesley affirms that God is the Creator, infinite in wisdom, power and goodness and as such, he could easily remove all sin and pain in a moment, but to do so would be to counteract himself and all he has been doing since creating us. God's wisdom, power and goodness are seen in governing us as humans made in his image, so he will not destroy our understanding, will or liberty and therefore cannot save us by compulsion or overruling our freedom.[67] This underscores the importance of not only having choice, but being able to actually exercise it, and the more one actively chooses the relationship with God, the deeper and richer the transformation of character. For Wesley this means that however salvation in Christ is affected, it must enable the restoration of choice that had been forfeited in the Fall. So "how can all men be made holy and happy while they continue as men?" Wesley says that God does not take away our understanding or affections, "least of all did he take away your liberty, your power of choosing good or evil; he did not *force* you; but being *assisted* by his grace you...*chose* the better part."[68] This assistance Wesley calls preventing (prevenient) grace, and it restores to humanity the ability to choose a relationship with God again, "without depriving any of them of that liberty which is essential to a moral

---

[63] *Works* 2, "God's Love to Fallen Man," 429.

[64] *Works* 2, "God's Love to Fallen Man," 430.

[65] *Works* 2, "God's Love to Fallen Man," 431.

[66] *Works* 2, "God's Love to Fallen Man," 432-33.

[67] *Works* 2, "On Divine Providence," 541. Wesley does allow for "exempt cases" where the power of grace Works irresistibly but only for a time; see *Works* 2, "The General Spread of the Gospel," 489.

[68] *Works* 2, "The General Spread of the Gospel," 489.

Agent."[69] God's grace is "that energy which works in us every right disposition, and then furnishes us for every good word and work." For "we have nothing which we have not received . . . the very first motion of good is from above, as well as the power which conducts it to that end."[70] He agrees with Augustine's statement that "he that made us *without ourselves* will not save us *without ourselves*."[71] Salvation is essentially "the Spirit of God renewing men in that image of God wherein they were created."[72] The initiative always lies with God and "it is God that worketh both inward and outward holiness."[73] Wesley is optimistic about the power of God's grace in relation to sin: "The loving knowledge of God, producing uniform, uninterrupted holiness and happiness, shall cover the earth, shall fill every soul of man."[74] When asked about people who have had no contact with Christians, Wesley says God "can take them by his Spirit" (as he did Ezekiel), or by "his angel", as he did Philip, "and set them down wheresoever it pleaseth him. Yea, he can find a thousand ways, to foolish man unknown. And he surely will."[75]

Salvation and Love

Wesley articulates the goal of salvation in Christ as: "'thou shalt love the Lord they God with all thy soul, and thy neighbour as thyself'. The Bible declares, 'Love is the fulfilling of the Law,' 'the end of the commandment,' of all the commandments which are contained in the oracles of God."[76] In his landmark sermon, "The Circumcision of the Heart," Wesley clearly sees love as the evidence of a 'perfect' life:

> add love, and thou hast the 'circumcision of the heart'. ...it is the essence, the spirit, the lie of all virtue. It is not only the first and great command [Matt. 22:38], but it is all the commandments in one. Whatsoever things are just, whatsoever tings are pure, whatsoever things are amiable or honourable; if there be any virtue, if there be any praise, they are all comprised in this one word—love. In

---

[69] *Works* 2, "The General Spread of the Gospel," 489. On prevenient grace, see J. Gregory Crofford, *Streams of Mercy: Prevenient Grace in the Theology of John and Charles Wesley* (Lexington: Emeth Press, 2010); Charles A. Rogers, "The Concept of Prevenient Grace in the Theology of John Wesley" (PhD thesis, Duke University, 1967).

[70] *Works* 3, "On Working Out Our Own Salvation," 203. See n. 24 on prevenient grace.

[71] *Works* 2, "The General Spread of the Gospel," 490. See also *Works* 2, "The Imperfection of Human Knowledge," 584.

[72] *Works* 3, "On Working Out Our Own Salvation," 200.

[73] *Works* 3, "On Working Out Our Own Salvation," 202.

[74] *Works* 2, "The General Spread of the Gospel," 488-89.

[75] *Works* 2, "The General Spread of the Gospel," 497.

[76] *Works* 3, "On Laying the Foundation of the New Chapel," 585. See also *Works* 3, "Of Former Times," 448, 453.

this is perfection and glory and happiness. [This is] [t]he royal law of heaven and earth...[77]

He put the question to his own Methodists: "Are you an happy partaker of this scriptural, this truly primitive religion? Are you a witness of the religion of love? Are you a lover of God and all mankind?"[78] If so, then

> let our whole soul pant after a general revival of pure religion and undefiled, of the restoration of the image of God, pure love, in every child of man. Then let us endeavour to promote...this scriptural, primitive religion; let us with all diligence diffuse the religion of love among all we have any intercourse with; let us provoke all men...to love and to good works; always remembering these deep words (God engrave them on our hearts!), 'God is love; and he that dwelleth in love, dwelleth in God, and God in him.' [1 Jn. 4:16][79]

Salvation is primarily all about re-establishing a relationship of love with both God and the neighbour, rather than a correct belief system, pattern of worship or code of conduct. The focus on love is clearly seen in his sermon "Catholic Spirit," where he notes the "royal law" of love that is due to all, but "there is a peculiar love which we owe to those that love God." This is the 'new commandment' of John 13:34-35 (and re-emphasised in 1 Jn. 3:11, 16; 4:7-8).[80]

So, if love is at the heart of salvation, what exactly is its nature and how do we experience it for ourselves and exercise it toward others? As a pastoral theologian, Wesley did not give a lot of attention to speculative and philosophical matters, but focused on the practical understanding and application of theology. This is equally true of his approach to understanding the nature of love. His clear preference is to describe love in action from Scripture—both in terms of the life of the Father, the Son and the Holy Spirit and the life of the disciples. He adds further illustrations from the lives of the Fathers and the great saints of the church, as well as his own Methodists.[81] In an early sermon "The Love of God" (1733) we find a brief formal explanation of what he understood by love. He mentions three interlinked components: obedience, desire and love itself. Love can be divided into love of complacency or delight and love of gratitude or benevolence.[82] The love for God as "delight" has to do with our enjoyment of God for who he is in himself; as "gratitude" it has to do with what he is to us—our Creator, Redeemer and Sustainer. The

---

[77] *Works* 1, "The Circumcision of the Heart," 407.

[78] *Works* 3, "On Laying the Foundation of the New Chapel," 592.

[79] *Works* 3, "On Laying the Foundation of the New Chapel," 592.

[80] *Works* 1, "The Witness of our own Spirit," 302-303.

[81] Wesley was particularly fond of both the Sermon on the Mount (Matt. 5-7) and I Cor. 13 to describe love; see the relevant passages in *Notes* (NT).

[82] *Works* 4, "The Love of God," 333. See n. 11 where Outler traces this understanding back to Aquinas.

second element is the desire of enjoying him, where the desire flows from love and increases as love increases. These are not to be confounded "As if love and desire were all one, whereas *desire* is as essentially distinct from the love that produces it as is any fruit from the tree upon which it grows."[83] The third element is obedience to God (1 Jn. 5:3).[84] It is this combination of delight and gratitude that carry us forward to please and obey God, enabling us to become one with him and to love him totally. Wesley also referred in the sermon to the love of "complacence" which is the natural affection we have for mankind, especially our fellow-Christians.[85] However, we are not to love anyone or anything else as much as we love God, and none that are contrary to the love of God.[86] God is not only the principal "but the only object of our love" in an absolute sense. This does not exclude the love of neighbour: "we cannot suppose any love forbidden by God which necessarily flows from this love of him."[87] This means that "whatever love tends to the love of God is no more forbidden than that which flows from it."[88] This is made even clearer in "The Circumcision of the Heart" where he explicitly links the love of God with the love of neighbour and God's good creation:

> it implies that we 'love our brother also'. Not yet does it forbid us...to take pleasure in anything but God. To suppose this is to suppose the fountain of holiness is directly the author of sin, since he has inseparably annexed pleasure to the use of those creatures which are necessary to sustain the life he has given us. … The one perfect good shall be your ultimate end. One thing shall ye desire for its own sake—the fruition of him that is all in all. One happiness shall ye propose to your souls, even an union with him that made them, the having 'fellowship with the Father and the Son', the being 'joined to the Lord in one Spirit'. One design ye are to pursue to the end of time—the enjoyment of God in time and eternity. Desire other things so far as they tend to this. Love the creature—as it leads to the Creator. But in every step you take be this the glorious point that terminates your view. Let every affection, and thought, and word, and work be subordinate to this. Whatever ye desire or fear, whatever ye seek or shun, whatever ye think, speak, or do, be it in order to your happiness in God, the sole end as well as source of your being.[89]

---

[83] *Works* 4, "The Love of God," 333.

[84] *Works* 4, "The Love of God," 332.

[85] *Works* 4, "The Love of God," 335.

[86] *Works* 4, "The Love of God," 333.

[87] *Works* 4, "The Love of God," 334.

[88] *Works* 4, "The Love of God," 335.

[89] *Works* 1, "The Circumcision of the Heart," 408. See Outler n.78 on participation and enjoyment of God. Note also Susannah's advice to John on the nature of sin in an earlier letter. See also *Works* 4, "The Love of God," 335. In n. 20 Outler points out that this is one of the oldest and constant themes in the Christian tradition from Origen through Augustine, Bonaventure and the Cambridge Platonists.

It is because of this that Wesley defines the essence of sin as the desire of the flesh, the desire of the eye and the pride of life focused on the creation and the creature, rather than the Creator (from 1 Jn. 2:16).[90] That is why it is inadequate to simply do good, abstain from evil and use God's ordinances, even when they are done with all sincerity.[91] All of our thoughts, words and actions must flow from God's love experienced and returned: "But we must love God before we can be holy at all, this being the root of all holiness. Now we cannot love God till we know he loves us: 'We love him, because he first loved us.'"[92] This is only possible by faith in Christ, and this faith is not simply intellectual assent to a set of propositional facts "but likewise the revelation of Christ in our hearts: a divine evidence or conviction of his love, his free unmerited love to me a sinner; a sure confidence in his pardoning mercy, wrought in us by the Holy Ghost..."[93] The evidence we are not self-deceived comes from keeping his commandments: "Love rejoices to obey, to do in every point whatever is acceptable to the Beloved. A true lover of God hastens to do his will on earth as it is done in heaven."[94] He goes on to say: "Thou dost not keep his commandments; therefore thou lovest him not, neither art thou partaker of the Holy Ghost."[95] It is faith that purifies the heart by God's power and "fills it with love stronger than death both to God and to all mankind—love that doth the works of God, glorying to spend and to be spent for all men, and that endureth with joy, not only the reproach of Christ, the being mocked, despised, and hated of all men, but whatsoever the wisdom of God permits the malice of men or devils to inflict; whosoever has this faith, this 'working by love', is not *almost* only, but *altogether* a Christian."[96] 1 Corinthians 13 shows "the highest of all Christian graces is properly and directly the love of our neighbour." And this is affirmed in the whole Bible "that works springing from this love are the highest part of the religion therein revealed."[97] This life of love was not merely to be demonstrated in our life with God or our fellow-Christians:

---

[90] *Works* 1, "The Almost Christian," 138. This trilogy is used very commonly by Wesley. See n. 38 and his agreement with Augustine; "The Way to the Kingdom," 226-27 and n. 64.

[91] *Works* 1, "The Almost Christian," 136.

[92] *Works* 1, "The Witness of the Spirit, II," 290.

[93] *Works* 1, "The Circumcision of the Heart," 405. The quoted section was added in 1748 to reflect his changed understanding of 'faith' by 1738. See also *Works* 1, "The Almost Christian," 138-39.

[94] *Works* 1, "The Spirit of Bondage and of Adoption," 280.

[95] *Works* 1, "The Spirit of Bondage and of Adoption," 281.

[96] *Works* 1, "The Almost Christian," 139. See also *Works* 1, "The Witness of our own Spirit," 304.

[97] *Works* 3, "The Reward of Righteousness," 405.

First, let *love* not visit you as a transient guest, but be the constant ruling temper of your soul. See that your heart be filled at all times and on all occasions with real, undissembled benevolence, not to those only that love *you*, but to every soul of man. Let it pant in your heart, let it sparkle in your eyes, let it shine on all your actions. Whenever you open your lips, let it be with love, and let there be in your tongue the law of kindness.[98]

The goal of pleasing those who do not yet know Christ is "to save their souls, to hold them up in love and holiness."[99] The goal of any friendship is "to love them as ourselves (for they also are included in the word 'neighbour'); to bear them real goodwill; to desire their happiness as sincerely as we desire the happiness of our own souls." In a sense to honour them as creatures "who are capable of knowing, of loving, and of enjoying him [God] to all eternity."[100]

Salvation and Holiness

In his critical early sermon "The Circumcision of the Heart" (1733) Wesley defines holiness as that "which directly implies the being cleansed from sin... and by consequence the being endued with those virtues which were also in Christ Jesus, the being so 'renewed in the image of our mind' as to be 'perfect, as our Father in heaven is perfect'."[101] Such a change is only possible by the power of the Holy Spirit through faith.[102] This was not some strange cultic emphasis, for he reminds us that "All the liturgy of the Church is full of petitions for that holiness without which the Scripture everywhere declares, no man shall see the Lord."[103] In the Church of England 'The Collect for Purity,' which is prayed at every Communion Service, asks God to "Cleanse the thoughts of our hearts, by the inspiration of thy Holy Spirit, that we may perfectly love thee, and worthily magnify thy holy name."[104] Wesley points out that the last clause focuses on "all outward holiness," while the petition to

---

[98] *Works* 3, "On Pleasing All Men," 422. See also 425, 426.

[99] *Works* 3, "On Pleasing All Men," 417. See also 416, 423.

[100] *Works* 3, "On Friendship with the World," 130.

[101] *Works* 1, "The Circumcision of the Heart," 402-03. It was updated in 1748 and Wesley still considered it the standard in 1778 – see Outler's Introduction, 401. Some recent resources that deal with Wesley's understanding of holiness and Christian perfection in greater depth are: Diane Leclerc, *Discovering Christian Holiness: The Heart of Wesleyan-Holiness Theology* (Kansas City: Beacon Hill Press of Kansas City, 2010); McEwan, *Wesley as a Pastoral Theologian*; T. A. Noble, *Holy Trinity: Holy People: The Historic Doctrine of Christian Perfecting* (Eugene: Cascade Books, 2013); Edgardo A. Colón-Emeric, *Wesley, Aquinas and Christian Perfection: An Ecumenical Dialogue* (Waco: Baylor University Press, 2009).

[102] *Works* 1, "The Circumcision of the Heart," 404.

[103] *Works* 4, "Hypocrisy in Oxford," 398.

[104] *Works* 4, "Hypocrisy in Oxford," 398. From the *Book of Common Prayer*, "Communion, Collect for Purity"; see n. 35.

cleanse the heart "contain the negative branch of inward holiness, the height and depth of which is purity of heart by the inspiration of God's Holy Spirit." The remaining words on love "contain the positive part of holiness, seeing this love, which is the fulfilling of the law, implies the whole mind that was in Christ."[105] He notes that many preach as if Christian holiness were a purely negative thing—getting to heaven by what we don't do. Some see it as merely an outward thing of doing good and using the means of grace; some add orthodoxy of opinions and zeal for church constitution and state.[106] These are all good things, but profit us nothing without the love of God in them.[107] You may have the outward signs of religion without the inward, but not vice versa, "For though the form may be without the power, yet the power cannot be without the form."[108] The key evidence is the presence of love in our hearts, that desires only God and happiness in God, and truly loving the neighbour.[109] In his sermon on "The Spirit of Bondage and of Adoption" Wesley outlines why it is that those outside of Christ don't find holiness an appealing prospect. Such a person is not responding to God's grace in a positive way and neither fears nor loves him. Wesley believes that such a person (the "natural man") "has no conception of that evangelical holiness without which no man shall see the Lord; nor of the happiness which they only find whose 'life is hid with Christ in God'."[110] He believes that such people have "a kind of joy," "pleasure," "worldly happiness," or "liberty,"[111] but it is just enough to blind them to the rich and enduring happiness only available to those who love God. However, as God's grace receives a positive response and the person opens up their life to God's love, then the Holy Spirit "sheds the love of God abroad in their hearts, and the love of all mankind; thereby purifying their hearts from the love of the world, from the lust of the flesh, the lust of the eye, and the pride of life."[112]

To be born again is to begin the relationship with Christ that will enable the believer to live in the power of God's love. Restoring the relationship with God is not just about forgiveness and pardon; it is also about changing our heart's inclination from loving the creation above the Creator, to loving the Creator above the creation. This misplaced love is a critical issue, "the resolving of which very nearly concerns both his present and eternal happiness."[113] Wesley

---

[105] *Works* 4, "Hypocrisy in Oxford," 398.
[106] *Works* 4, "Hypocrisy in Oxford," 398.
[107] *Works* 4, "Hypocrisy in Oxford," 399.
[108] *Works* 4, "Hypocrisy in Oxford," 400.
[109] *Works* 1, "The Almost Christian," 141.
[110] *Works* 1, "The Spirit of Bondage and of Adoption," 251.
[111] *Works* 1, "The Spirit of Bondage and of Adoption," 253.
[112] *Works* 1, "The Spirit of Bondage and of Adoption," 262-63. See also *Works* 1, "The Circumcision of the Heart," 413.
[113] *Works* 1, "On Sin in Believers," 317.

clarifies that by this remaining sin "I here understand inward sin: any sinful temper, passion, or affection; such as pride, self-will, love of the world, in any kind or degree; such as lust, anger, peevishness; any disposition contrary to the mind which was in Christ."[114] For those who trust in Christ and have found new life in him and the love of God is poured into the heart by the Spirit, there is a very real deliverance from the power of sin. Wesley believed that as long as the believer walks in love, which they may always do, they have power over both outward and inward sin, even though both Scripture and experience demonstrate that sin remains in the heart.[115] Because the essence of salvation is a restored relationship and Christ is present with the believer, then: "Where the sickness is, there is the physician... Christ indeed cannot *reign* where sin *reigns*; neither will he *dwell* where any sin is *allowed*. But he *is* and *dwells* in the heart of every believer who is fighting against all sin."[116] Dealing with this requires what Wesley called "the repentance of believers," which is a "kind of self-knowledge."[117] It has to do with the "conviction of sin which *remains* in our heart" such as pride and self-will. However, "A will every man must inevitably have, as long as he has an understanding. This is an essential part of human nature, indeed of the nature of every intelligent being."[118] Wesley notes that Jesus had a human will but this was always subject to the will of the Father, but this is no longer true for us because we choose what is pleasing to our nature rather than to God. This is a type of idolatry and so directly contrary to the love of God (loving the world more than loving God).[119] "He may feel in a thousand ways a desire of earthly things or pleasures. In the same proportion, he will forget God, not seeking his happiness in him, and consequently being a 'lover of pleasure more than a lover of God'."[120] Wesley also links the pride of life with a desire to be praised or to fear condemnation and other tempers "which are as contrary to the love of our neighbour as these are to the love of God?"[121] He then lists things like jealousy, evil surmisings, suspicion, envy, resentment, revenge, and covetousness; it also attaches to our words and actions through sins of omission, doing works of mercy and works of piety with mixed motives, and a range of other defects. In all of these we are utterly helpless to change ourselves.[122] Only the Lord can change the heart; only then is "the leprosy cleansed... the evil root, the carnal mind, is destroyed and inbred

---

[114] *Works* 1, "On Sin in Believers," 320.

[115] *Works* 1, "On Sin in Believers," 320-23.

[116] *Works* 1, "On Sin in Believers," 323. See n. 43 with the emphasis on the interpersonal and therapeutic views of salvation against all its forensic alternatives; see also *Works* 1, "The Circumcision of the Heart," 404 and n. 25.

[117] *Works* 1, "The Repentance of Believers," 336.

[118] *Works* 1, "The Repentance of Believers," 337.

[119] *Works* 1, "The Repentance of Believers," 337-38.

[120] *Works* 1, "The Repentance of Believers," 338.

[121] *Works* 1, "The Repentance of Believers," 339.

[122] *Works* 1, "The Repentance of Believers," 339-45.

sin subsists no more. But if there be no such second change, if there be no instantaneous deliverance after justification, if there be none but a gradual work of God (that there is a gradual work none denies) then we must be content, as well as we can, to remain full of sin till death."[123] What God promises, he will do but we must long for the faith "that the great physician, the lover of my soul, is willing to 'make me clean'." And he will do it *now*.[124] "Through him [Christ] I cannot only overcome, but expel all the enemies of my soul. Through him I can 'love the Lord my God with all my heart, mind, soul, and strength'; yea, and walk in holiness and righteousness before him all the days of my life."[125] In response to faith "the heart is cleansed from all sin, and filled with pure love to God and man. But even that love increases more and more, till we 'grow up in all things unto him that is our head', 'till we attain the measure of the stature of the fullness of Christ'."[126]

This fullness of love Wesley terms "Christian Perfection" and it is clearly defined in terms of our present human condition, not our condition before the fall or after resurrection.[127] Wesley states that before the fall we were like the angels but not now; "the highest perfection which man can attain while the soul dwells in the body does not exclude ignorance and error, and a thousand other infirmities."[128] Our ability to think, evaluate and judge is compromised by our current bodily existence, and from wrong judgments, wrong words and actions flow, as well as wrong affections. "Mistake as well as ignorance is, in our present state, inseparable from humanity... And a mistake in judgment may occasion a mistake in practice, yea, naturally leads thereto." So an error in judging another person leads to treating them more or less affectionately than he deserves.[129] It is important to note that ignorance and error are infirmities and not sins. This is a critical point in Wesley's understanding and one which we will examine more thoroughly later. In the light of our present bodily reality, we need the merits of Christ's death every moment "for innumerable violations of the Adamic as well as the angelic law. It is well therefore that we are not now under these, but under the law of love... This is now, with respect to us, the perfect law. But even against this, through the present weakness of our understanding, we are continually liable to transgress. Therefore every man living needs the blood of atonement, or he could not stand before God."[130]

---

[123] *Works* 1, "The Repentance of Believers," 346.

[124] *Works* 1, "The Repentance of Believers," 348.

[125] *Works* 1, "The Repentance of Believers," 350.

[126] *Works* 3, "On Working Out Our Own Salvation," 204.

[127] This is dealt with in some detail in *Works* 13, "Thoughts on Christian Perfection," 57-80; "Further Thoughts Upon Christian Perfection," 95-131 and especially " "A Plain Account of Christian Perfection," 132-91.

[128] *Works* 3, "On Perfection," 73. See n. 12. See also *Works* 2, "The End Of Christ's Coming," 482-84.

[129] *Works* 2, "On the Fall of Man," 406.

[130] *Works* 3, "On Perfection," 73-74.

Wesley stresses that the whole basis of our restored relationship is God's grace and it is never our achievement:

> Yea, suppose God has now thoroughly cleansed our heart, and scattered the last remains of sin; yet how can we be sensible enough of our own helplessness, our utter inability to all good, unless we are every hour, yea, every moment, endued with power from on high? Who is able to think one good thought, or to form one good desire, unless by that Almighty power which worketh in us both to will and to do of his good pleasure? We have need even in this state of grace to be thoroughly and continually penetrated with a sense of this. Otherwise we shall be in a perpetual danger of robbing God of his honour, by glorying in something we have received as though we had not received it.[131]

Salvation and Happiness

In his sermon "Original Sin" Wesley notes how many of the ancients pictured humanity as having all virtue and happiness in their make up or at least in their own power because all human beings are self-sufficient and their destiny lies in their own hands.[132] He commented that many Christians in his own day agreed with this judgement, and how much more would this be true today, especially with the strong individualism present in Western cultures. He affirmed that the ancient writers, both heathen and Christian, have shown that happiness goes with virtue and misery with vice.[133] The issue is then a matter of what you believe the virtuous life to be and whether or not you pursue it. Wesley was confident that the answer was not to be found in the power of reason because our sin-affected intellect and education would be insufficient to define virtue and how to acquire it. While reason has its place in Wesleyan theology, it is fatal to over-value it.[134] Critically, it cannot produce the love of God and since this is "the very essence of virtue, it follows that virtue can have no being unless it spring from the love of God. Therefore as reason cannot produce this love, so neither can it produce virtue... It cannot give happiness, since separate from these [faith, hope, love, virtue] there can be no happiness for any intelligent creature. It is true, those who are void of all virtue may have

---

[131] *Works* 3, "Of the Church," 53-54.

[132] *Works* 2, "Original Sin," 172.

[133] *Works* 2, "The End Of Christ's Coming," 471. For a recent overview of the way that western philosophy and theology have understood the nature of happiness see Ellen T. Charry, *God and the Art of Happiness* (Grand Rapids: Wm. B. Eerdmans, 2010).

[134] *Works* 2, "The Case of Reason Impartially Considered," 600. Neither is 'truth' a sufficient ground for virtue: see *Works* 3, "An Israelite Indeed," 279-82. On the place of reason in Wesley's theology, see Stephen W. Gunter, W. Stephen, Scott J. Jones, Ted A. Campbell, Rebekah L. Miles, and Randy L. Maddox, *Wesley and the Quadrilateral: Renewing the Conversation* (Nashville: Abingdon Press, 1997).

pleasures such as they are; but happiness they have not, cannot have."[135] This implies that happiness is clearly related to the choice we make regarding God and our relationship with him which, as we have already seen, is a key point in the Wesleyan theological framework. That raises the question of the pursuit of happiness and whether it is legitimate. He comments on the common experience of those who seek happiness: "Pursuing happiness, but never overtaking it? And who can blame you for pursuing it? It is the very end of your being. The Great Creator made nothing to be miserable, but every creature to be happy in its kind."[136] This is confirmed by God's pronouncement that all of his creation was "very good" (Gen. 1:31). This would not be a true statement "had not every intelligent creature—yea, everyone capable of pleasure and pain—*been happy in answering the end of its creation* [emphasis mine]."[137] Note the important point made in the final phrase of this statement: genuine, lasting happiness is only found in fulfilling the purposes for which we were created, which is to love God and neighbour. This means that unhappiness is an unnatural state and it makes it right for us to long for deliverance from it. Wesley's observation is that sadly we are "taking a wrong way to a right end:... [seeking] happiness in your fellow-creatures instead of your Creator."[138]

> The seeking happiness in what gratifies either the desire of the flesh, by agreeably striking upon the outward senses; the desire of the eye, of the imagination, by its novelty, greatness, or beauty; or the pride of life, whether by pomp, grandeur, power, or the usual consequence of them, applause and admiration: 'is not of the Father...but of the world'—it is the distinguishing mark of those who will not have him reign over them.[139]

He concludes that neither the pleasures of the world nor the religion of the world (opinions, outward duties) can make us happy because God is spirit and to be worshipped in spirit and truth: "In this alone can you find the happiness you seek—in the union of your spirit with the Father of spirits; in the knowledge and love of him who is the fountain of happiness, sufficient for all the souls he has made."[140] Wesley is adamant that "as there is but one God in heaven above and in the earth beneath, so there is only one happiness for created spirits, either in heaven or earth. This one God made our heart for

---

[135] *Works* 2, "The Case of Reason Impartially Considered," 598. See also *Works* 3, "An Israelite Indeed," 280.

[136] *Works* 3, "Spiritual Worship," 100. See also *Works* 1, "The Righteousness of Faith," 213.

[137] *Works* 3, "Spiritual Worship," 100.

[138] *Works* 3, "Spiritual Worship," 101.

[139] *Works* 1, "The Circumcision of the Heart," 409. See also *Works* 3, "The Danger of Riches," 234.

[140] *Works* 3, "Spiritual Worship," 101.

himself; and it cannot rest till it resteth in him."[141] In this same sermon he gives the example of his own experience: he was miserable and unhappy until he knew God "the source of present as well as eternal happiness."[142] And this "happy knowledge of the true God" is simply the Christian religion. This is not defined in notions (faith), duties, outward actions, but "it properly and directly consists in the knowledge and love of God, as manifested in the Son of his love, through the eternal Spirit. And this naturally leads to every heavenly temper, and to every good word and work."[143] The clear implication is that unless a person is "born again none can be happy even in this world. For *it is not possible in the nature of things that a man should be happy who is not holy* [emphasis mine]... [because] all unholy tempers are uneasy tempers"—malice, hatred, envy, jealousy, revenge and the "softer passions"[144] Wesley actually pairs "holiness and happiness" frequently and it is one of the most characteristic of the phrases that he uses to describe the Christian life.[145] Every desire that is not according to the will of God eventually brings sorrow, as does pride, self-will and idolatry. As long as these reign there can be no happiness, and they do reign till our nature is changed.[146] Wesley affirms that only the Christian can be truly happy and the unhappy are not truly Christian: "for if religion and happiness are in fact the same, it is impossible that any man can possess the former without possessing the latter also... [these] are utterly inseparable."[147]

It is at this stage that we inevitably ask the question: what is the nature of this happiness that we are to experience—is it a feeling, an emotion, a state, or what? To explore this fully is beyond the scope of this book, but there are a number of points that need to be made.[148] In his sermon "The General

---

[141] *Works* 3, "Spiritual Worship," 97. See also *Works* 3, "Spiritual Worship," 97-98; *Works* 2, "The End Of Christ's Coming," 478-81.

[142] *Works* 3, "Spiritual Worship," 98.

[143] *Works* 3, "Spiritual Worship," 99. See also *Works* 3, "Spiritual Worship," 101.

[144] *Works* 2, "The New Birth," 195.

[145] See *Works* 1, "Upon our Lord's Sermon on the Mount, VI," 582.

[146] *Works* 2, "The New Birth," 196.

[147] *Works* 3, "Spiritual Worship," 100. Wesley does allow for temptation and "deep nervous disorders," but generally "whoever is not happy, yea, happy in God, is not a Christian." See also *Works* 2, "The New Birth," 200.

[148] As was mentioned earlier in the chapter, an examination of Wesley's understanding of happiness, including such associated terms as feelings, desires, pleasures, and emotions, can be found in Lancaster, *The Pursuit of Happiness*. Being an 18th century person, Wesley has a very limited conception of the psychology of our emotional life, and his use of the language of the passions, tempers and affections reflects his historical setting, with all its limitations from a current perspective. An excellent study of this subject is found in Gregory S. Clapper, *John Wesley on Religious Affections: His Views on Experience and Emotion and Their Role in the Christian Life and Theology* (Metuchen: Scarecrow Press, 1989); Clapper, *The Renewal of the Heart is the Mission*

Deliverance" Wesley states that God made us capable of knowing, loving, and obeying him, and this we were able to fulfil: "This was the supreme perfection of man, as it is of all intelligent beings—the continually seeing and loving and obeying the Father of the spirits of all flesh. *From this right state, and right use of all his faculties, his happiness naturally flowed* [emphasis mine]."[149] Happiness is clearly tied to a state of being in a right relationship with God, from which flows the right exercise of all our God-given abilities. In his sermon "On Love" he makes the point that

> Without love nothing can so profit us as to make our lives happy. By happiness I mean, not a slight, trifling pleasure, that perhaps begins and ends in the same hour; but such a state of well-being as contents the soul and gives it a steady, lasting satisfaction. But that nothing without love can profit us as to our present happiness will appear from this single consideration: you cannot want it in any one single instance without pain; and the more you depart from it the pain is the greater.[150]

Wesley is confident that we will have a sense, an awareness, of this happiness not only because of the way we are created, but also through the direct witness of the Holy Spirit. This assurance is not simply a feeling, but a deep, settled consciousness of the rightness of our relationship with God and living in harmony with God's plans and purposes.[151] This means that we are not primarily talking about emotions, feelings or desires—though they are associated with both the right relationship and the right exercise of our abilities, and are an essential part of our humanity. There are times when happiness (as Wesley understands it) is accompanied by positive emotions, but our sense of living before God with integrity can still exist when experiencing negative emotions. This is something that will be explored further in later chapters.

Wesley's judgement that only Christians are truly happy is at odds with the verdict of society, both in his own day and in ours. Many see Christianity as essentially negative and restrictive, while Christians are viewed as miserable and unhappy. He thinks this is because many do not truly understand what it is and see it merely a long list of rules and regulations, duties and obligations. According to Scripture "it lies in one single point: it is neither more nor less than love—it is love which 'is the fulfilling of the law', 'the end of the commandment'. Religion is the love of God and our neighbour—that is every

---

of the Church: Wesley's Heart Religion in the Twenty-First Century (Eugene: Wipf & Stock, 2010); Anthony J. Headley, *Getting It Right: Christian Perfection and Wesley's Purposeful List* (Lexington: Emeth Press, 2013).

[149] *Works 2*, "The General Deliverance," 439.

[150] *Works 4*, "On Love," 386. See also 383; *Works 3*, "The Danger of Riches," 242.

[151] The witness of the Spirit in relationship to our emotions is dealt with in chapters 4 and 5 of this book. The Spirit's witness and the link with human experience is examined in some detail in McEwan, *Wesley as a Pastoral Theologian*.

man under heaven. This love, ruling the whole life, animating all our tempers and passions, directing all our thoughts, words, and actions, is 'pure religion and undefiled'."[152] Experiencing and living in the power of such love cannot be 'misery':

> Is it misery to love God? To give him my heart who alone is worthy of it? Nay, it is the truest happiness, indeed the only true happiness which is to be found under the sun. So does all experience prove the justness of that reflection which was made long ago: 'Thou has made us for thyself; and our heart cannot rest until it resteth in thee.' Or does anyone imagine the love of our neighbour is misery, even the loving man as our own soul? So far from it that next to the love of God this affords the greatest happiness of which we are capable.[153]

He then deals with the common objection raised in his day (and still current in our day) that loving God this way would be destructive of our happiness since it would deprive us of the innocent pleasures of life and leave us with very little enjoyment. Our happiness is not just tied to our love for God alone and in isolation from the rest of his creation:

> Not that we are to love or delight in none but him. For he hath commanded us not only to love our neighbour—that is, all men—as ourselves; to desire and pursue their happiness as sincerely and steadily as our own; but also to love many of his creatures in the strictest sense—to delight in them, to enjoy them—only in such a manner and measure as we know and feel not to indispose but to prepare us for the enjoyment of him.[154]

So while we cannot find genuine happiness in any creature (as experience shows), anything that promotes loving God is to be enjoyed.[155] Wesley affirms

> The entire love of God...is in no wise destructive of that happiness which our blessed religion was designed to establish. So far from it that love, entire love, is the point wherein all the lines of our holy religion centre. This is the very happiness which the great Author of it lived and died to establish among us. And a happiness it is, worthy of God!... A happiness not built on imagination, but real and rational; a happiness that does not play before our eyes at a distance, and vanish when we attempt to grasp it, but such as will bear the closest inspection and the more it is tried will delight the more.[156]

---

[152] *Works* 3, "The Important Question," 189. See also *Works* 2, "The Case of Reason Impartially Considered," 600.

[153] *Works* 3, "The Important Question," 189. See also *Works* 3, "Spiritual Worship," 102.

[154] *Works* 4, "On Love," 383; see also 384.

[155] *Works* 4, "The Love of God," 340-41. Wesley notes that enjoyment itself cannot support us in the troubles and pain we experience in this present life; see p. 342.

[156] *Works* 4, "The Love of God," 343.

Some ask if this happiness is to last all through our present life on earth and Wesley admits that in many it does not, but this is not inevitable. Wesley is confident that God wills our happiness to continue, but it is not automatic. He refers to Jude 21, where we are urged to "keep" ourselves in the love of God. This re-emphasises the co-operative nature of God's grace: "Accordingly, whoever improves the grace he has already received, whoever increases in the love of God, will surely retain it. God will continue, yea, will give it more abundantly."[157] If this is true for love, it is also true for holiness and happiness. Careful reflection on what Wesley says demonstrates that happiness is not actually the goal of our Christian life. God does desire for us to be happy, but happiness itself cannot be pursued directly—this belongs to love alone. Wesley makes it clear that it is love alone that will "infallibly lead you to happiness both in this world and in the world to come."[158]

God and Humanity: the New Creation

Though God's work of salvation in this present life is able to deliver us from the reign of sin in our hearts, it does not bring about a full deliverance from all the consequences of personal and social sin, let alone the devastation wrought on the rest of God's created order. There is clearly an 'already—not yet' tension in Wesley's understanding of Christ's work. We already experience a great deliverance from the power of sin but it is not yet a final deliverance, in which all things will be made new. This new creation will have no end and it will be "either a happy or a miserable eternity" based on our own choice.[159] Wesley is convinced that none need be rejected, for God wants all to experience this life of eternal love, holiness and happiness "by repentance to faith in a bleeding Lord; by faith to spotless love, to the full image of God renewed in the heart, and producing all holiness of conversation."[160] Given his understanding of being created in God's image and the correlation of love and liberty, he is absolutely sure that an eternity apart from God for any human being is the consequence of their own choice and not a divine decree: "it is impossible this should be the lot of any creature but by his own act and deed."[161] He often reminded his hearers how foolish it is to prefer temporal things to eternal, yet in our natural state this is what we do; "the very disease of our nature is the loving the creature above the Creator."[162] It is the gift of faith

---

[157] *Works* 3, "An Israelite Indeed," 284.
[158] *Works* 3, "The More Excellent Way," 263. See also *Works* 3, "An Israelite Indeed," 283.
[159] *Works* 2, "On Eternity," 365.
[160] *Works* 1 "The Great Assize," 374.
[161] *Works* 2, "On Eternity," 366.
[162] *Works* 4, "The Love of God," 338. See n. 37 that looks at the essence of sin as a disease.

that opens our eyes and understanding to see God and the things of God, so the earthly things that are seen are not "his aim, the object of his pursuit, his desire, or happiness," but those things that are as yet unseen but are no less certain because of the faithfulness of God.[163] When Christ returns everyone will rise with their own body, though it will be changed in properties; only then will the corruptible put on incorruption, and the mortal put on immortality (1 Cor. 15:53),[164] and the physical side of our life will be in total harmony with the spiritual side. The body will no longer be a hindrance to the full expression of love to God and neighbour. It is only after the day of resurrection and the renewal of all God's created order that we will be in an environment free from all destructive natural forces and weather patterns, with no more disasters, scarred environments, or violence.[165] There will be no more death, sin, sorrow, or pain, but "a deep, an ultimate, an uninterrupted union with God," a "constant communion," and a "continual enjoyment" of the Triune God "and of all creatures in him!" It is only then that we will be able to experience in full all the benefits of Christ's salvation personally, corporately and environmentally: "Hence will arise an unmixed state of holiness and happiness far superior to that which Adam enjoyed in paradise." [166] It is this vision of the goal of human existence that puts everything into perspective and helps to illuminate much of John Wesley's pastoral guidance for a people who often experienced a great deal of personal pain and suffering during their earthly life. It is to this that we now turn.

---

[163] *Works* 2, "On Eternity," 367-69.

[164] *Works* 1 "The Great Assize," 358.

[165] *Works* 2, "The New Creation," 500-510.

[166] *Works* 2, "The New Creation," 510. In Wesley's reading of Scripture, even the animal creation will be restored in glory and perhaps even lifted higher; see *Works* 2, "The General Deliverance," 440-50.

Chapter 3:

Experiencing of the Life of God in the Soul

John Wesley believed that the fullest picture of the Christian life is given by Christ in the Sermon on the Mount and he wrote a series of sermons from these chapters to illustrate this. As we examine them we can see how Wesley presented the strong relational note that underscores the whole exposition, and in what way love, holiness and happiness are interlinked in the Christian life. Many Christians wonder how realistic it is for ordinary people to experience such a life of grace while dealing with the reality of personal and corporate sinfulness. During the course of Wesley's ministry he became convinced that the promises of God could and would be fulfilled in the lives of his people before death and that a life of pure love for God and neighbour was genuinely possible by God's grace alone. He was equally convinced that this life of pure love is also a holy and happy life. This chapter examines Wesley's understanding of the nature of the life of God in the soul, what it looks like in practice, and how we may experience it for ourselves.

The Nature of the Life of God in the Soul

In writing to his nephew Samuel Wesley in 1790, John expressed his deep concern about his life, particularly his lack of religion: "I do not mean external religion, but the religion of the heart;… *that life of God in the soul of man*, [emphasis mine] the walking with God and having fellowship with the Father and the Son."[1] The life he envisioned for his relative was not simply a compilation of moral and spiritual qualities drawn from a range of Biblical texts. Wesley believed that in the Sermon on the Mount (Matt. 5-7) God has given us an accurate portrayal of the Christian life and we are not to be satisfied with anything less. What the Lord required, he also enabled by his grace and through the gift of the Holy Spirit.

Upon our Lord's Sermon on the Mount

This series of 13 sermons was written over the period 1748-1750 and the intention is to show us "the whole plan of his [Christ's] religion, to give us a full prospect of Christianity, to describe at large the nature of that holiness without which no man shall see the Lord."[2] In Wesley's analysis the Sermon

---

[1] *Letters* (Telford) VIII: 218.
[2] *Works 1*, "Upon our Lord's Sermon on the Mount, I," 473.

divides into 3 sections: Ch. 5 is the "sum of all true religion" in 8 principles; Ch. 6 gives the rules for right intention and Ch. 7 cautions against the main hindrances of religion as well as an application of the whole.[3] He introduces his commentary on these chapters by noting the purpose for the whole discourse: "To bless men, to make men happy was the great business for which our Lord came into the world."[4] In many ways the key to the whole picture of the holy life is found in Matthew 5:3-12, and the eight 'blessings' given there which direct us to the only true source of happiness—Jesus Christ himself and compliance with his will for us.[5] In his commentary on these verses, Wesley leaves us in no doubt that the Christian life and the authentically happy life are one and the same thing. He affirms that "blessed" should be translated "happy" in every case, and it is then linked with both holiness and love.

He begins by telling us that "'Blessed (or happy) are the poor in spirit.' Happy are the mourners, the meek; those that hunger and thirst after righteousness; the merciful, the pure in heart: happy in the end and in the way; happy in this life and in life everlasting!"[6] He wants to be sure that we take notice that the first beatitude addresses "poor in spirit"—not the poor in outward circumstances, who may be far from happy.[7] Living in the 18th century, Wesley was faced with the ugly reality of extreme poverty and its consequences; he knew only too well the debilitating impact this had on personal and community life. However, the poor in spirit "whatever their outward circumstances are, have that disposition of heart which is the first step to all real, substantial happiness, either in this world or that which is to come."[8] As we saw in the previous chapter, he situates happiness in a relationship with God and neighbour, not in circumstances. The "kingdom of heaven" is within us and it is righteousness, peace and joy in the Holy Spirit; the life of God in the soul; the mind that was in Christ, "the image of God stamped upon the heart, now renewed after the likeness of him that created it? What is it but the love of God because he first loved us, and the love of all mankind for his sake."[9] It is "the first springing up of those rivers of pleasure which flow at God's right hand for evermore."[10] This is a far cry from the picture of Christianity as a life of misery and it confirms that life in Christ is essentially positive and attractive, rather than negative and repellent. However, it does not give the Christian grounds for complacency, let alone pride. Rather it should provoke a deep sense of Christian humility, "which flows from a sense of the

---

[3] *Works 1*, "Upon our Lord's Sermon on the Mount, I," 474-75.

[4] *Notes* (NT), Matt. 5:2.

[5] *Notes* (NT), Matt. 5:2.

[6] *Works 1*, "Upon our Lord's Sermon on the Mount, I," 474.

[7] *Works 1*, "Upon our Lord's Sermon on the Mount, I," 475.

[8] *Works 1*, "Upon our Lord's Sermon on the Mount, I," 476.

[9] *Works 1*, "Upon our Lord's Sermon on the Mount, I," 481.

[10] *Works 1*, "Upon our Lord's Sermon on the Mount, I," 481.

love of God, reconciled to us in Christ Jesus."[11] The reference to mourning in
v. 4 has to do with

> the conviction we feel of inbred sin is deeper and deeper every day. The more we
> grow in grace the more do we see of the desperate wickedness of our heart. The
> more we advance in the knowledge and love of God, through our Lord Jesus
> Christ…, the more do we discern of our alienation from God, of the enmity that is
> in our carnal mind, and the necessity of our being entirely renewed in
> righteousness and true holiness.[12]

The danger is that the Christian under conviction will ignore the promptings of
the Spirit or reject them and so begin to lose the close relationship they have
with God.[13]

In describing meekness, Wesley is careful not to identify it as some sort of
spinelessness or the absence of strong affections; "It does not destroy but
balance the affections, which the God of nature never designed should be
rooted out by grace, but only brought and kept under due regulations."[14] He
does not see the Christian life as one in which our emotional life is stunted and
denied; rather, it is to flourish under the power and direction of the Spirit. He
goes on to say that the meek are zealous for God,

> But their zeal is always guided by knowledge, and tempered in every thought and
> word and work with the love of man as well as the love of God. They do not
> desire to extinguish any of the passions which God has for wise ends implanted in
> their nature. But they have the mastery of all; they hold them in subjection and
> employ them only in subservience to those ends. And thus even the harsher and
> more unpleasing passions are applicable to the noblest purposes. Even hate and
> anger and fear, when engaged against sin, and regulated by faith and love, are as
> walls and bulwarks to the soul, so that the wicked one cannot approach to hurt it.[15]

This is of major importance because so often the passions are seen as
problematic, if not inherently evil. Wesley does not see even the passions of
hate, anger and fear as intrinsically evil and therefore to be eradicated or
lamented. He appears to be comfortable with the notion that if we did not
"hate" sin and its effects then we would be less than pleasing to God. The
problem is not the passion, but to whom and to what they are directed. So anger
against sin is permissible because even Jesus did this; however, like Jesus, we
are to be grieved for the sinner while angry at the sin.[16] This is easier said than

---

[11] *Works 1*, "Upon our Lord's Sermon on the Mount, I," 482.
[12] *Works* 1, "Upon our Lord's Sermon on the Mount, I," 482-83.
[13] *Works* 1, "Upon our Lord's Sermon on the Mount, I," 483-85. It is also to be our
attitude when we see the state of those living without Christ; see p. 486.
[14] *Works* 1, "Upon our Lord's Sermon on the Mount, II," 489.
[15] *Works* 1,, "Upon our Lord's Sermon on the Mount, II," 490.
[16] *Works* 1, "Upon our Lord's Sermon on the Mount, II," 491-92. See 492, n. 20.

done and in the next chapter we will examine the practical pastoral advice that Wesley offers concerning it. Righteousness is then defined as "every holy and heavenly temper in one; springing from as well as terminating in the love of God our Father and redeemer, and the love of all men for his sake."[17] He affirms that righteousness is essentially a relational quality and not compliance with laws, rules or regulations. He believes that just as hunger and thirst are our strongest appetites and they cannot be satisfied with anything other than food and drink, so it is with righteousness: "Give me love or else I die!"[18] This implies that a person thirsty for God cannot be satisfied "with what the world accounts religion, as with what they account happiness."[19] Lest the Christian then fall into the trap of seeing spiritual development primarily in terms of cultivating personal spiritual practices, another element in the character of the meek is that they do not shirk some of the more difficult tasks that arise because we are to love our neighbours. Wesley says that God does not excuse a deficiency in some duties simply because we do well in others: *"performing our duty to God will not excuse us from our duty to our neighbour* [emphasis mine]; that works of piety, as they are called, will be so far from commending us to God if we are wanting in charity, that on the contrary that want of charity will make all those works an abomination to the Lord."[20] This underscores the centrality of life in community if the life of God is to flourish in our souls. The solitary life focused on private spiritual exercises, or Christians choosing to cultivate their personal devotional life rather than ministering to the neighbour is, in effect, a denial of the clear teaching of the Sermon. This continues the strong focus on relationships with other people that are so important to Wesley's understanding of salvation and it is the key to his interpretation of the next verses. The quality of mercy is vital because those who truly love their neighbour will want them to know God. Wesley notes that this love is so important that Paul gives a full account of its qualities in 1 Corinthians 13:1-4 and Romans 12:20-21.[21] "And the greater his love, the more he does rejoice in the blessings of all mankind, the farther is he removed from every kind and degree of envy toward any creature."[22] The pure in heart are those who through faith in Christ are purified and cleansed "from every desire but to please and enjoy God, to know and love him more and more, by that hunger and thirst after righteousness which now engrosses their whole soul: so that now they

---

[17] *Works* 1, "Upon our Lord's Sermon on the Mount, II," 495. Also see n. 42.

[18] *Works* 1, "Upon our Lord's Sermon on the Mount, II," 496.

[19] *Works* 1, "Upon our Lord's Sermon on the Mount, II," 496. The world sees religion as do no harm, abstain from outward sin, do good, and use the means of grace. Wesley's "General Rules" are simply moralistic outside of faith; see n. 45.

[20] *Works* 1, "Upon our Lord's Sermon on the Mount, II," 493.

[21] *Works* 1, "Upon our Lord's Sermon on the Mount, II," 499.

[22] *Works* 1, "Upon our Lord's Sermon on the Mount, II," 500.

love the Lord their God with all their heart, and with all their soul, and mind, and strength.[23] But even this is linked with the love of neighbour:

> How excellent things are spoken of the love of our neighbour! It is 'the fulfilling of the law', 'the end of the commandment'. Without this all we have, all we do, all we suffer, is of no value in the sight of God. But it is the love of our neighbour which springs from the love of God; otherwise itself is nothing worth.[24]

The peacemaker is "one that being filled with the love of God and of all mankind cannot confine the expressions of it to his own family, or friends, or acquaintances, or party; or to those of his own opinions; no, nor those who are partakers of like precious faith; but steps over all these narrow bounds that he may do good to every man; that he may some way or other manifest his love to neighbours and strangers, friends and enemies."[25] Of course, not everyone receives this love gladly, and so persecution is inevitable, though this is always a matter of God's providential governance.[26]

In the next section of the Sermon (vv.13-16) he returns again to the observation that religion is not just a matter of the heart and the images of salt, light and city imply an outward life with others: "Christianity is essentially a social religion, and that to turn it into a solitary one is to destroy it."[27] Wesley goes on to explain: "When I say this is essentially a social religion, I mean not only that it cannot subsist so well, but that it cannot subsist at all without society, without living and conversing with other men."[28] He affirms the necessity of solitude at times and our devotional life makes this essential (even for extended periods), but this must not lead to the neglect of the people and situations wherein God has placed us.[29] Wesley makes the point that the religion of the Sermon "cannot subsist without society...[because] several of the most essential branches thereof can have no place if we have no intercourse with the world."[30] As we have seen, we need other people if we are to become truly meek, make peace or do good, etc. To those who want to turn Christianity into a solitary, inward and private experience, he writes:

> it is most true that the root of all religion lies in the heart, in the inmost soul; that this is the union of the soul with God, the life of God in the soul of man. But if this root be really in the heart it cannot but put forth branches. And these are the

---

[23] *Works* 1, "Upon our Lord's Sermon on the Mount, III," 511.

[24] *Works* 1, "Upon our Lord's Sermon on the Mount, III," 510.

[25] *Works* 1, "Upon our Lord's Sermon on the Mount, III," 518.

[26] *Works* 1, "Upon our Lord's Sermon on the Mount, III," 523.

[27] *Works* 1, "Upon our Lord's Sermon on the Mount, IV," 533. See also *Works* 13, "The Preface to *Hymns and Sacred Poems*", 37-39.

[28] *Works* 1, "Upon our Lord's Sermon on the Mount, IV," 533-34.

[29] *Works* 1, "Upon our Lord's Sermon on the Mount, IV," 534-37.

[30] *Works* 1, "Upon our Lord's Sermon on the Mount, IV," 537.

several instances of outward obedience, which partake of the same nature with the root, and consequently are not only marks or signs, but substantial parts of religion.[31]

However, to turn it only into an outward religion of social work without a "root" is equally worthless because God is only pleased with outward service that arises from the heart. As Wesley says, while "love is all in all," its very nature it leads us to obedience and action:[32]

> To glorify him therefore with our bodies as well as with our spirits, to go through outward work with hearts lifted up to him, to make our daily employment a sacrifice to God, to buy and sell, to eat and drink to his glory: this is worshipping God in spirit and in truth as much as praying to him in the wilderness.[33]

What is more, we cannot ever act on the basis of our judgement as to whether the people we are called to serve are going to be finally lost or saved and use this to determine if we will or will not help them. We are commanded to feed the hungry and clothe the naked no matter the outcome, and we will be condemned if we do not. Given some of the emphases we meet with in missions and evangelism about only going to the receptive people and the accompanying focus on success judged by numbers, this is an aspect of Wesley's understanding of the Christian life that is too easily lost. God generally changes hearts using people, so we are to do all we can as if we could change them, and then leave the outcome to God.[34]

Just as the love of Christ requires us to be active in service to the neighbour, it also requires us to give careful attention to our own morals and behaviour. This is where our current obsession with love as a feeling leads us into potentially fatal error. We seem to think that as long as I feel good about you and feel good about myself, then anything goes, and it is really no one else's business. However, the love of God is not merely a feeling, nor is it divorced from the character and nature of God. No relationship can flourish if the freedom of one party continually damages the other. You can't go on a journey together and genuinely share companionship on the way without a common destination and having the needed resources to actually get there. To walk with Christ and to enter the Kingdom requires certain character traits and without them entry into the presence of God at the end of time is not going to be a positive experience. As Wesley has constantly emphasised, the focus in Christianity is the heart and this is essentially summed up in terms of love for God and all mankind.[35] Wesley believed that Jesus came to retain the "moral

---

[31] *Works* 1, "Upon our Lord's Sermon on the Mount, IV," 541-42.

[32] *Works* 1, "Upon our Lord's Sermon on the Mount, IV," 542.

[33] *Works* 1, "Upon our Lord's Sermon on the Mount, IV," 544.

[34] *Works* 1, "Upon our Lord's Sermon on the Mount, IV," 546.

[35] *Works* 1, "Upon our Lord's Sermon on the Mount, V," 571.

law" in the Ten Commandments and this is seen in the next section of the Sermon (vv. 17-48). This law was written on our hearts at creation as an intrinsic element of our nature that truly reflected the character of God and God's love. While it is now defaced by sin, it cannot be wholly blotted out while we have any sense of good and evil. In fact, it applies to the whole race at all times, since the nature of humanity and our relationships are set by God's creative act.[36] This means that law and gospel are intimately linked together and are always in agreement. The commandments relate to the law, and the gospel relates to the promises; to love God as a commandment is part of the law, while as part of the gospel it is a promise.[37] So "every command in Holy Writ is only a covered promise."[38] Wesley says that Ch. 5 "has laid before us those dispositions of soul which constitute real Christianity: the inward tempers contained in that holiness 'without which no man shall see the Lord'—the affections which, when flowing from their proper fountain, from a living faith in God through Jesus Christ, are intrinsically and essentially good, and acceptable to God."[39]

Wesley now turns his attention to Ch. 6 to show how our actions may be in harmony with this character, both in terms of "works of piety" and "works of mercy."[40] These are two very important categories for Wesley, with the former referring to those actions that are largely directed toward God and the latter to those actions largely directed towards the neighbour. They are intimately connected as we saw in the illustration given earlier of the root and the branches. If they are not, then "Any temporal view, any motive whatever on this side eternity, any design but that of promoting the glory of God, and the happiness of men for God's sake, makes every action, however fair it may appear to men, an abomination unto the Lord."[41] Prayer is one of the major works of piety and it discloses the true inclinations of our hearts: "And indeed our prayers are the proper test of our desires, nothing being fit to have a place in our desires which is not fit to have a place in our prayers; what we may not pray for, neither should we desire."[42] This means that prayer is not primarily to inform God about our desires, but to uncover in ourselves the true nature of them, to fix the sense of the wants more deeply in our hearts, and increase the sense of our dependence on God who alone is able to supply them. It is not so much to move God to give to us, but to change us so that we are willing and ready to receive from him.[43]

---

[36] *Works* 1, "Upon our Lord's Sermon on the Mount, V," 551-52.
[37] *Works* 1, "Upon our Lord's Sermon on the Mount, V," 554.
[38] *Works* 1, "Upon our Lord's Sermon on the Mount, V," 554-55.
[39] *Works* 1, "Upon our Lord's Sermon on the Mount, VI," 573.
[40] *Works* 1, "Upon our Lord's Sermon on the Mount, VI," 573.
[41] *Works* 1, "Upon our Lord's Sermon on the Mount, VI," 576.
[42] *Works* 1, "Upon our Lord's Sermon on the Mount, VI," 578.
[43] *Works* 1, "Upon our Lord's Sermon on the Mount, VI," 577.

The sermon on Matthew 6:19-23 has Wesley reflecting on "pure intention"; what the eye is to the body, intention is to the soul. So a "single eye" is focused on God and Christ Jesus: "to know him with suitable affections, loving him as he hath loved us; to please God in all things; to serve God (as we love him) with all our heart and mind and soul and strength; and to enjoy God in all and above all things, in time and in eternity."[44] The biblical image of light indicates both a true divine knowledge and holiness: "It is by faith that the eye of the mind is opened to see the light of the glorious love of God. And as long as it is steadily fixed thereon on God in Christ, reconciling the world unto himself, we are more and more filled with the love of God and man, with meekness, gentleness, long-suffering; with all the fruits of holiness, which are, through Jesus Christ, to the glory of God the Father."[45] As is so common in Wesley, it also implies "happiness as well as holiness. How sweet and pleasant to see Christ and to walk in the light as God is in the light 'rejoicing evermore, praying without ceasing, and in everything giving thanks, *enjoying* whatever is the will of God concerning him in Christ Jesus."[46] He believes there is no medium between the single and the evil eye, any more than there is between purity and impurity. The advertising claims of something being '99% pure' is simply to state it is, in fact, impure. In Wesley's opinion, the evil eye is to "aim at any other end than God; if we have any view but to know and love God, to please and serve him in all things; if we have any other design than to enjoy God, to be happy in him both now and for ever."[47] He believes that without this singleness of focus, there can be no lasting peace or contentment. One of the hard tests of our intentions has to do with how we accumulate and spend money. He is adamant that we ought to pay our bills, and should provide "such things as are needful for the body" like food, clothing and the means to provide them. This also involves providing for our children and household in one's lifetime, as well as making suitable provision for their welfare after our death. However, these provisions need to be "necessaries" and not "delicacies or superfluities." Of course, this raises the issue of how to decide what is necessary and what is not? This is something to which we will return later. It is important to note that for Wesley the heart of the issue is not wealth as such, but the "desire" for it. This desire is often driven by the belief that we can trust wealth to help us with life's problems and provide for our happiness.[48] However, it is only God who can meet these needs and Wesley reiterates, "O trust in him for happiness as well as for help. All the springs of happiness are in him."[49] God alone is the sufficient source,

---

[44] *Works* 1, "Upon our Lord's Sermon on the Mount, VIII," 613.

[45] *Works* 1, "Upon our Lord's Sermon on the Mount, VIII," 614.

[46] *Works* 1, "Upon our Lord's Sermon on the Mount, VIII," 615.

[47] *Works* 1, "Upon our Lord's Sermon on the Mount, VIII," 615.

[48] *Works* 1, "Upon our Lord's Sermon on the Mount, VIII," 616-25.

[49] *Works* 1, "Upon our Lord's Sermon on the Mount, VIII,"626.

who of his own rich and free mercy holds them out to us as in his own hand, that reserving them as his gift, and as pledges of his love, we may 'enjoy all' that we possess. It is his love gives a relish to all we taste, puts life and sweetness into all, while every creature leads us up to the great Creator, and all earth is a scale to heaven. He transfuses the joys that are at his own right hand into all he bestows on his thankful children; who, having fellowship with the Father and his Son Jesus Christ, enjoy him in all and above all.[50]

This returns us to the centrality of trust in a relationship. This has its beginning as we believe in him "as a loving, pardoning God.... And thus to believe in God implies to *trust* in him as our strength, without whom we can do nothing, who every moment endues us with power from on high, without which it is impossible to please him."[51] It is also to trust in God "as our happiness; as the centre of spirits, the only rest of our souls; the only good who is adequate to all our capacities, and sufficient to satisfy all the desires he hath given us."[52] Once again, trust is a related to both love and happiness:

Now, to love God in the manner the Scripture describes, in the manner God himself requires of us, and by requiring engages to work in us, is to love him as the one God; that is, 'with all our heart, and with all our soul, and with all our mind, and with all our strength'. It is to desire God alone for his own sake, and nothing else but with reference to him; to rejoice in God; to delight in the Lord; not only to seek, but find happiness in him; to enjoy God as the chiefest among ten thousand; to rest in him as our God and our all—in a word, to have such a possession of God as makes us always happy.[53]

Such a relationship is inherently transformative: "Now God is love; therefore they who resemble him in the spirit of their minds are transformed into the same image.... Their soul is all love....they are like him, loving unto every man, and their mercy extends to all his works."[54] From this love flows obedience: "the performing all the ordinary actions of life with a single eye and a pure heart—offering them all in holy, fervent love, as sacrifices to God through Jesus Christ."[55] That is why those trusting in riches while claiming to love and trust God end up with the worst of both worlds: "How uncomfortable a condition must he be in, who, having the fear but not the love of God, who serving him, but not with all his heart, has only the toils and not the joys of religion. He has religion enough to make him miserable, but not enough to

---

[50] *Works* 1, "Upon our Lord's Sermon on the Mount, VIII'" 626. See also *Works* 1, "Upon our Lord's Sermon on the Mount, X," 653.

[51] *Works* 1, "Upon our Lord's Sermon on the Mount, IX," 635.

[52] *Works* 1, "Upon our Lord's Sermon on the Mount, IX," 635.

[53] *Works* 1, "Upon our Lord's Sermon on the Mount, IX," 635.

[54] *Works* 1, "Upon our Lord's Sermon on the Mount, IX," 636.

[55] *Works* 1, "Upon our Lord's Sermon on the Mount, IX," 636-37.

make him happy: his religion will not let him enjoy the world, and the world will not let him enjoy God."[56]

Finally, in the two sermons that deal with Ch. 7 Wesley highlights the practical application of the material from the previous two chapters. In particular he sees our propensity to judge one another in harsh and negative ways as a major hindrance to holy living: "there is no situation of life, nor any period of time, from the hour of our first repenting and believing the gospel till we are made perfect in love, wherein this caution is not needful for every child of God."[57] The issue is not judging as such, but "thinking of another in a manner that is contrary to love."[58] This requires that we are not to judge another harshly since that tends to undermine whatever good is in them and it shows a lack of love. "Love will not infer from a person's falling once into an act of open sin that he is accustomed so to do, that he is habitually guilty of it."[59] Likewise, for prayer to be effective, we must live in love with all: "Confirm your love towards one another and towards all men. And love them, not in word only, but in deed and in truth. Therefore all things whatsoever ye would that men should do to you, do even so unto them; for this is the law and the prophets."[60] This is the "royal law" of Christ, a pure and genuine morality. "But none can ever walk by this rule (nor ever did from the beginning of the world), none can love his neighbour as himself, unless he first love God. And none can love God unless he believe in Christ, unless he have redemption through his blood, and the Spirit of God bearing witness with his spirit that he is a child of God. Faith therefore is still the root of all, of present as well as future salvation."[61]

That is why it is essential for everyone to "Believe in him [Christ], and thy faith will work by love. Thou wilt love the Lord thy God because he hath loved thee; thou wilt love thy neighbour as thyself. And then it will be thy glory and joy to exert and increase this love, not barely by abstaining from what is contrary thereto—from every unkind thought, word, and action—but by showing all that kindness to every man which thou wouldst he show unto thee."[62] The danger is that we can settle for doing all the outward works of a Christian and still be turned away by Christ on the day of judgement: "for your heart was not right toward God. Ye were not yourselves meek and lowly; ye were not lovers of God and of all mankind; ye were not renewed in the image of God. Ye were not holy as I [Christ] am holy. . . . Ye are transgressors of my

---

[56] *Works* 1, "Upon our Lord's Sermon on the Mount, IX," 637-38.

[57] *Works* 1, "Upon our Lord's Sermon on the Mount, X," 651.

[58] *Works* 1, "Upon our Lord's Sermon on the Mount, X," 654.

[59] *Works* 1, "Upon our Lord's Sermon on the Mount, X," 655.

[60] *Works* 1, "Upon our Lord's Sermon on the Mount, X," 660.

[61] *Works* 1, "Upon our Lord's Sermon on the Mount, X," 662.

[62] *Works* 1, "Upon our Lord's Sermon on the Mount, X," 663.

law—my law of holy and perfect love."[63] The one who does get to enter heaven is the one who thirsts only for God, who loves God and all mankind, and from this does good to all.[64]

> He knows God: his Father and his friend, the parent of all good, the centre of the spirits of all flesh, the sole happiness of intelligent beings. He sees, clearer than the light of the noonday sun, that this is the end of man: to glorify him who made him for himself, and to love and enjoy him forever. And with equal clearness he sees the means to that end, to the enjoyment of God in glory; even now to know, to love, to imitate God, and to believe in Jesus Christ whom he hath sent.[65]

Such a person can confess Galatians 2:20: "'The life I now live': namely, a divine, heavenly life, a life which is 'hid with Christ in God' [Col. 3:3]. I now live, even in the flesh, a life of love, of pure love both to God and man; a life of holiness and happiness, praising God and doing all things to his glory."[66] This essentially defines what Wesley meant by Christian perfection: "How desirable is the happiness here described! How venerable, how lovely the holiness! This is the *spirit* of religion; the quintessence of it. These are indeed the fundamentals of Christianity!"[67]

Experiencing the Life of God in the Soul

In 1731 Wesley wrote to Mary Pendarves asking what she thought about his walk with God and in it he declares:

> My present sense is this. I was made to be happy; to be happy I must love God; in proportion to my love of whom my happiness must increase. To love God I must be like him, holy as he is holy; which implies the being pure from vicious and foolish passions and comprises in the word charity. In order to root these out of my soul and plant these in their stead I must use, (1), such means as are ordered by God, (2), such as are recommended by experience and reason.... I lay it down for a rule that I can't be too happy or therefore holy.[68]

The three qualities of love, holiness and happiness are intimately interlinked in his description of the Christian life and are clearly the goal he has in mind. Several years later (1737) we find Mary Chapman telling him that it seemed to her that his religion was without cheer or friendliness. He replies, "I am convinced, as true religion or holiness cannot be without cheerfulness, so steady cheerfulness,...cannot be without holiness or true religion." We are to

---

[63] *Works* 1, "Upon our Lord's Sermon on the Mount, XIII," 690-91.

[64] *Works* 1, "Upon our Lord's Sermon on the Mount, XIII," 691.

[65] *Works* 1, "Upon our Lord's Sermon on the Mount, XIII," 692.

[66] *Works* 1, "Upon our Lord's Sermon on the Mount, XIII," 693.

[67] *Works* 1, "Upon our Lord's Sermon on the Mount, III," 530.

[68] *Works* 25: 293-94. See also *Works* 25: 321.

enjoy "the truly innocent pleasures of life" which do not hinder a greater good or promote evil.[69]

> And this I know is the will of God concerning me: that I should enjoy every pleasure that leads to my taking pleasure in him, and in such a measure as most leads to it. I know that, as to every action which is naturally pleasing, it is his will that it should be so; therefore in taking that pleasure, so *far* as it tends to this end (of taking pleasure in God), I do his will. Though therefore that pleasure be in some sense distinct from the love of God, yet is the taking of it by no means distinct from his will.[70]

The only thing needful is to do God's will, which is our renewal in the image of God "in faith and love, in all holiness and happiness."[71] In the same year he writes to William Wogan, re-emphasising that "religion is love and peace and joy in the Holy Ghost; that as it is the happiest, so it is the cheerfullest thing in the world; that [it] is utterly inconsistent with moroseness, sourness, severity, and indeed with whatever is not according to the softness, sweetness, and gentleness of Jesus Christ."[72] These references illustrate how his own spiritual journey during the Oxford and Georgia years (1725-1737) had the one goal in mind and was consistent with that outlined in the early letter to his mother in 1725 quoted in chapter 1. What was to change following his return from Georgia has to do with his understanding and experience of faith.[73]

RELATIONSHIP, FAITH AND TRUST

If it is a relationship of love that lies at the heart of Christianity, then central to the formation and development of a healthy relationship is trust. This comes to the fore in Wesley's own understanding as he returned to England in 1738, following his time in Georgia. In the important sermon "Salvation by Faith" (June 1738), he reminds us that all the blessings of God come us through grace alone: "grace is the source, faith the condition, of salvation."[74] Faith is faith in Christ and God through Christ; "it is not barely a speculative, rational thing, a

---

[69] *Works* 25: 502.

[70] *Works* 25: 502-03. Wesley gives the example of eating—which he does with pleasure—see p. 502.

[71] *Works* 25: 503.

[72] *Works* 25: 500.

[73] This finds its focus on the events leading up to and following his spiritual experience at Aldersgate on May 24, 1738. There is a great deal of debate about the meaning and significance of this event. See, for example, Kenneth J. Collins, *John Wesley: A Theological Journey* (Nashville: Abingdon Press, 2003); Gunter et al, *Wesley and the Quadrilateral*; Randy L. Maddox, ed., *Aldersgate Reconsidered* (Nashville: Abingdon Press, 1990).

[74] *Works* 1, "Salvation by Faith," 118.

cold, lifeless assent, a train of ideas in the head; but also a disposition of the heart."[75] After quoting from Romans 10:9-10, he goes on to say:

> Christian faith is then not only an assent to the whole gospel of Christ, but also a full reliance on the blood of Christ, a trust in the merits of his life, death, and resurrection; a recumbancy upon him as our atonement and our life, as given for us, and living in us. It is a sure confidence which a man hath in God, that through the merits of Christ his sins are forgiven, and he reconciled to the favour of God.[76]

However, faith is not the goal of the gospel: "Yea, all the glory of faith before it is done away arises hence, that it ministers to love. It is the great temporary means which God has ordained to promote that eternal end. . . . Love existed from eternity, in God, the great ocean of love. Love had a place in all the children of God, from the moment of their creation. They received at once from their gracious Creator to exist, and to love."[77] Wesley believes that before the Fall, Adam walked with God by sight and not by faith—and certainly not faith in the particular sense linked with salvation. He goes on to say: "man being then pure from every stain of sin, holy as God is holy. But love even then filled his heart. It reigned in him without a rival. And it was only when love was lost by sin that faith was added...to restore man to the love from which he was fallen."[78] It was not needed before that since there was no failure of "confidence in redeeming love.... Faith then was originally designed of God to re-establish the law of love....it is the grand means of restoring that holy love wherein man was originally created."[79] By this faith we are saved from both the guilt and the power of sin. Wesley was confident that the one born of God does not commit habitual sin (sin that reigns) or wilful sin, since we continually desire the holy and perfect will of God.[80] Nor does such a person "sin by infirmities, whether in act, word, or thought; for his infirmities have no concurrence of his will; and without this they are not properly sins."[81] Even at this early stage he sees clearly that relationships are broken when one or both parties is deliberately intent on harming it; a healthy, loving relationship can and will survive unintentional blunders and failings arising from a limited understanding and faulty judgement.

Wesley is in no doubt of the absolute fixity of God's love for us and that "the grace or love of God, whence cometh our salvation, is free in all, and free

---

[75] *Works* 1, "Salvation by Faith," 120.
[76] *Works* 1, "Salvation by Faith," 121. See n. 35 & 36 and language of the homily 'Of Faith'; faith as assent versus faith as trust. See also *Works* 1, "The Marks of the New Birth," 418-19; *Works* 1, "The Way to the Kingdom," 230-31.
[77] *Works* 2, "The Law Established through Faith, II," 39.
[78] *Works* 2, "The Law Established through Faith, II," 40.
[79] *Works* 2, "The Law Established through Faith, II," 40.
[80] *Works* 1, "Salvation by Faith," 123-24.
[81] *Works* 1, "Salvation by Faith," 124.

for all."[82] This emphasises that love cannot, by its very nature, be selective. Thus the doctrine of predestination "tends to destroy the comfort of religion, the happiness of Christianity" since it takes away hope in God's promises and tends to destroy "Christian holiness, happiness, and good works."[83] He is deeply convinced that without an assurance that God's love is for us all, as are the promises of salvation, then there are no grounds for "Christian happiness."[84] Without this assurance we are not able to freely love and serve the neighbour, "For whatever lessens our love must so far lessen our desire to do them good."[85] He is sure that "if any man truly love God he cannot but love his brother also. Gratitude to our Creator will surely produce benevolence to our fellow-creatures. If we love him, we cannot but love one another, as Christ loved us."[86] If we find this difficult, then he says "Beg that he [God] would give you more love; and love will make the labour light."[87] Wesley affirms that it is generally God's "pleasure to work by his creatures: to help man by man."[88] This is further explained when he writes: "the grand reason why God is pleased to assist men, rather than immediately by himself, is undoubtedly to endear us to each other by these mutual good offices, in order to increase our happiness both in time and eternity."[89] All of this underscores that being a Christian is not simply about a private, personal, inward relationship with God; it essentially and unequivocally includes the love of neighbour, and without the relationship with neighbour no one can truly have the character that God seeks to form. As was said earlier, the love of God is not simply a feeling or emotion divorced from character. God's love perfectly expresses his nature and character, and love is inherently transformative because you cannot be in a genuine relationship without being impacted by it. In this case, we experience and share the love of the Creator and we cannot remain in that relationship without it changing us. To reject the workings of love is to reject the one who shares that love with us, leading to the loss of the relationship if we persist in it. Given our sinfulness, we no longer intuitively know how to live in love with God nor how to share that love with the neighbour. We need to be shown the true state of our heart and this, Wesley believes, is the function of the law.

---

[82] *Works* 3, "Free Grace," 544.
[83] *Works* 3, "Free Grace," 551.
[84] *Works* 3, "Free Grace," 549.
[85] *Works* 3, "Free Grace," 551.
[86] *Works* 3, "On Family Religion," 336. See also *Works* 2, "The Law Established through Faith, II," 42.
[87] *Works* 3, "On Family Religion," 341.
[88] *Works* 3, "On the Education of Children," 349.
[89] *Works* 3, "Of Good Angels," 15.

THE LAW OF GOD

In his sermon "The Original, Nature, Properties, and Use of the Law" (1750), Wesley says Romans 7:12 refers to the moral law and its origins are in eternity, not with Moses or Noah.[90] When God created the angels "he endued them with understanding to discern truth from falsehood, good from evil; and as a necessary result of this, with liberty, a capacity of choosing the one and refusing the other." This enabled them to offer God "a free and willing service"; he also gave them a law, "a complete model of all truth...and of all good...to make way for a continual increase of their happiness; seeing every instance of obedience to that law would both add to the perfection of their nature and entitle them to an higher reward."[91] It is this law that was also given to human beings: "he gave this free, intelligent creature the same law...engraven on his heart by the finger of God," so it is "coeval with his nature." We rebelled and almost lost the law from the heart, but God through Christ "in some measure re-inscribed the law on the heart of his dark, sinful creature."[92] Wesley believes that it is this law that was subsequently written on tablets of stone for Moses, but it cannot be known fully by us till the work of the Spirit reveals it to us through faith in Christ.[93] The law is a picture of Christ,[94] who is the model of what it means to be a human being. The law is used to convince the world of sin through the work of the Holy Spirit "who can work it without any means at all, or by whatever means it pleaseth him.... But it is the ordinary method of the Spirit of God to convict sinners by the law. It is this which, being set home on the conscience, generally breaketh the rocks in pieces."[95] As Wesley said, we need first to convince people that they are sick before they will turn to the Physician.[96] The law illuminates the true nature of our heart and it also brings us to Christ so that we may live. Wesley says it is true that in "both these offices it acts the part of a severe schoolmaster. It drives us by force, rather than draws us by love. And yet love is the spring of all. It is the spirit of love which, by this painful means, tears away our confidence in the flesh...."[97] Finally, it is the law that keeps us alive and prepares us for deeper life in God, convincing us of remaining sin and keeping us close to God, so that we will increasingly transformed into the image of Christ. It is Christ himself who empowers us to be able to do what is commanded and confirms our hope

---

[90] *Works* 2, "The Original, Nature, Properties, and Use of the Law," 6.

[91] *Works* 2, "The Original, Nature, Properties, and Use of the Law," 6.

[92] *Works* 2, "The Original, Nature, Properties, and Use of the Law," 7. The moral law is thus both divine gift and prevenient grace—see n.10.

[93] *Works* 2, "The Original, Nature, Properties, and Use of the Law," 8.

[94] *Works* 2, "The Original, Nature, Properties, and Use of the Law," 9.

[95] *Works* 2, "The Original, Nature, Properties, and Use of the Law," 15. See also *Works* 2, "The Law Established through Faith, I," 22.

[96] *Works* 2, "The Law Established through Faith, I," 23.

[97] *Works* 2, "The Original, Nature, Properties, and Use of the Law," 16.

of attaining it by his grace. In a memorable turn of phrase, Wesley says it is a "divine mirror" that shows the depth of sin and sends us to Christ for the cure.[98] Through Christ we can be freed form the power of sin and then we need to "stand fast in this liberty…. Stand fast in loving God with all thy heart and serving him with all thy strength. This is perfect freedom; thus to keep his law and to walk in all his commandments blameless."[99]

We make the law void if we teach faith supersedes the necessity of holiness or misrepresent what it means to be under a covenant of grace and not works. Wesley says that *only* Adam was under a covenant of works and that was *before* the Fall: "He was fully and properly under that covenant, which required perfect, universal obedience, as the one condition of acceptance, and left no place for pardon, upon the very least transgression."[100] This has not been required of any sinful human being since: "the manner of their acceptance is this: the free grace of God, through the merits of Christ, gives pardon to them that believe with such a faith as, working by love, produces all obedience and holiness."[101] He points out that it is a false belief that "faith supersedes the necessity of holiness…or that Christian liberty is a liberty from any kind or degree of holiness—so perverting those great truths that we are now under the *covenant of grace* and not of *works*" or that it excuses a lower standard of holiness.[102] Preaching should seek

> to produce all manner of holiness, negative and positive, of the heart and of the life…. In order to this we continually declare…that faith itself, even Christian faith, the faith of God's elect, the faith of the operation of God, still is only the handmaid of love. As glorious and honourable as it is, it is not the end of the commandment. God hath given this honour to love alone. Love is the end, the sole end, of every dispensation of God, from the beginning of the world to the consummation of all things. And it will endure when heaven and earth flee away; for 'love' alone 'never faileth'. Faith will totally fail; it will be swallowed up in sight, in the everlasting vision of God.[103]

Some say we can sin because grace abounds, but the Christian "obeys, not from the motive of slavish fear, but on a nobler principle, namely, the grace of God ruling in his heart, and causing all his works to be wrought in love."[104] Wesley asks, "Is love a less powerful motive than fear? If not, let it be an invariable rule, 'I will do nothing, now I am *under grace* which I durst not have done

---

[98] *Works* 2, "The Original, Nature, Properties, and Use of the Law," 16-18.

[99] *Works* 2, "The Original, Nature, Properties, and Use of the Law," 19.

[100] *Works* 2, "The Law Established through Faith, I," 27.

[101] *Works* 2, "The Law Established through Faith, I," 27.

[102] *Works* 2, "The Law Established through Faith, II," 33.

[103] *Works* 2, "The Law Established through Faith, II," 38.

[104] *Works* 2, "The Law Established through Faith, I," 29-30.

when *under the law'*."[105] So while we are justified by faith alone, good works must follow faith otherwise we are still in our sins; there is no righteousness or holiness before faith, but holiness must follow it.[106]

In early1770 Wesley wrote to a nobleman (perhaps the Earl of Dartmouth) about two different "ranks" of Christians, both of whom may be in the favour of God. The "lower" rank avoid all known sin, do much good, and use all the means of grace but have little of the life of God in the soul and are much conformed to the world. The "higher" rank make the Bible their whole rule of life and their sole aim is to do the will of God and be conformed to his image. In the steady pursuit of this they deny themselves and take up their cross daily, keeping a singular focus to attain most of the mind of Christ and to please him the most. He told the nobleman that he needed someone to encourage him for without it he will stop short—not of heaven "but of that degree of holiness, and consequently of happiness both in time and eternity, which is now offered to your acceptance."[107] This is a significant insight into Wesley's pastoral heart: being a Christian is not merely about escaping from condemnation, but is about living the most loving, the holiest and therefore the happiest life possible on earth in preparation for its continuance in heaven. Wesley denies that we need to sin in order to exalt righteousness by faith, otherwise it would be beneficial to have sin in heaven.[108] In the same vein, he wrote to Elizabeth Hardy and quoted a long list of texts that reject the notion of a sinning religion: "not only abundance of particular texts, but the whole tenor of Scripture declares, Christ came to 'destroy the works of the devil, to save us from our sins'—all the works of the devil, all our sins, without any exception or limitation.... But it is at least as much for His glory to cleanse us from them all before our death as after it."[109] Nevertheless, "For as long as we are in the body, we are liable to mistake and to speak or act according to that mistaken judgement. Therefore we cannot abide the rigor of God's strict justice, but still need mercy and forgiveness."[110] Exactly how this works out in practice is the focus of his pastoral advice, but he is in no doubt that the goal is scriptural and true to God's intentions in the provision of salvation through Christ.

---

[105] *Works* 2, "The Law Established through Faith, I," 31. This is equally true for sins of omission.
[106] *Works* 2, "The Law Established through Faith, I," 28.
[107] *Letters* (Telford) V: 173.
[108] *Letters* (Telford) III: 380-81.
[109] *Letters* (Telford) IV: 12.
[110] *Letters* (Telford) IV: 13.

A LIFE OF PURE LOVE[111]

As we have seen, Wesley believed that the life of God in the soul impacts both our being and our doing. God's desire is to transform us into the image of Christ by experiencing the love of God and then to live out that love in relationship with himself and the neighbour, by the right use of all the faculties with which God has endowed us. In a letter written to his niece, Sarah Wesley, in 1781, he notes that almost everyone feels the desire to flee from the "wicked world" and be at rest. "But it is not a wilderness that can give rest any more than a populous city. 'God hath made our heart for Himself, and it cannot rest till it resteth in Him.' You want only that one point, love—to love *Him* because He first loved *us*."[112] And it is love that is the fulfilling of the law that applies to us all since the Fall."[113] In the extended correspondence with 'John Smith' beginning in 1745, Wesley devotes much attention to love and the relationship with God and neighbour.[114] He reminds him that living a "good life" is not enough; these people "have not 'inward holiness'. They love the world, they love money. They love pleasure, or praise. Therefore, the love of God is not in them; nor consequently the Christian love of their neighbour."[115] He re-emphasises that "'Love is the fulfilling of the law.' I believe this love is given in a moment. But about this I contend not. Have this love, and it is enough. For this I will contend till my spirit returns to God."[116] This is "the very foundation of Christianity" and says "for it is true that from May 24, 1738, 'wherever I was desired to preach, *salvation by faith* was my only theme' (i.e., such a love of God and man as produces all inward and outward holiness, and springs from a conviction wrought in us by the Holy Ghost of the pardoning love of God)."[117] This encounter with God's love must be "felt" in the heart.[118]

> We mean that inspiration of God's Holy Spirit whereby he fills us with righteousness, peace, and joy, with love to him and to all mankind. And we believe it cannot be, in the nature of things, that a man should be filled with this peace and joy and love by the inspiration of the Holy Ghost without perceiving it, as clearly as he does the light of the sun.[119]

---

[111] There is some debate as to the best adjective to attach to love when referring to God's love. A number of scholars prefer the adjective 'holy' and while Wesley certainly uses this, he uses 'pure' much more frequently.

[112] *Letters* (Telford) VII: 58. See also *Letters* (Telford) VII: 267-68.

[113] *Works* 3, "On Patience," 174-75.

[114] 'John Smith' is the pseudonym adopted by one of Wesley's correspondents.

[115] *Works* 26: 202.

[116] *Works* 26: 159.

[117] *Works* 26: 183. See also *Works* 25: 670.

[118] *Works* 25: *Works* 25: 577-78.

[119] *Works* 26: 181-82.

In Wesley's own spiritual journey this experience of the love of God did not come easily. For instance, at the end of 1738 Wesley writes: "I can't yet love anyone as I ought, because I can't love our blessed Lord, *as I ought*. My heart is cold and senseless. It is indeed a heart of stone. O when will he take it out of the midst of me, and give me a heart of flesh? Pray for me…that our God would give me a broken heart, and a loving heart, a heart wherein his Spirit may delight to dwell."[120] Samuel Wesley Jnr. was less convinced of the central place of love and their correspondence reflects this. In particular Samuel mentions those of a melancholic and gloomy disposition, who constitutionally can't be changed without a miracle.[121] This is a telling point and it took many years before John himself was clear that love is not merely a human feeling or disposition. If it is God's love poured into our hearts by the Holy Spirit, then our own temperament is not the determining factor. Later he would acknowledge that this witness of the Spirit varies and it is not inconsistent with doubt, but faith, hope and love are totally the gift of God, and cannot arise from our own natural power.[122] It is grace that is the gift of God and he defined it as "that power of God which worketh in us both to will and to do of His good pleasure" and this is seen both by outward works and by being inwardly felt (specifically love, joy, peace): "men are satisfied they have grace, first by feeling these, and afterward by their outward actions."[123] In a series of letters to Dr. Henry Stebbing he points out that from this experience of grace "will spring many other things which till then he experienced not, as the love of God shed abroad in his heart, that peace of God which passeth all understanding, and joy in the Holy Ghost, joy, though not *unfelt*, yet *unspeakable* and full of glory."[124] These inward fruits of the Spirit must be felt: "When the Holy Ghost hath fervently kindled your love towards God, you will know these to be very sensible operations." Just as we hear and feel the wind by bodily organs, so we experience the work of the Spirit "by feeling it in your soul," as well as by outward effects.[125] He goes as far as saying, "Faith is seeing God; love is feeling God."[126] This experienced reality is tied to the direct witness of the Spirit and this must precede the testimony of our own spirit:

> We must be holy in heart and life before we can be conscious that we are so. But we must love God before we can be holy at all, this being the root of all holiness.

---

[120] *Works* 25: 584.

[121] *Works* 25: 613. See also 594, 598, 599-600, 645-47, 694.

[122] *Works* 26: 199.

[123] *Letters* (Telford) IV: 332.

[124] *Works* 25: 671.

[125] *Works* 25: 672. See also *Works* 26: 108. For an examination of the nature of 'experience' in Wesley, see Isabel Rivers, *Reason, Grace, and Sentiment: A Study of the Language of Religion and Ethics in England 1660-1780*. Vol. 1, *Whichcote to Wesley* (Cambridge: Cambridge University Press, 1991).

[126] *Works* 26: 108.

> Now we cannot love God till we know he loves us: 'We love him, because he first
> loved us.' And we cannot know his love to us till his Spirit witnesses to our
> spirit.... Since therefore the testimony of his Spirit must precede the love of God
> and all holiness, of consequence it must precede our consciousness thereof.[127]

It is the constant refrain of his letters concerning his people and their
experience—either commenting on how God's love fills their heart or else
praying for God to do this work.[128] Love filling the heart can be envisioned in
two distinct but interrelated ways. The first involves our capability to love—our
inclination to love God and neighbour as we ought. It is the work of the Holy
Spirit to create and shape this inclination as God always intended, rather than it
being directed in selfish and self-centred ways due to our sinfulness. The
second element is our capacity to receive and to give love. I Corinthians 13:8
reminds us that love will never end. This means our capacity for love will
continue to expand, both in terms of being filled with the love of the infinite
God in an ever-increasing measure, and the depths of love that we can then
share with the neighbour. Through the work of the Spirit, our capacity to
receive and give love, as well as our inclination to share love with both God
and neighbour may always increase. Wesley said to one of his correspondents:

> It comforts me to hear that your love does not decrease: I want it to increase daily.
> Is there not height and depth in Him with whom you have to do, for your love to
> rise infinitely higher and to sink infinitely deeper into Him than ever it has done
> yet?[129]

If this is to become our reality, then the first step is to repent. Wesley defines
this as knowing ourselves a sinner, governed by a perverse and distorted will,
alienated affections, and with our passions out of kilter. This is all tied to the
heart, and it can be summed up as the lust of the flesh, the lust of the eye and
the pride of life.[130] Scripture and experience both teach us that we cannot
change ourselves: "For so long as the tree remains evil, it cannot bring forth
good fruit."[131]

As the Holy Spirit begins his work in us and we are born again, then "There
is in that hour a general change from inward sinfulness to inward holiness. The

---

[127] *Works* 1, "The Witness of the Spirit, II," 290. See n. 17 for Outler's comments.
Wesley agrees that God may give this assurance gradually or in an instant; see *Works*
26: 157.

[128] See, for example, *Works* 25: 602-603.

[129] *Letters* (Telford) III: 217.

[130] *Works* 1, "The Way to the Kingdom," 226. In n. 64 Outler comments that 1 Jn 2:16 is
Wesley and Augustine's comprehensive definition of sin as an overreach of what are in
themselves innocent appetites and we are responsible for this. He then gives a long list
of sermons where this triad appears as well as in some of the letters.

[131] *Works* 1, "The Way to the Kingdom," 229.

love of the creature is changed into the love of the Creator, the love of the world into the love of God. Earthly desires, the desire of the flesh, the desire of the eyes, and the pride of life, are in that instant changed by the mighty power of God into heavenly desires."[132] This process of sanctification is explicitly tied to love: "Love is the sum of Christian sanctification: it is the one *kind* of holiness which is found, only in various degrees, in the believers who are distinguished by St. John into 'little children, young men, and fathers'. The difference between one and the other properly lies in the degree of love."[133] Wesley strongly believed that the doctrine of the "necessity of sinning" is "directly subversive of all holiness."[134] As we have seen, if we do not have a confidence in the power of God's grace to deal with the sin issue, then we will always be limiting God's work in our lives. There should be an increase in love from the first experience till a person is "thoroughly convinced of inbred sin, of the total corruption of his nature, to take it all away, to purify his heart and cleanse him from all unrighteousness" in order to love God with all our heart and soul.[135] Prior to this our holiness was mixed, as was our love and our will, but now "His whole soul is now consistent with itself: there is no jarring string. All his passions flow in a continued stream, with an even tenor to God."[136] Wesley goes on to say:

> there is no mixture of any contrary affections—all is peace and harmony. After being filled with love, there is no more interruption of that than the beating of his heart. And continual love bringing continual joy in the Lord, he rejoices evermore. He converses continually with the God whom he loves, unto whom in everything he gives thanks. And as he now loves God with all his heart, and with all his soul, and with all his mind, and with all his strength, so Jesus now reigns alone in his heart, the Lord of every motion there.[137]

He was confident that by grace alone, it is possible to love God with all our heart and serve him with all our strength and this is Christian perfection. In a letter to William Dodd in 1756 Wesley wrote, "When I began to make the Scriptures my study (about seven-and-twenty years ago), I began to see that Christians are called to *love God with all* their *heart* and to *serve Him with all their strength*; which is precisely what I apprehend to be meant by the scriptural term Perfection."[138] He reminded Walter Churchey in 1771 that "Entire

---

[132] *Works* 3, "On Patience," 174.

[133] *Works* 3, "On Patience," 175. See n. 44 on kind and degrees.

[134] *Letters* (Telford) III: 170.

[135] *Works* 3, "On Patience," 175.

[136] *Works* 3, "On Patience," 176.

[137] *Works* 3, "On Patience," 176.

[138] *Letters* (Telford) III: 157. See also *Letters* (Telford) III: 168; *Works* 2, "Christian Perfection," 104. Wesley's use of the term perfection caused endless debate with his

sanctification, or Christian Perfection, is neither more nor less than *pure love*
[emphasis mine]—love expelling sin and governing both the heart and life of a
child of God. The Refiner's fire purges out all that is contrary to love, and that
many times by a pleasing smart. Leave all this to Him that does all things well
and that loves you better than you do yourself."[139] God's love is 'pure' because
it is unmixed with any other motive, intention, or desire. Our human love is
corrupted by selfishness and self-centredness, though it is still capable of great
service and sacrifice by God's prevenient grace. Thus Wesley's concern in his
sermon on Matthew 6:19-23 for the "single eye" that we mentioned earlier.
This is then linked to holiness: "I still think that perfection is only another term
for holiness, or the image of God in man. God *made man perfect*, I think, is just
the same as He made him *holy*, or in *His own image*."[140]

Wesley admits that "Scriptures are silent upon the subject" of whether this
work of grace is gradual or instant, a process or a crisis. He allows for freedom
of opinion on this as long as we desire this experience of grace.[141] His own
inquiries led him to record that "every one of these...has declared that his
deliverance from sin was instantaneous, that the change was wrought in a
moment. ...[so] I cannot but believe that sanctification is commonly, if not
always, an *instantaneous* work."[142] However we understand it, it is always by
faith alone and not of works. So we need to believe God's promise, believe he
is able and he is willing "today" to fill the heart with love, expelling all sin. We
will then, in the Scriptural sense, be perfect (1Thess. 5:23), which refers "not so
much to the kind as to the degree of holiness. As if he [Paul] had said, 'Ye shall
enjoy as high a degree of holiness as is consistent with your present state of
pilgrimage.... loving him with all your heart (which is the sum of all
perfection)."[143] At this point we need to remind ourselves that there is a
difference between humanity as originally created, as fallen, as saved by grace
and as finally resurrected and glorified. Therefore, Wesley says:

> We expect to be 'made perfect in love', in that love which 'casts out' all painful
> 'fear', and all desire but that of glorifying him we love, and of loving and serving
> him more and more. We look for such an increase in the experimental knowledge
> and love of God our Saviour as will enable us always to 'walk in the light, as he is
> in the light'. We believe the whole 'mind' will be in us 'which was also in Christ
> Jesus'; that we shall love every man so as to be ready 'to lay down our life for his

---

critics, as well as within Methodism itself. He says he personally continues to use it
because it is scriptural, though he is not fond of it; see *Letters* (Telford) III: 167.

[139] *Letters* (Telford) V: 223. See also *Letters* (Telford) VI: 178.

[140] *Letters* (Telford) III: 168. See also *Letters* (Telford) V: 140-41.

[141] *Works* 3, "On Patience," 177.

[142] *Works* 3, "On Patience," 178. See also *Letters* (Telford) V: 333.

[143] *Works* 3, "On Patience," 179.

sake', so as by this love to be found freed from anger and pride, and from every unkind affection.[144]

He clearly limits perfection in this life to love—the love of God received in its fullness and shared by grace with the neighbour. While we are alive on earth there is no "absolute perfection" and no "perfection of degrees"; perfection in Wesley's sense always involves the possibility of continued increase, in both the knowledge and love of God.[145] He writes repeatedly that there is no perfection in knowledge or freedom from ignorance in this life, nor from the mistakes that arise from them. Since we are not God, we cannot ever have knowledge that is perfect in extent (though we can be sure of things essential to salvation), and this limitation leads to misjudgements of people and actions, as well as our understanding and application of Scripture.[146] Likewise, in this life, we are not free from bodily infirmities.[147] The physical nature of the body living in a disordered and corrupted environment makes it liable to weakness, sickness, disorder, pain, and death.[148] Even mature Christians deal with the consequences of weak and limited understanding: confusion, inaccuracy, mistakes, false judgments, wanderings of imagination, and so "the corruptible body press down the soul! And how many are the temptations which we have to expect, even from these innocent infirmities!"[149] There are "a thousand nameless defects either in conversation or behaviour. These are the infirmities which are found in the best of men in a larger or smaller proportion. And from these none can hope to be perfectly freed till the spirit returns to God that gave it."[150] These inward or outward imperfections are not of a moral nature and so are not sin because there is no condemnation for things we have no power to help; "There is no guilt, because there is no choice."[151] He reminded James Hervey that even when we are perfect in love "we should still need His Spirit, and consequently His intercession, for the continuance of that love from moment to moment. Beside, we should still be encompassed with infirmities and liable to mistakes, from which words or actions might follow, even though the heart was all love, which were not exactly right. Therefore in all these

---

[144] *Works* 2, "Satan's Devices," 140. See also *Works* 3, "On Perfection," 70-71.

[145] *Works* 2, "Christian Perfection," 105-105.

[146] *Works* 2, "Christian Perfection," 100-102.

[147] For an excellent, but short, examination of Wesley's understanding of infirmities and their relationship to sin, see Colin N. Peckham, *John Wesley's Understanding of Human Infirmities* (Ilkeston: The Wesley Fellowship, 1997).

[148] *Works* 3, "On Temptation," 159.

[149] *Works* 3, "On Temptation," 160. See also *Works* 2, "Wandering Thoughts," 130-37. Outler sees this as an important sermon on the limits of perfection, along with "On Sin in Believers" and "The Repentance of Believers."

[150] *Works* 2, "Christian Perfection," 103.

[151] *Works* 1, "The First-fruits of the Spirit," 41.

respects we should still have need of Christ's priestly office."[152] Furthermore, there is no freedom from temptation (even Jesus faced this). He reminded Joseph Algar that "by not 'going on to perfection' all believers will grow dead and cold; and then they are just ripe for levity, tattling, and evil-speaking, which will soon destroy all the life of God out of their souls." So he was to preach perfection as strongly and explicitly as possible.[153] Even those who had already experienced perfect love dare not rest on their current experience. He told Mrs. Pawson in 1789 that she had a special ministry to those enjoying or seeking perfect love and "You do well strongly to insist that those who do already enjoy it cannot possibly stand still. Unless they continue to watch and pray and aspire after higher degrees of holiness, I cannot conceive not only how they can go forward but how they can keep what they have already received." This was a point to be much insisted upon both in public and private, "that all who have tasted of the pure (love) of God should continually grow in grace, in the image of God, and in the knowledge of our Lord Jesus Christ."[154] In summary, Christian perfection is a gift of God's grace received by faith alone and the immediate "fruit" of this faith is power over sin, peace, hope and joy.[155] As a result of this, "Whether they are in ease or in pain, in sickness or health, in abundance or want, they are happy in God."[156]

Wesley is equally clear that "The necessary fruit of this love of God is the love of our neighbour, of every soul which God hath made."[157] Commenting on those who believe that keeping the outward commandments is sufficient, Wesley says:

> That the love of God is not an affection of the soul, but merely an *outward service*? And that the love of our neighbour is not a disposition of the heart, but barely a course of *outward works*? To mention so wild an interpretation of the Apostle's words [1 Jn. 5:3] is sufficiently to confute it. The plain indisputable meaning of that text is: 'this is the' sign or proof of the 'love of God', of our keeping the first and great commandment—to keep the rest of his commandments. For true love, if it be once shed abroad in our heart, will constrain us to do; since whosoever loves God with all his heart cannot but serve him with all his strength.

---

[152] *Letters* (Telford) III: 380.

[153] *Letters* (Telford) VII: 109. See also *Letters* (Telford) V: 276; *Letters* (Telford) VI: 66.

[154] *Letters* (Telford) VIII: 184. Wesley wrote in a letter to Adam Clarke in 1790: "Last week I had an excellent letter from Mrs. Pawson (a glorious witness of full salvation), showing how impossible it is to retain pure love without growing therein." See *Letters* (Telford) VIII: 249.

[155] *Works* 1, "The Marks of the New Birth," 419-25.

[156] *Works* 1, "The Marks of the New Birth," 422. See also 425.

[157] *Works* 1, "The Marks of the New Birth," 426. See n. 66 where the love of God is the substance of inward holiness and love of neighbour in the substance of outward holiness.

A second fruit then of the love of God (so far as it can be distinguished from it) is universal obedience to him we love, and conformity to his will; obedience to all the commands of God, internal and external; obedience of the heart and of the life, in every temper and in all manner of conversation.[158]

So the mark of a genuine Christian "is so to love God, who hath thus loved you, as you never did love any creature: so that ye are constrained to love all men as yourselves; with a love not only ever burning in your hearts, but flaming out in all your actions and conversations, and making your whole life one 'labour of love', one continued obedience to those commands, 'Be ye merciful, as God is merciful; 'Be ye holy as I the Lord am holy;' 'Be ye perfect, as your Father which is in heaven is perfect.'"[159] He emphasises that faith is "productive of all Christian *holiness*" rather than "Christian *practice*." This is because some are prone to rest in an "*outside* religion" rather than a "*heart*" religion.[160] A clear example of this is seen in 1771 when he reminded John Valton that "The most prevailing fault among the Methodists is to be *too outward* in religion. We are continually forgetting that the kingdom of God is *within us*, and that our fundamental principle is, We are saved by faith, producing all *inward* holiness, not by any externals whatever."[161] He also warned his people to be careful not to talk of a justified or sanctified "state" as it tends to lead people "to trust in what was done in one moment" whereas "Every hour God is more or less pleased with us according to the whole of our inward and outward behaviour."[162]

Wesley confidently proclaims that "true religion, or a heart right toward God and man, implies happiness as well as holiness," for it is linked to peace and joy in the Holy Spirit.[163] So both holiness and happiness are the "immediate fruit of God's reigning in the soul."[164] As we have seen, this centres on loving God totally (inward holiness) and our neighbour as ourselves (outward holiness). In a letter to Mrs. Woodhouse, Wesley affirms that "there is no happiness without Him for any child of man."[165] He is clearly claiming that we, by God's grace alone, may fulfil the Great Commandment to love God and neighbour; such a life is therefore holy, and consequently happy. The three are inseparably and intimately linked, so that you cannot truly experience the one without experiencing the other. Wesley can confidently say to Thomas Rutherford in 1881, "I wish Isabella and you much happiness, which you

---

[158] *Works* 1, "The Marks of the New Birth," 427.

[159] *Works* 1, "The Marks of the New Birth," 428.

[160] *Works* 26: 179.

[161] *Letters* (Telford) V: 289.

[162] *Letters* (Telford) V: 265.

[163] *Works* 1, "The Way to the Kingdom," 223. See also n. 31 and the other sermons listed by Outler.

[164] *Works* 1, "The Way to the Kingdom," 224.

[165] *Letters* (Telford) V: 174. Apparently her husband did not approve of Methodism.

cannot fail of if you have much holiness. Therefore the certain way to make each other happy is to strengthen each other's hands in God."[166] It is the quality of the life with God that is the determining factor, and not outward circumstances. In a letter to Jane Bisson (later Mrs. Cock) in 1783, he can write: "It gives me much pleasure to find you are still happy in God, leaning upon your Beloved. O may you increase therein more and more! May you be more and more holy, and you will be more and more happy."[167] That this was not expected to be a momentary experience is underscored by another letter to her four years later: "I rejoice to hear that you are still happy in God; and trust that happiness will never cease but rather increase more and more till your spirit returns to God. Be assured there is no necessity that it ever should cease. He is willing to give it you always; and *He can purify you by the fire of His love as well as by the fire of afflictions* [emphasis mine]. Do not therefore expect or desire affliction, but let the joy of the Lord be your strength.[168] This underscores Wesley's expectation that our experience of happiness in God need never cease and spiritual formation does not require us to experience suffering. On the other hand, happiness was not just to be the experience of those who were living without affliction. For example, Wesley encourages Miss Cummins (clearly a woman in very poor health) to use the time she has left wisely and reminds her "what are called pleasures and diversions can give you no solid happiness" because she was created for better things—a life with God.[169] Then he asks if she is afraid to die, is she "happy in God," can she say, "I have nothing need, beneath, above, Happy, happy in Thy love?"[170] Wesley expected a positive answer to his question. This seems to be completely unrealistic to many in the light of everyday human experience. How can anybody be happy when personally experiencing pain, suffering and grief, or when empathising with others going through such things? If in the past Wesley had trouble with the word perfection, today it would be with the word happiness because of the way we commonly understand it. It is little wonder that this question occupies much of Wesley's pastoral correspondence. Before turning to this material in the next two chapters, it is important to be reminded that his understanding of love, holiness and happiness are all within the context of a relationship with God, and subsequently with neighbour. It is the quality of the relationship that is critical; if this is poor, then all his claims fall to the ground.

---

[166] *Letters* (Telford) VII: 72.

[167] *Letters* (Telford) VII: 189. See also *Letters* (Telford) V: 337.

[168] *Letters* (Telford) VIII: 4-5.

[169] *Letters* (Telford) VI: 30.

[170] *Letters* (Telford) VI: 31.

Chapter 4

Spiritual Formation:
Challenges to Developing the Life of God in the Soul

In a letter to James Barry in 1787, Wesley quotes a London preacher to the effect that if you try and take away a child's rattle it will become angry and probably try to scratch or bite you. However, if you first offer the child something better, it will throw away the rattle itself.[1] As many parents will know, getting the baby to part with its plaything is easier said than done. It is often a mystery as to what motivates the child to reach out for the new item and let go of the old; what seems to work in one situation will not work in the next. Simply saying that something is 'bad' rarely works, nor does seeking to remove it by force—even if the thing is actually harmful or dangerous to the child's welfare. As a loving parent we try to find the thing that will appeal to our child so that it prefers to have the new item rather than the one it already has. We need to find something that is appealing to the senses, is more desirable than the current item, and holds out the promise of greater pleasure. If this is a problem for a parent, it is even more of a problem for the person seeking to help another cultivate the life of God in the soul.

Wesley believed that in our current human condition nothing "is more natural to us than to seek happiness in the creature instead of the Creator."[2] If we are 'happy' with our current sources of pleasure and satisfaction, we are not going to be easily induced to give them up—even if it is harmful to our well-being. Seeking to change people's addiction to drugs (legal or otherwise) by simply saying it is 'bad for you' or trying to change behaviour by the power of the law is rarely successful in the short term, let alone for the long term. Merely providing information and education is ineffective; authorities must try to find that which is more appealing and has a more desirable outcome, both personally and relationally. Car companies rarely bother providing us with reams of facts and figures as to why their car is better than the others—it is by creating a desire associated with the perceived benefits of ownership that entice us to change. As we noted earlier, "No man loves God by nature.... What we love, we delight in: but no man has naturally any delight in him. We take no pleasure in him at all; he is utterly tasteless to us."[3] Though in the initial glow of our new relationship with God, this may seem to be a thing of the past, it

---

[1] *Letters* (Telford) VIII: 12.
[2] *Works* 2, "Original Sin," 179-80.
[3] *Works* 2, "Original Sin," 178.

soon re-emerges and we discover that we are not as easily parted from this yearning as we think. What is it that will resonate with us and cause us to investigate whether life in God will be more satisfying than our present experience and will then keep us motivated to develop the relationship to its full potential? This raises the whole issue of motivation. If our present experience fails to deliver what it apparently promised, then we will seek for someone or something else to provide the missing satisfaction. If we are going to consider God as the answer to our present dissatisfaction, then we need to consider two key elements: our openness to the possibility that God will satisfy the heart (motivation) and our willingness to trust that God genuinely cares for us (providence). We briefly examine both of these before turning to Wesley's pastoral advice in which he identifies some of the critical hindrances to living in love with God and neighbour.

Motivation

The Psalmist reminds us, "Taste and see that the Lord is good" (Ps. 34:8, NIV). So what would induce us to try the 'taste test'?[4] We are tempted to try some new taste if we are hungry, inquisitive, or intrigued by a new experience. Boredom and restlessness also make us open to new possibilities. It is at this point that we come to Wesley's oft-quoted statement from Augustine: "Thou hast made us for thyself; and our heart cannot rest until it resteth in thee."[5] This human desire for 'rest' is a deep theological conviction for Wesley and it is the basis for his confidence in the appeal of the gospel. Ultimately, rest and happiness are one and the same in Wesley's understanding, since when our hearts are truly at rest in God, we are truly happy. This keeps it centred on love and relationships, as this is the creational framework for human existence. Hebrews 11:25 (NIV) makes reference to the enjoyment of "the fleeting pleasures of sin" and this reminds us that, like the child with the rattle, we are initially easily amused by anything that catches our attention; but the verse (and Augustine) reminds us it does not ultimately last. Our Creator God has so made us that nothing outside of a loving relationship with him and the neighbour can fully and finally satisfy and enable us to live without shame, guilt or regret.

This can be illustrated by his correspondence with his nephew, Charles Wesley, who was making a name for himself as a court organist. He tells him that he is now at a critical point: "just launching into life, and ready to fix your choice, whether you will have God or the world for your happiness. Scripture and reason tell you now, what experience will confirm, if it pleases God to

---

[4] For an examination of the role of desire in our motivation, see James K. A. Smith, *Desiring the Kingdom: Worship, Worldview, and Cultural Formation* (Grand Rapids: Baker Academic, 2009).

[5] *Works* 3, "The Important Question," 189. Some other examples can be found in *Works* 3, "Spiritual Worship," 97, 102; *Works* 2, "The End Of Christ's Coming," 478-81.

prolong your life—that He made your heart for Himself, and it cannot rest till it rests in Him."[6] The world will try to divert him from this truth and the example of those around him will certainly make an impression and incline him to think as they do. It will only be the depth of his relationship with God that keeps him safe in such an environment: "And as your *business* rather than your *choice* calls you into the fire, I trust that you will not be burnt; seeing He whom you desire to serve is able to deliver you even out of the burning fiery furnace."[7] It is the human desire for happiness that Wesley identifies as the critical motivation, and he narrows down our myriad choices to two: God or the world that he created. The immediate appeal is certainly strongest from the world and all it offers in terms of pleasure and satisfaction. Human experience demonstrates that pleasurable experiences and abundant possessions only go so far in meeting the deepest needs of our heart. Happiness is not ultimately to be found in an 'I—it' connection, where the 'it' can be any experience, thing, or person that we use as an object for our own selfish pleasure. We see every day how people can be reduced to objects that we use for our own satisfaction, with pornography being but one example. Happiness can only truly be found in an "I—thou" connection, where the 'thou' is another person with whom we have a genuine loving relationship. People can live with many disadvantages in life if they know they are loved, and can love others in return.

The very notion of loving God, finding pleasure and delight in him above all of his creation is decidedly 'unnatural' and 'unappealing' to us in our present condition because of sin, which is essentially to love the creature more than the Creator. We are now convinced that the fullness of life, pleasure and delight are found in using people or material things to provide us with gratifying experiences that we can obtain on our own terms. This must change if we are to progress in our life with God and with the neighbour. Wesley's mother, Susanna, had advised him that the best way to develop his own spiritual life would be to meditate more on the love of God, for if we lose God "we lose all good, all happiness, all peace, all pleasure, health and joy; all that is either good in itself, or can be good for us."[8] She told him that we cannot truly know what love is until we are united to God "and there read its wondrous nature in the clear mirror of Uncreated Love!"[9] It is only as we encounter God himself through the ministry of the Holy Spirit that we can experience the true nature of love, without the damage and distortion created by our self-centredness. Wesley wholeheartedly agreed with this and in his extensive pastoral correspondence, as well as his more formal writings, reminded everyone that it is God himself and our relationship with him that lies at the heart of the whole

---

[6] *Letters* (Telford) VII: 81.
[7] *Letters* (Telford) VII: 81.
[8] *Works* 25: 384.
[9] *Works* 25: 217.

Christian religion. So the place to begin is with the quality and depth of our relationship with God himself.

> But what is it to love God? Is not to love anything the same as habitually to delight in it? Is not then the purport of both these injunctions this, that we delight in the Creator more than his creatures? That we take more pleasure in him than in anything he had made? And rejoice in nothing so much as in serving him? That (to take Mr. Pascal's expression) while the generality of men use God and enjoy the world, we on the contrary only use the world while we enjoy God.[10]

Providence

As we saw in chapter 2, Wesley believed God had created us as free creatures, with the power to exercise real choices. This had to remain true even after we had sinned, and God remains committed to dealing with us as free agents and will not coerce or overrule our choices, as that would be a violation of love. This leaves us with a conundrum—how does the Sovereign Creator interact with his creation in such a way that his own intentions and purposes are fulfilled while respecting the freedom of the human race? The two ends of the spectrum are usually rejected by Christians: God as Sovereign directly causes all things (fatalism) or God is powerless to deal with the creatures he made and is at the mercy of their decisions and actions (chaos). Our understanding of the nature of God will incline us to settle closer to one end of the spectrum or the other, but most Christians freely confess that God's governance of his creation remains essentially a mystery. The New Testament language of God as our Loving Father and Christians as his beloved children gives us some grounds for trying to understand divine providence in relational terms. Family relationships cannot be truly loving and healthy if the parent forces the child to conform 100% to their will, nor can a genuine relationship exist if the child acts in ways that are totally rebellious and destructive. A loving parent desires that their child will develop their full potential while still maintaining a deep relationship of love. However, genuine love must respect the choices the child makes and that means also accepting the consequences of their choice—both for them and the parent. A parent will try to prevent the child making a wrong or destructive choice by sharing their own wisdom and taking appropriate action. What is appropriate for a toddler and what is appropriate for a mature adult cannot be the same if we are to respect their personhood. We try to avert the consequences or minimise the harm that follows a wrong choice, but the more the child is fully responsible for their choices, the more they need to face the outcomes or their personal freedom is violated. The parent's love does not cease just because the consequences might be destructive and love will always seek a way to redeem the situation without destroying the child's liberty.

---

[10] *Works* 25: 270.

Wesley deals with the subject of providence extensively in his formal writings and his correspondence. In the sermon "On Divine Providence" (1786) we find his mature reflection on the topic.[11] He admits that divine providence will always be a mystery to us, but the clearest account of it is found in the Scriptures. The particular text of the sermon (that the very hairs of our head are numbered by God) implies that "nothing is small that concerns the happiness of any of his creatures."[12] Wesley affirms that there is both a general providence (God's governance of the creation as a whole) and a particular providence (God's care of the individual person, especially the Christian).[13] God, in his omnipresence, also sustains and preserves every element of his creation, and watches over every aspect of it. He knows "all the connections, dependencies, and relations, and all the ways wherein one of them can affect the other."[14] As a loving God, he is not unmoved by what he sees, nor does he remain uninvolved when things go wrong. As Wesley says, the Scripture assures us that even if a mother would forget her children, God will never forget us, though this is often hard to believe in a world filled with pain and misery.[15] We are called to trust that God "is infinite in wisdom as well as power; and all his wisdom is continually employed for the good of all his creatures."[16] As we saw earlier, God could have removed all pain and suffering by his own omnipotent power, but to do so would have necessitated overruling our liberty and destroying the very nature of love.[17] God governs all his creation, including humanity, in ways that are true to his nature as love and the attendant freedom that belongs to all healthy relationships. He knows everything that we experience and is with us through them all, watching over "every circumstance that relates either to their souls or bodies, either to their inward or outward state, wherein either their present or eternal happiness is in any degree concerned."[18] This is true for humanity in general, but especially for those who have responded to his loving grace and become Christians.[19] Wesley closes his sermon by saying that what we learn from this understanding of providence is "to put our whole trust in him who hath never failed them that seek him" and to be thankful for his

---

[11] *Works* 2, "On Divine Providence," 2: 535-50. Outler points out that he used the text Lk. 12:7 at least 45 times between 1744 and 1785; see his introductory comment on 534. See also *Works* 3, "Spiritual Worship," 91-94; *Works* 4, "On Guardian Angels," 225-35; *Works* 2, "Thoughts Upon God's Sovereignty," 548-50; *Works* (Jackson) XI, "Serious Thoughts Occasioned by the Late Earthquake at Lisbon," 1-13.

[12] *Works* 2, "On Divine Providence," 537.

[13] *Works* 2, "On Divine Providence," 543-50.

[14] *Works* 2, "On Divine Providence," 539.

[15] *Works* 2, "On Divine Providence," 539. The reference is to Isa. 49:15.

[16] *Works* 2, "On Divine Providence," 540.

[17] See also *Works* (Jackson) XI, "An Estimate of the Manners of the Present Times," 160.

[18] *Works* 2, "On Divine Providence," 543.

[19] *Works* 2, "On Divine Providence," 541-43.

providential care.[20] This requires that we walk closely with God, not presuming on his provision by being careless, indolent or slothful, and doing all we can to take care of ourselves and others.[21]

Rules, Regulations and Relationships

In the sermon "The First-fruits of the Spirit" (1746) Wesley points out that if we walk after the Spirit in our hearts and lives, we are taught of him to love God and neighbour "with a love which is as 'a well of water springing up into everlasting life'. And by him they are led into every holy desire, into every divine and heavenly temper, till every thought which arises in their heart is holiness unto the Lord."[22] It all sounds so simple! It is very easy to miss the critical condition: it is only "if" we walk after the Spirit. Wesley is confident that the limiting factor does not lie with God's grace, but with our failure to cooperate with the grace God gives and consequently falling back into lives of defeat. Becoming more like our Lord and Saviour Jesus Christ is certainly not automatic, nor is it a simple list of do's and don'ts that can be followed thoughtlessly and without much effort.

For many in the church a list of rules and regulations to follow does seem to be the most straightforward way of advancing our Christian life and demonstrating to others that we are being transformed. At first glance Wesley and his Methodists seem to embrace endless lists of things to do or not do, say or not say, and places to go or not go. We read his "General Rules of the United Societies" and see a list similar to other lists about character and behaviour. Wesley himself never regarded them as a comprehensive and infallible set of rules to be simply put into practice: "These are the General Rules of our societies; all of which we are taught of God to observe, even in his written Word, the only rule, and the sufficient rule, both of our faith and practice. And all of these we know his Spirit writes on every truly awakened heart."[23] The foundation here is clearly Scripture, but Scripture illuminated by the Holy Spirit. And we need this illumination because "the Scripture, in most points, gives only general rules; and leaves the particular circumstances to be adjusted by the common sense of mankind."[24] In order to apply any particular rule, the Christian is to consider the outcome in their personal life and in the life of the neighbour. We are to make use of the reason God has given to us personally and as a community, as well observing the practical outcomes in other people and communities. There is always a danger of replacing a dependency on the

---

[20] *Works* 2, "On Divine Providence," 548.
[21] *Works* 2, "On Divine Providence," 549.
[22] *Works* I, "The First-fruits of the Spirit," 236.
[23] *Works*, 9:73.
[24] *Works*, 9:263.

work of the Spirit with a mechanical application of the general rules.[25] This makes it important to consult with those experienced in the ways of God over such questions.[26] We need to ask if this is an "appointed means which it generally pleases God to bless."[27] The lives of the members of the societies were significant as models for seekers to follow and as sources of spiritual experience and encouragement.[28] Our conscience is also important in decision-making, as long as it is formed and evaluated by Scripture.[29] The Christian needs to keep in balance the evidence of the internal assurance and the outward change to minimise self-delusion.

Wesley reminds Ann Foard that "we are continually forming general rules from our own particular experience."[30] This arises when I assume, either consciously or unconsciously, that the things which so helpfully shaped my life would also be best to shape yours, without taking any account of the fact that we are different people with different experiences, strengths and weaknesses. The danger is equally acute for communities, when those in one cultural setting assume their way is God's way for all cultural settings. In both cases, the possibility of being self-deluded about the benefits of our regime is never seriously considered. Just because I find it difficult to regulate my time on Facebook and have found the only way to deal with it is to ban it completely, does not mean that everyone has difficulty in regulating their time and perhaps for them it does not need to be banned but simply controlled.

The imposing of rules on ourselves and on others as the surest guide to holy living is made more difficult if we believe that God intends for us to be happy and to enjoy the life that he has given us. How do we decide what is legitimate pleasure and what is not? In an early letter to John concerning the writings of Thomas à Kempis, Susanna wrote:

> I take Kempis to have been an honest, weak man, that had more zeal than knowledge, by his condemning all mirth or pleasure as sinful or useless, in opposition to so many direct and plain texts of Scripture. Would you judge of the lawfulness or unlawfulness of pleasure, of the innocence or malignity of actions? Take this rule. Whatever weakens your reason, impairs the tenderness of your conscience, obscures your sense of God, or takes off your relish of spiritual things; in short, whatever increases the strength and authority of your body over your mind; that thing is sin to you, however innocent it may be itself. And so on the contrary.[31]

---

[25] *Letters* (Telford), 5: 344. See also *Letters* (Telford), 6: 263; 7: 224.

[26] *Letters* (Telford), 5: 278; 6: 58, 126, 127, 178, 239.

[27] *Letters* (Telford), 5: 237.

[28] See for example *Letters* (Telford), 5: 261-62, 290; 7: 167.

[29] *Letters* (Telford), 5: 302-303. See also *Letters* (Telford), 5: 277-78.

[30] *Letters* (Telford) IV: 269.

[31] *Works* 25:166.

His mother's advice makes the point that Christianity cannot finally be reduced to a set of mechanical rules and regulations to be applied indiscriminately to all people, without losing its essential nature. John, in his early years, tried to live an authentic Christian life by a very careful observance of rules of conduct, personal devotion and worship practices, but found it to be a failure, however, this does not negate the need for guidance and advice in seeking to be like Christ. John's correspondence was filled with the wisdom he had gained as the leader and spiritual guide of the Methodist people and what follows is an examination of some of the critical hindrances to living in love with God and neighbour.

Spiritual Idolatry: the Desire of the Flesh, the Desire of the Eye, and the Pride of Life

In his sermon "Spiritual Idolatry" Wesley establishes the close connection between idolatry and love: "As there is no firm foundation for the love of our brethren except the love of God, so there is no possibility of loving God except we 'keep ourselves from idols'."[32] The phrase from 1 John 2:16 is very commonly quoted by Wesley as a major hindrance to the full life of God in the soul. The context of the verse shows the focus is on the only God who is

> the end of all the souls he has made, the centre of all created spirits—'and eternal life,' the only foundation of present as well as eternal happiness. To him therefore alone our heart is due. And he cannot, he will not quit his claim, or consent to its being given to any other.... And to give our heart to any other is plain idolatry. Accordingly, whatever takes our heart from him, or share it with him, is an idol; or, in other words, whatever we seek happiness in, independent of God.[33]

Wesley defines "the desire of the flesh" as "seeking happiness in the gratification of any or all of the external senses," especially taste, smell, and feeling. The "desire of the eye" is "seeking happiness in gratifying the imagination" and it is also tied to the pursuit of novelty in the form of diversions and amusements.[34] The "pride of life" is seeking praise or being proud. In short, "to seek happiness" in any desire, any object, any human person is idolatry.[35] This comprehensive definition avoids the common caricature that idolatry is tied to worshipping some form of natural or carved image. It reminds us that even worthy things, such as our love for others and the goodness of creation can become idolatrous if they displace the primacy of

---

[32] *Works* 3, "Spiritual Idolatry," 103.

[33] *Works* 3, "Spiritual Idolatry," 104-105.

[34] *Works* 3, "Spiritual Idolatry," 106-08. See also *Works* 2, "The Wisdom of God's Counsels," 560-61.

[35] *Works* 3, "Spiritual Idolatry," 109.

loving God from the heart.[36] They become idolatrous when we seek our happiness in them alone.[37] To avoid this, we must "be deeply convinced that none of them bring happiness."[38] None of them can bring true and lasting contentment and "discontent is incompatible with happiness." Universal experience "clearly proves that as God made our hearts for himself, so they cannot rest till they rest in him."[39]

In October 1732 his mother, Susanna, approved his stance against anything that increases "the lust of the flesh, the lust of the eye, and the pride of life"; this included such diversions as horse racing, masquerades, balls, plays, and operas. While it was not impossible to be religious and attend these, she pointed out that no "serious Christian" would do so and no one who loved God would find any relish for such vain amusements.[40] A little later she commends him on his spiritual practices and that he should continue to "renounce all insubordinate love of the world, and to love and obey God with all his strength."[41] John's struggles with this led him to go to Georgia as a missionary to the Indian tribes and he sought to justify his choice by saying it would enable him to escape the types of temptations found in England by going to a group uncorrupted by English society. He believed this would enable him to more easily mortify the lust of the eye, the lust of the flesh and the desire for sensual pleasures. Their simple food would prevent him seeking that happiness in food and drink which God had designed to be found only in faith, love and joy in the Holy Spirit. He affirmed that there was no hope of real holiness in England due to the temptation to take the easy road.[42] He was to discover that changing your geographic location and community did not change the nature and force of temptation to idolatry. Self-indulgence can be found in any circumstance, situation or community because it is essentially a matter of the heart and not a matter of external location.[43]

---

[36] *Works* 3, "Spiritual Idolatry," 106-108. See also *Works* 2, "The Wisdom of God's Counsels," 560-61.

[37] *Works* 3, "Spiritual Idolatry," 109.

[38] *Works* 3, "Spiritual Idolatry," 111.

[39] *Works* 3, "Spiritual Idolatry," 112. See also 113-14.

[40] *Works* 25: 345. See Susanna's 'rules' on discerning sin and a letter to Mary Pendarves on p. 277.

[41] *Works* 25: 354.

[42] *Works* 25: 439-41. See Emilia Wesley's letter of August 13, 1735 in which she claims he lost Mrs. Chapone because he denied the place of human love; 430-31. See also the letter to Samuel Wesley Jnr. with its special mention of the lusts of the flesh, of the eye and the pride of life; *Works* 25: 444.

[43] *Works* 3, "On God's Vineyard," 515. He gives a long list of the things that please the eye on 516.

Lifestyle

One of the areas of life where our desires become most evident is our chosen lifestyle or the one that we yearn to have and will spend our time, effort and money to acquire. Beneath the specific items that Wesley often lists is a deep concern for the implications of the lifestyle chosen by those who identify themselves as Christians. He saw this as the litmus test of the depth of their understanding and subsequent commitment to the relationship with God and neighbour. For example, he warned Ebenezer Blackwell about his business taking away his focus on God: "Are not even lawful, nay necessary, things at other times a grievous hindrance, especially when we undertake them without any suspicion of danger, and consequently without any prayer against that danger?"[44] The danger was that things which are lawful and necessary rarely lead to an examination of the heart and so can easily slip into idolatry. As the Methodist movement sought to honour God and be faithful stewards of God's blessings, many became rich and successful business people. He warned his people that if we slide "into the love of the world, by the same degrees that this enters in, the love of God will go out of the heart."[45] This was easy to say but often hard to do in practice, so he regularly offered advice on how to distinguish a godly use of God's provision from an idolatrous one. He reminds Samuel Furly that while Jesus explicitly required the rich young ruler to sell all he had in order to escape covetousness (Matt. 19:16-22), "we are nowhere commanded so to do. Let any man show the contrary if he can."[46] In the case of Judith Madan, who was a wealthy woman, the two easy options were to dispose of all her wealth and live in poverty, or to simply keep things as they were because her wealth was a blessing from God. Wesley is aware that neither of these options will actually glorify God.

> You are not at liberty to choose what is, absolutely speaking, the most excellent way—which is to cut off all superfluity of every kind, to expend all our time and all our substance in such a manner as will most conduce to the glory of God and our own eternal happiness. Nor is it easy to say how far you may vary from this. Something must be allowed to the circumstances you are in. But who can say how much? Only the Spirit of God, only the unction from above which teacheth us of all things.[47]

She was in a situation where she had certain obligations and was therefore not free to suit only herself by disposing of all her wealth beyond her own necessities, nor could she simply keep the status quo without sinning. It is important to notice that he does not offer her a simple set of rules and

---

[44] *Letters* (Telford) III: 216.

[45] *Works* 2, "The Wisdom of God's Counsels," 560-61. See also *Letters* (Telford) IV: 88.

[46] *Works 26*: 557.

[47] *Works 26*: 440-41.

regulations to follow or a formula to apply. She must rely on the wisdom and guidance of the Holy Spirit, who will take into account her circumstances. He does advise her, however, to redeem as much time as she can "from fashionable folly" and indicates such things as fashionable dress, useless diversions and trifling conversation.[48] In a later sermon, he will try and clarify that the problem with fashion is our desire to be admired and praised by others, rather than seeking to please God alone.[49] The danger is how much our use of money is governed by covetousness. That is why he warns Miss Johnson that her recent substantial inheritance brings danger and, depending on her use of the gift, "You may be hereby far more happy or far more miserable in eternity!"[50] On the other hand, he can advise Mrs. Hall that God, who knows what is best, withheld prosperity to save her from pride, self-will and the hurtful desires that come with abundance. But even with the little she has, she is to "Be good and do good to the utmost of your present power, and then happy are you."[51]

An interesting insight into how Wesley counselled people over their lifestyle is seen in his correspondence with Sir James Lowther. Lowther was deeply concerned about his spiritual life because he was very wealthy and feared he loved the world more than God. Wesley reminds him that God is "the sole proprietor of all things"; he is therefore God's "steward," who is called to take care of business and use the money wisely, because the danger of loving money more than God is always present.[52] He sought to show Lowther the difference between "worldly and Christian prudence"; worldly prudence either seeks worldly ends (riches, honour, ease, pleasure), or pursues Christian ends on worldly maxims or by worldly means, thinking that the more power, money, learning or reputation we have, the more good we can do. Wesley says that if a Christian follows this line of thinking he will decline slowly into worldly prudence: "He will use more or less of conformity to the world, if not in sin, yet in doing some things that are good in themselves, yet (all things considered) are not good to him; and perhaps at length using guile or disguise; simulation or dissimulation; either seeming to be what he is not, or not seeming to be what he is."[53] Once again we see a similar perspective to that offered by Susanna Wesley on the nature of sin: it cannot be exactly defined, but is tied to what can damage the relationship with God and neighbour. Christian prudence seeks Christian maxims by Christian means. This keeps us relying on God and not human power to achieve outcomes that both glorify God and help our neighbour. It reminds us that God uses the weak, the foolish, and the poor to

---

[48] *Works* 26: 441.
[49] *Works* 3, "On Dress," 252-254.
[50] *Letters* (Telford) IV: 59.
[51] *Letters* (Telford) III: 199.
[52] *Works* 26: 543-45.
[53] *Letters* (Telford) IV: 63.

achieve his aims.[54] Given the popularity of the 'wealth and prosperity gospel' in western nations and our propensity to cultivate relationships with wealthy Christians and Christian organisations to fund our ministry projects, Wesley's concerns are certainly relevant to our own day. He encourages Lowther to practice discerning the voice of God by following the one rule (the Word of God) with the one guide (the Holy Spirit).[55] Human advice is always going to be limited because "General rules cannot reach all particular cases, in some of which there is such a complication of circumstances that God alone can show what steps we should take."[56] There is always a danger of getting guidance from people who can hardly be impartial one way or the other on such issues, so Lowther must himself read the Scripture, prayerfully meditate on its content and seek God's wisdom directly by the ministry of the Holy Spirit.[57] Pastorally, Wesley recognized that there would always be differing opinions on any proposed course of action due to our limited understanding of God and his ways. Therefore it was important to in the end to follow our own conscience on practical matters just as much as it was on doctrinal matters.[58]

Wesley does not see poverty as a virtue in and of itself, nor does it automatically wean us from covetousness and the misuse of God's resources. The general principles of how to avoid the trap of idolatry were laid down in a sermon entitled "The Use of Money" (1760). He saw no inherent problem with the proper use and *gain* of money and told people that they were free to do this as long as it did not hurt the neighbour by damaging their body (the sale of harmful substances) or their soul (by the promotion of temptation and sin).[59] Then they were to *save* all they can by not wasting money merely to gratify the desire of the flesh, the desire of the eye or the pride of life. Finally, and most importantly for their spiritual welfare, they were to *give* all they can for the service of God and the neighbour.[60] Wesley believed that the creation was "very good" and its use was to promote "the glory of God in the happiness of his intelligent creatures,"[61] but he was concerned with the deceitfulness of riches, with people gaining and saving all they could but not faithfully giving back to God. This is tied to the depth of relationship we have with God and with the neighbour. The shallower the relationship, the less we will be inclined to give; the deeper the relationship the more we will want to give. As Wesley

---

[54] *Letters* (Telford) IV: 63.

[55] *Letters* (Telford) IV: 64.

[56] *Letters* (Telford) IV: 66.

[57] *Letters* (Telford) IV: 66. See also his advice to his brother's widow in *Letters* (Telford) VIII: 76.

[58] *Works*, 2:86. See also *Works*, 20: 122. More information on Wesley's understanding and use of private judgement can be found in Leon O. Hynson, "The Right of Private Judgement," *Asbury Theological Journal* 60, no. 1 (Spring, 2005).

[59] *Works* 2, "The Use of Money," 270-72.

[60] *Works* 2, "The Use of Money," 273-80.

[61] *Works* 2, "The Wisdom of God's Counsels," 552.

said, we need wisdom so that we neither harm those for whom we are responsible, nor endlessly indulge our selfish desires through our stewardship of God's good gifts.

Wesley saw relationships as essential to our spiritual wellbeing and he regularly advised his people on how to nourish and nurture their family, church and community life. An unhealthy relationship could become a snare in our walk with God and he told Ebenezer Blackwell that his friendships might be hindering his progress in holiness because he is "carrying a right principle too far? I mean, a desire to please all men for their good. Or is it a kind of shame? The being ashamed, not of sin, but of holiness, or of what conduces thereto?" He asks him to reflect upon whether he was spending too much time with non-Christians, seeking to please them and in the process giving way on many areas of Christian practice? Wesley warned him that giving way on one point leads to another till all is lost.[62] Another area of concern was that of marriage and family. Wesley affirmed that spouses and children "ought to love one another tenderly: they are commanded to do so. But they are neither commanded nor permitted to love one another idolatrously!" What he identifies here is the danger that "they seek their happiness in the creature, not in the Creator." [63] This is a very subtle temptation and one that in our day, with its emphasis on the power of romantic love, is even harder to escape. In some western cultures we seem to have elevated the family to the status of an idol, alongside the notion of the perfect partner who will bring us total fulfilment. Of course, when this does not happen, then we simply look for some other relationship to try and fill the void. Wesley expressed his concern for Ann Taylor and her proposed marriage precisely on these grounds. From a young age she had a desire to love and serve God, but the "real temptation will be, especially while you are young, to seek happiness in some creature."[64] He goes on to talk about those who think happiness is found in marriage to a particular person:

> Vain thought! Happiness is not in man; no, nor any creature under heaven.... When you begin to know God as *your* God, then, and not before, you begin to be happy; but much more when you love Him. And as you increase in loving faith your happiness will increase in the same proportion. Steer steady to this point. Keep the issues of the heart! By Almighty grace keep yourself from idols.[65]

He advises her to find one or two Christian friends with whom she can discuss her situation, while keeping up private prayer and reading the Bible.[66] However, a Christian marriage could be a real source of blessing and he told Jane Bisson: "It gives me much pleasure to find you are still happy in God, leaning upon

---

[62] *Works* 26: 505. See also *Works* 26: 542.

[63] *Works* 3, "Spiritual Idolatry," 111. See also *Letters* (Telford) VIII: 152.

[64] *Letters* (Telford) VII: 374.

[65] *Letters* (Telford) VII: 374.

[66] *Letters* (Telford) VII: 374.

your Beloved. O may you increase therein more and more! May you be more and more holy, and you will be more and more happy!"[67] In a later letter he tells her "I am glad, however, that you are still happy in God. If you had married an ungodly man, it would certainly have been a sin. But it was no sin to marry a child of God…. And surely, if you pray mightily for him, the Lord will hear your prayer, and supply whatever is yet wanting in his faith, till he is *happy and holy and perfect in love* [emphasis mine]."[68] Wesley's own marriage was not a success and he seems at times to value the single life over that of marriage, but towards the close of his own life and ministry, he can affirm that it is no bar to a life of love, holiness and happiness.[69]

Doctrinal Opinions and Divisions in the Church

As we learn about God and his work in the world, we form opinions about many matters of doctrine, worship practice, and lifestyle. In many areas we find common ground across the denominational spectrum but in others we are divided, sometimes amicably and sometimes not. Our differing opinions can become barriers to fellowship and lead to a loss of relationship. Wesley strongly affirmed: "It is the glory of the people called Methodists that they condemn none for their opinions or modes of worship. They think and let think, and insist upon nothing but faith working by love."[70] When he asks about how the work of God is progressing in a place, his key questions are: "Do they love one another? Are they all of one heart and soul? Do they build one another up in the knowledge and love of our Lord Jesus Christ?"[71] This should be a central feature of Wesleyan spirituality today—keeping the primary focus on love and relationship by looking for ways to work together rather than focusing on the inevitable differences of opinion and looking for ways to separate. This does not mean ignoring differences or pretending they don't exist; nor does it mean being one thing in public settings and another in private conversations.

Wesley believes that the rule for judging right and wrong is the Scripture, with the good being those things clearly advocated by Scripture and the bad those things it forbids; everything else is a matter of indifference.[72] He reminds his people that this is not "speculative latitudinarianism" (indifference to all opinions), nor "practical latitudinarianism" (indifference to public worship and how it is conducted), nor an "indifference to all congregations" (wandering

---

[67] *Letters* (Telford) VIII: 97.

[68] *Letters* (Telford) VIII: 128. See also *Letters* (Telford) VIII: 159; *Letters* (Telford) VII: 143.

[69] For example, see *Letters* (Telford) IV: 220.

[70] *Letters* (Telford) VII: 190. For Wesley's understanding of opinions in relationship to essential doctrines, see chapter 2. See also *Works* 25: 573; *Works* 26: 160.

[71] *Works* 25: 582.

[72] *Works* 1, "The Witness of our own Spirit," 302-303.

from church to church with no ties of fellowship).[73] Each person needs to be fixed on their religious principles, firmly adhering to their understanding of worship and tied to one local congregation, while embracing as brothers and sisters in Christ all others; "This is catholic or universal love….catholic love is catholic spirit."[74] He is convinced that the real cause of separation in the church is a lack of love: "It is the nature of love to unite us together, and the greater the love the stricter the union. And while this continues in its strength nothing can divide those whom love has united. It is only when our love grows cold that we can think of separating from our brethren." When we separate from each other, we break the law of love and all the commandments to love.[75] It is from this lack of love that unkind tempers, evil surmising, uncharitable judging, offence, anger, resentment, bitterness, malice, and hatred arise. This inward state then becomes the outward evidence of speech and action.[76]

Some of the most debated issues in Wesley's long ministry arose between those who were Arminian in their doctrinal orientation and those who were Calvinistic.[77] As early as 1745 Wesley strongly believed that even clear denominational differences are not as important "as the loving of one another with a pure heart fervently, and not forsaking, much less refusing, the assembling of ourselves *together*."[78] In a series of letters to the Reverend Gilbert Boyce (a Baptist pastor) he deals with the issue of strongly held opinions that become the source of division within the Church, and therefore harm both its witness and its fellowship. Wesley believed that a difference of opinion between them need not cause a break, even though neither was likely to change their views. He affirms that God's primary focus is our salvation, and "To this immediate end of renewing each soul in love, and the whole mind which was in Christ, he has pointed out several means, many of which we cannot use, at least not fully, without joining together. A company of men joining together for this purpose we are accustomed to call a church." He admits that he has both likes and dislikes about things in his own Church of England but "I have not found any community who (in my apprehension) come so near the Scripture plan, or so nearly answer the original design of a church, as the people called Methodists," though he absolutely denies that the Church

---

[73] *Works* 2, "Catholic Spirit," 92-94. In the sermon Wesley gives a long list of orthodox beliefs that are shared by all who belong to the one, holy, apostolic, catholic church—so he is not advocating that any belief system will do, nor are we to be indifferent to the beliefs outlined in the ecumenical creeds; see 81-87.

[74] *Works* 2, "Catholic Spirit," 94.

[75] *Works* 3, "On Schism," 64.

[76] *Works* 3, "On Schism," 65.

[77] More information on this issue can be found in Allan Coppedge, *John Wesley in Theological Debate* (Wilmore: Wesley Heritage Press, 1987); McGonigle, *Sufficient Saving Grace.*

[78] *Works* 26: 124. See also 128-30; 132-36, 157-58.

of England or the Methodists are "the" true church.[79] When it comes to the critical issue of baptism, he says that he does not believe the "mode of baptism" is "necessary to salvation," or even baptism at all, otherwise the Quakers are damned. He thinks that trying to persuade someone of a particular mode of baptism is poor employment and it is far better "by the grace of God, in persuading them to love God with all their hearts, and their neighbour as themselves."[80] He told Mrs. Turner: "the kingdom of God is not opinions (how right so ever they be), but righteousness and peace and joy in the Holy Ghost.... Shall we for opinions destroy the work of God, or give up love, the very badge of our profession? Nay, by this shall men know that we belong to the Lover of Souls, to Him who loved us and gave Himself for us."[81] He share with her the example of his own relationship with George Whitefield and Richard Hill, both staunch Calvinists.[82] He reminded Alexander Clark that Methodist preachers have a right to preach their doctrines just as Lady Huntingdon's (Calvinists) do theirs: "But I blame all even that speak the truth otherwise than *in love*. Keenness of spirit and tartness of language are never to be commended. It is only *in meekness* that we are to instruct those that oppose themselves. But we are not allowed upon any account whatever to return evil for evil or railing for railing."[83] Wesley is honest enough to admit this is hard to avoid, sometimes even for things of an "indifferent nature." He confesses he also finds it hard to proportion his own zeal according to the occasion or to temper it with prudence.[84] Towards the end of his life (1788) Wesley warned John Mann: "Whatever opposers you meet with—Calvinists, Papists, Antinomians, and any other—have a particular care that they do not take up too much either of your time or thoughts. You have better work: keep to your one point, Christ dying for us and living for us."[85]

Both the Calvinists and the Arminians belonged to the evangelical wing of the Protestant church and so they actually held many things in common, centred on the Protestant Reformation and its later developments. One group who were viewed with considerably more suspicion by most people of Wesley's day were the Roman Catholics—and this was only strengthened by the two Jacobite uprisings in the 18th Century that sought to return a Catholic monarch to the throne.[86] In 1784 Wesley finds himself writing about his nephew Charles who had become a Roman Catholic. Perhaps surprisingly, given his historical

---

[79] *Works* 26: 419. See also *Works* 2, "The Reformation of Manners," 302.

[80] *Works* 26: 425-26.

[81] *Letters* (Telford) V: 339.

[82] *Letters* (Telford) V: 340.

[83] *Letters* (Telford) VI: 276. See also *Letters* (Telford) VIII: 96.

[84] *Works* 26: 197.

[85] *Letters* (Telford) VIII: 69.

[86] For more on Wesley's relationship with Roman Catholicism in the 18th century see David Butler, *Methodists and Papists: John Wesley and the Catholic Church in the Eighteenth Century* (London: Darton, Longman and Todd, 1995).

situation, the key question for Wesley is not his opinions and modes of worship, but where is his heart? Genuine religion is defined as "Happiness in God, or in the knowledge and love of God. It is 'faith working by love', producing 'righteousness and peace and joy in the Holy Ghost.' In other words, it is an heart and life devoted to God." If Charles has this experience, then he will not finally perish notwithstanding his current opinions and modes of worship, even though Wesley sees them as a hindrance to his Christian life.[87] If Charles does not have this heart religion, then he doubts he ever will, given where he now belongs and worships.[88] In other words, some settings in Wesley's view were more likely to enable a genuine heart experience with God, but that does not mean we should therefore condemn them for perceived errors. He states we ought to love people even when they hold (in his opinion) erroneous views: "really invincible ignorance never did nor ever shall exclude any man from heaven," but those clearly knowing the gospel must be born again.[89] When James Barry asked him if you can be a Roman Catholic and be saved, Wesley gave a carefully nuanced response. He likens the question to asking if a person can dance or play cards and be saved. Wesley says that possibly Barry could, but he can't and that is as much as can safely be said. Even then, we ought not to share this opinion with those outside of Christ, as it will only anger and not convince them. While Methodists don't dance or play cards, they must make allowances for those outside the movement, otherwise he would be sending his own parents to hell who did both of these things and yet "died in the full assurance of faith." Wesley reminds Barry that God has given the Methodists a large measure of the light and he expects them to use all the light granted, but to deal tenderly with those who have not.[90] In other words, Wesley is sure of the light he has received on salvation and is aware of God's requirements for him, but he dare not extend those demands to another, who must be left to God's own judgement.

Even when dealing with those who don't hold orthodox Christian beliefs and who actively oppose the Methodist doctrines, Wesley advises that while the preacher needs to guard his people against such a person, "Nevertheless I advise you and all our preachers never oppose him openly. Doing thus would only give the unawakened world an advantage against you all." They must not speak severely or contemptuously of the man in mixed company: "You must use no weapons in opposing him but only those of truth and love." Preachers should privately advise those who have been influenced by him and set them right as soon as possible.[91] Sometime the opposition to Methodism became

---

[87] *Letters* (Telford) VII: 216.

[88] *Letters* (Telford) VII: 217. See a similar letter to his nephew Samuel Wesley, *Letters* (Telford) VII: 230-31.

[89] *Works* 26: 198.

[90] *Letters* (Telford) VIII: 12.

[91] *Letters* (Telford) VIII: 13.

more strident and he advised Charles Atmore not to take any notice of those who are opposing the work, "only be loving and courteous to any of them when they come in your way. If you and your people have more life of God in yourselves than them, you infallibly will prevail. You should continually exhort them all to this."[92] In other words, the best argument anyone can offer is a better life! Sometimes the opposition actually resulted in persecution of various kinds. John Crook had informed Wesley about the opposition stirred up by the local bishop and one of the clergy, leading to outbreaks of persecution. Wesley advises him to stay faithfully at his post and to be patient: "Beware of despising your opponents! Beware of anger and resentment! Return not evil for evil or railing for railing."[93] His advice to Matthew Lowes sums up his whole pastoral approach to those who differed from him: "What would one not do (except sin) that brotherly love may continue!"[94]

Spiritual Issues and Practices

One of the areas in our life with God that often causes a great deal of angst arises when we compare our own experience with that of another person— someone we know personally or we have heard their story on the media, from church history or the Bible itself. In the comparison we can be tempted to think we are so unspiritual that we give up or settle for a poor quality of relationship with God, or we think we are so spiritual that we become proud and neglectful. Sometimes we get very discouraged by our experience and think there must be something wrong with us and therefore God does not love us as he does those who clearly living a victorious life.

BEGINNING THE CHRISTIAN LIFE

Today there are so many programs on offer to be used in evangelism and all of them carry the expectation of a reasonably swift response. Many churches still offer the type of service that gives an invitation to come forward and receive Christ following the gospel message. The expectation is for the person to come forward, pray and receive new life in Christ there and then. Many can testify to the effectiveness of such methods. Wesley was certainly no stranger to effective gospel preaching and many thousands began their life in Christ during the services and meetings offered by the Methodists. However, what happens when your spiritual journey does not fit the usual pattern? Wesley's early correspondence with Lady Maxwell shows him ministering to one whose entry into new life in Christ was anything but swift, and who struggled with why God delayed in answering her prayer.[95] He puzzled over why it was so gradual rather

---

[92] *Letters* (Telford) VIII: 175.
[93] *Letters* (Telford) VI: 228.
[94] *Letters* (Telford) IV: 57. See also *Letters* (Telford) VIII: 150.
[95] *Letters* (Telford) IV: 253.

than instantaneous (as it has been for so many). He urged her to continue to simply trust Christ and the work of grace would be done. His confidence rests on the fact that "Christ is yours; He hath loved you; He hath given Himself for you. Therefore you shall be holy as He is holy, both in heart and in all manner of conversation."[96] Over the next several years he noted how she was progressing in her walk with God, though it still seemed very gradual. He continued to urge her to believe "today" and not to give up hope.[97] He reiterates that God's grace is sufficient for her even in this protracted waiting period, as long as she can answer positively the question: "Are not you still determined to seek your happiness in Him, and to devote to God all you have and all you are?"[98] The question of timing was also of concern to a Mr. Alexander: "It is very certain your day of grace is not passed: if it were, you would be quite easy and unconcerned. It is plain the Lover of souls is still striving with you and drawing you to Himself."[99] Wesley firmly believed that faith, hope and love are completely the gift of God, and are not in our natural power.[100] We cannot believe "when" we will, only "if" we will, and therefore the timing of God's gift of faith is always a mystery.[101] This means that we can never demand God give us faith, nor is it automatic once we have fulfilled a set of conditions, or carried out a series of spiritual exercises. In an age of 'easy believism' we struggle to comprehend how God could possibly withhold faith from those who meet the criteria required, and so are easily turned back from our relationship with God in order to explore an alternative we think will provide a shorter way to happiness.

Sometimes our struggles come because of our understanding of Scripture. Wesley's niece, Sarah Wesley, struggled with her inner life and often felt emotionally dead and cold, even when participating in the Lord's Supper. She wondered if this was God's judgement on her because of the way she interpreted 1 Corinthians 11:27: was God withholding his presence from her because she was "eating and drinking unworthily"? Wesley told her that this passage dealt with the particular sin of one group eating and drinking before the other, and so one group was hungry and the other drunk. He assures her that she is in no danger of this and that God was working in his own way. When she comes to the Table God does not give her joy or sweetness, nor contrition and brokenness, since neither of these would suit his design. He thinks that God leaves her with a dull, unfeeling heart so she may know herself better in order to know him and in due course he will deliver her if she remains faithful. Wesley admits that this lack of emotional sensation is difficult to deal with and

---

[96] *Letters* (Telford) IV: 308-09.

[97] *Letters* (Telford) IV: 317.

[98] *Letters* (Telford) V: 48.

[99] *Letters* (Telford) VII: 196.

[100] *Works* 26: 199.

[101] *Letters* (Telford) VI: 287.

so he urged her to find a close Christian friend to share her journey because it
would be too hard alone.[102] Sarah also struggles to resign her will to God's will,
and wonders if this is the problem limiting her walk with God. Wesley assures
her that "if we were first to resign our will to God in order to be in favour with
Him, our case would be desperate: nay, but you shall first be conscious of His
favour, and then be resigned to Him." She has to keep trusting that Christ loved
and died for her, so she can freely claim new life in him just as she is now.[103]
This is a critical point: if salvation is of grace by faith, then we actually cannot
surrender our will to him—it does not lie in our power to do so. We can, by
prevenient grace, choose to open up our life to the work of the Holy Spirit and
allow him to begin the process of transformation. Wesley reminds her that
"Without an endeavour to please God and to give up our own will, we never
shall attain his favour. But till we have attained it, till we have the Spirit of
adoption, we cannot actually give up our own will to Him."[104] In other words,
the desire to surrender must be present even though we cannot actually perform
it and God responds in grace to the one who takes this attitude and then his
grace makes possible the actual surrender. Wesley reminded Mary Cooke that
"There is an irreconcilable variability in the operations of the Holy Spirit on the
souls of men, more especially as to the manner of justification." For some it is
like an overwhelming power, for others a gentle and almost insensible way—
and she is one of the latter.[105] She must accept the mystery of God's grace at
work in her life, and use the grace given to her enabling her to receive more.[106]
This is a lesson we would do well to take to heart, given the sheer diversity of
human experience and the ways that God seeks to work in our lives.

THE EXPERIENCE OF CHRISTIAN PERFECTION

Wesley worked constantly with his own Methodist people to help them
understand the true nature of Christian perfection and how to enter into the
depth of relationship it represented. A very good example of this is the
extensive correspondence with Dorothy Furly and it illustrates many of the
issues faced by devoted Christians as they seek to experience the pure love of
God in their life. She evidently struggled with many doubts and fears
concerning the experience. Wesley reminds her that the obstacle is not her own
strength or even her worthiness: "what impotence in you can be a bar to the
almighty power of God? And what unworthiness can hinder the free love of
God? His love in and through Christ Jesus?... The Canaan of His perfect love is
open. Believe, and enter in!"[107] She must be grateful for what is now, rather

---

[102] *Letters* (Telford) VII: 53-54.
[103] *Letters* (Telford) VII: 66.
[104] *Letters* (Telford) VII: 74-75.
[105] *Letters* (Telford) VII: 298.
[106] *Letters* (Telford) VII: 303-304.
[107] *Letters* (Telford) III: 217.

than lamenting what is not yet. We do not improve our relationship with God by seeing the current relationship as faulty or inadequate. It is not all it shall be, but neither is it the emptiness of what was before the relationship began. The attitude needed to further enrich the relationship is exactly the same attitude that was required to begin it—an acknowledgement that it is by his grace and love alone that we are transformed. None are ever worthy of God's love, but that does not mean we are then worthless. Christ did not die for the worthless; he died for the unworthy, and the present quality of our life can never be a barrier to his working.

A little later he writes again and assures her that temptation itself does not weaken us unless we yield to it. However, the experience may leave "heaviness and soreness…upon the spirit till there is a fresh discovery of the love of God."[108] We are all prone to link our emotional state to our spiritual state and believe that the former is an accurate measure of the latter. This is an issue to which we shall return later, but Wesley admits that it often takes a renewed sense of God's love before our depression will lift. He wonders is Dorothy is truly being open with him about her spiritual life and invites her to write both to him and to Sarah Crosby as friends. Through such a sharing "It will again bring the promise of holiness near; which, indeed, always seems to be far off when we give way to any known sin, when we in any way grieve the Spirit of God. There may be some rare cases wherein God has determined not to bestow His perfect love till a little before death; but this I believe is uncommon: He does not usually put off the fulfilling of His promises."[109] He tells her to be encouraged and to keep seeking God's grace. This is to be an active waiting upon God and not a passive waiting for God to act, even though this involves some activities that she would rather avoid for the present."[110] Developing the life of God in the soul requires that we embrace the ministry opportunities that are set before us at this present moment, even if it would be our natural inclination to avoid this until we are 'more spiritual.' God's love is inherently active in reaching out to others and whatever measure of this love is in our hearts 'today' is sufficient for us to be actively involved in service to the neighbour. So while she is to be active in ministry and relationships, she is to be careful to avoid people and situations that have been occasions of sin.[111] Though it is only lightly touched on here, Wesley acknowledges that God can and does work in the afflictions of life and they are a means of uncovering such things as pride and stubbornness. This is not a statement about the universal benefit of suffering but the words of a pastor who knows the person well and can see what elements in their life are damaging the walk with God. In fact, in

---

[108] *Letters* (Telford) III: 219.

[109] *Letters* (Telford) III: 221.

[110] *Letters* (Telford) III: 221.

[111] *Letters* (Telford) III: 229. See also *Letters* (Telford) VII: 377-78.

1762 he has to warn her not to be hurt by many of the things in his brother's *Short Hymns*, as they tended to overemphasise the necessity of suffering.[112]

Early in 1758 he tells Dorothy that her expectation of a spiritual breakthrough was hindered by not "understanding the freeness of the gift of God. You are perpetually seeking for something in yourself to move Him to love and bless you. But it is not to be found there; it is in Himself and in the Son of His love. He did then give you a proof of this in that fresh evidence of pardon; and He is ready to give it to you again today, for He is not weary of well-doing."[113] She struggles to believe that God would freely purify her heart, and so is continually seeking to be or do something to earn God's favour (this may be the cause of an earlier reference to pride and stubbornness). Sometimes we refuse to believe God is being honest with us when he says he loves us just as we are and that something must change in us before we can experience such love. We stubbornly cling to the notion there is something we need to start doing or stop doing in order to be more acceptable to God. This is where the paradox of 'active waiting' on God that is such a critical element in Wesleyan spirituality is easily misunderstood. Wesley says, "All who expect to be sanctified at all expect to be sanctified by faith. But meantime they know that faith will not be given but to them that obey. Remotely, therefore, the blessing depends on our works, although immediately on simple faith."[114] In other words, we must walk in the grace and light we have (obedience) and more will be given; fail to walk in the grace and light given, and even what we do have will gradually slip away. He had earlier reminded to learn to be faithful in little things, especially conversation, and this was apparently not happening.[115]

By 1760 Dorothy was becoming involved in disputes with others over the experience of heart holiness. Wesley tells her this will only hurt her spiritual progress, reminding her that "God is Sovereign, in sanctifying as well as justifying. He will act when as well as how He pleases; and none can say unto him, What doest thou?"[116] By 1762 she seems to have been sanctified wholly but was troubled by the claims of some that it meant living almost in an angelic state.[117] Wesley has to remind her that sanctification is an instantaneous deliverance from all sin and a power to cleave to God, but even "in the lower degree" it does not exclude a useless thought or speaking a useless word. He says this would be inconsistent with living in a corruptible body, which makes

---

[112] *Letters* (Telford) IV: 189.

[113] *Letters* (Telford) IV: 5.

[114] *Letters* (Telford) IV: 71.

[115] *Letters* (Telford) III: 208.

[116] *Letters* (Telford) IV: 97.

[117] This was being claimed by some in the London Revival; particularly the supporters of Thomas Maxfield and George Bell. For further information on the perfectionist controversy see n. 2 in *Works*. 20: 406; n. 42 in *Works*, 21: 346; Rack, *Reasonable Enthusiast*, 333-42.

it impossible to always think aright. If Christian perfection implies this then it can't be experienced till after death. He tells her: "I want you to be all love. This is the perfection I believe and teach. And this perfection is consistent with a thousand nervous disorders, which that highly-strained perfection is not." If perfection is set too high so that none have ever attained it, it will effectively drive it out of the world.[118] In the last of his letters to her 1783, Wesley confirms how God has worked in her life: "You are enabled to give a very clear and standing proof that weakness of nerves cannot prevent joy in the Lord. Your nerves have been remarkably weak, and that for many years, but still your soul can magnify the Lord and your spirit rejoice in God your Saviour!"[119]

TEMPTATION AND SIN

Wesley consistently believes that we need liberty to be truly happy, because "only free agents can be perfectly happy, as without the possibility of choosing wrong there can be no freedom."[120] Making a real choice requires having genuine options from which to choose and that means we can be influenced (tempted) to believe one option is better than the other.[121] Making a wrong choice can lead to the loss of a close relationship with God: "A clear conviction of the love of God cannot remain in any who do not walk closely with God. And I know no one person who has lost this without some voluntary defect in his conduct; though perhaps at the time he was not conscious of it, but upon prayer it was revealed to him."[122] The phrase "at the time" underscores the importance of being aware of the subtlety of temptation and its attractiveness. A clear example of how this happens is given in Wesley's sermon "The Great Privilege of those that are Born of God." He uses the example of King David seeing Bathsheba in a state of undress and the king's immediate sexual attraction to her. Wesley says at this point it is only a temptation and the Holy Spirit is faithful to warn him of his danger. If he had immediately acted to remove the temptation by turning away and refocusing his mind, all would have been well: "But he yielded in some measure to the thought and the temptation began to prevail over him. Hereby his spirit was sullied. He saw God still; but it was more dimly than before. He loved God still, but not in the same degree, not with the same strength and ardour of affection."[123] David continued to ignore the voice of the Spirit "till nature was superior to grace, and kindled lust in his soul."[124] As a result of this, "Faith, the divine, supernatural intercourse with

---

[118] *Letters* (Telford) IV: 188.

[119] *Letters* (Telford) VII: 197. Apparently she had suffered from some form of debilitating illness for many years.

[120] *Works* 25: 267.

[121] *Works* 25: 267.

[122] *Letters* (Telford) III: 174.

[123] *Works* 1, "The Great Privilege of those that are Born of God," 439.

[124] *Works* 1, "The Great Privilege of those that are Born of God," 439.

God, and the love of God ceased together. He then rushed on as a horse into the battle, and knowingly committed the outward sin."[125] Wesley's analysis leads him to conclude that "some sin, of omission at least, must necessarily precede the loss of faith—some inward sin. But the loss of faith must precede the committing outward sin."[126] This is why simply having a rule or law does not of itself help. There was no law banning David from walking on his palace roof and no law banning Bathsheba from bathing on hers. It was the serendipitous conjunction of events that provided the occasion for the temptation, and we can never hedge ourselves around with enough rules and regulations to prevent things like this happening. Rather, we must keep "the loving eye of the soul…steadily fixed on God" and the temptation will lose its power. If we don't do this, then our own desire (which in itself is not sinful) draws us out of God "'caught by the bait' of present or promised pleasure" that is not consistent with our life in God. It is when we lose this inner struggle that the desire brings forth sin inwardly, and this inward sin destroys our faith [trust] and then outward sin follows.[127] This is much the same scenario that faced Adam and Eve in the Garden of Eden in Genesis 3. It was the attractiveness of the fruit that appealed to legitimate desires but the actual temptation was to satisfy them in a way that God had clearly forbidden. For life in God to flourish we need

> the continual inspiration of God's Holy Spirit: God's breathing into the soul, and the soul's breathing back what it first receives from God; a continual action of God upon the soul, the re-action of the soul upon God, manifested to the heart, and perceived by faith; and an unceasing return of love, praise, and prayer, offering up all the thoughts of our hearts, all the words of our tongues, all the works of our hands, all our body, soul, and spirit, to be an holy sacrifice, acceptable unto God in Christ Jesus.[128]

This "re-action of the soul" is absolutely necessary if we are to continue in God, "For it plainly appears God does not continue to act upon the soul unless the soul re-acts upon God."[129] God certainly initiates the relationship, but if we fail to respond positively and turn away to another source of love and happiness, the Spirit will gradually withdraw: "He will not continue to breathe into our soul unless our soul breathes toward him again."[130] Yielding to temptation not only leads to sin and condemnation, it also leads to the damaging of our relationship with God.

---

[125] *Works* 1, "The Great Privilege of those that are Born of God," 439-40. See Wesley's 9-point summary of this process and the further example of Peter at Galatia, 440-41.
[126] *Works* 1, "The Great Privilege of those that are Born of God," 441.
[127] *Works* 1, "The Great Privilege of those that are Born of God," 441-42.
[128] *Works* 1, "The Great Privilege of those that are Born of God," 442.
[129] *Works* 1, "The Great Privilege of those that are Born of God," 442.
[130] *Works* 1, "The Great Privilege of those that are Born of God," 442.

He told Peggy Dale that "the more vigorously you follow after Him the clearer will that unction be, without which it is not possible on some occasions to distinguish between temptations and sins."[131] This is particularly true when we are faced with sudden, intense temptations or to other unexpected events. He states that "it seems whenever a believer is by surprise overtaken in a fault there is more or less condemnation as there is more or less concurrence of his will. In proportion as a sinful desire or word or action is more or less voluntary, so we may conceive God is more or less displeased, and there is more or less guilt upon the soul."[132] If the surprise comes because we have been wilful and culpable in ignoring God's warnings about the situation, we experience proper guilt and condemnation because we could have acted to avoid being in that situation. Any failure to anticipate and shun problem situations when warned by God is "wilful sin." A genuinely unexpected and unforseen surprise brings grief and shame but no guilt or condemnation. Neither are we condemned for the tug of inward sin remaining as long as we do not give way to it.[133] If we go back to the incident mentioned before, where King David remained in Jerusalem and was therefore walking on the palace rooftop at the time when Bathsheba was bathing. Wesley would say he was wilfully guilty in his reaction to seeing her if God had challenged him about staying in the city. If that were not the case, then he did not wilfully contribute to the unexpected incident. His subsequent action though, was clearly to be condemned. This is one of those areas where the Christian caution about going to certain places, participating in certain events and adopting a certain lifestyle is seen by some non-Christians as a life-denying negativity. In fact, it is often a sensible precaution against getting caught in a powerful temptation that otherwise could be avoided.

WILDERNESS STATE

Wesley notes how many people wander in a barren landscape of endless temptation and torment after they become Christians. He defines this as a "wilderness state" and it results from the loss of "a sure trust in his love, and a liberty of approaching him with holy boldness." This leads to "the loss of love, which cannot but rise or fall at the same time, and in the same proportion, with true, living faith. Accordingly they that are deprived of their faith are deprived of their love of God also.... They are not now happy in God, as everyone is that truly loves him. They do not delight in him as in time past."[134] This downward spiral inevitably leads to a loss of joy in the Holy Spirit, accompanied by forfeiting our sense of pardon, hope, peace and power over sin, and a loss of love for the neighbour.[135] It is due to a sin of commission or omission

---

[131] *Letters* (Telford) V: 48.
[132] *Works* 1, "The First-fruits of the Spirit," 242.
[133] *Works* 1, "The First-fruits of the Spirit," 242-46.
[134] *Works* 2, "The Wilderness State," 206.
[135] *Works* 2, "The Wilderness State," 206-207.

(especially the latter in Wesley's opinion), resulting from ignoring the Holy Spirit's reproofs and checks which leads to a slow, gradual withdrawal of his loving presence.[136] This sad state of affairs is not caused by "the bare, arbitrary, sovereign will of God," for God rejoices in us and still yearns to give us the gifts of sanctification, peace, joy. Furthermore, "He never repenteth of that which he hath given, or desires to withdraw them from us. Therefore he never *deserts* us, as some speak: it is we only that *desert* him."[137]

This is a very important point for Wesleyan spirituality: the love of God does not wax and wane the way ours does, nor does God withdraw his love or his presence in order to teach us a lesson or to toughen us up. If we lose the awareness of his love and presence for any extended time, it is usually because we have moved away from him and rebuffed him. Wesley comments on the understanding of spirituality found amongst some Roman Catholic writers that it is more spiritual to have "naked faith" deprived of all sense of God's presence and comfort. That it is only in a state of spiritual "darkness" and "dryness" that we can be purified from pride, the love of the world and an inordinate self-love. This means that we should not expect nor desire to always walk in God's light.[138] He finds the same truth taught by some of the mystics who claim: "Is not the work of God in the heart most swiftly and effectually carried on during a state of inward suffering? Is not a believer more swiftly and thoroughly purified by sorrow than by joy? By anguish and pain and distress and spiritual martyrdoms than by continual peace?"[139] Wesley is adamant that this is *not* scriptural: "the Scripture nowhere says that the absence of God best perfects his work in the heart!"[140] In a letter to William Law, Wesley affirms that Paul inseparably links righteousness and peace and joy, and they promote growth "till the peace of God sanctifies us wholly. But if these things are so, then 'distress and coldness' [which Law said promote holiness] are' not 'better' than fervent love and joy in the Holy Ghost."[141] He goes on to say:

> the doctrine that it is better and more profitable for the soul to lose its sense of the love of God than to keep it is not only unscriptural but naturally attended with the most fatal consequences. It directly tends to obstruct, if not destroy, the work of God in the heart, by causing men to bless themselves in those ways which damp the fervour of their affections, and to imagine they are considerably advanced in grace when they have grieved, yea quenched, the Spirit.[142]

---

[136] *Works* 2, "The Wilderness State," 208-209.

[137] *Works* 2, "The Wilderness State," 208. See n. 36 on the "dark night of the soul" and "withdrawal."

[138] *Works* 2, "The Wilderness State," 212.

[139] *Works* 2, "The Wilderness State," 219.

[140] *Works* 2, "The Wilderness State," 219.

[141] *Letters* (Telford) III: 361.

[142] *Letters* (Telford) III: 361. See also *Works* 2, "The Wilderness State", 219-20;

He also rejects the mystic writers' notion that a true knowledge of ourselves, even after justifying faith, will bring a deep heaviness as we discover just how unlike God we are. Wesley acknowledges this may bring "heaviness" but never "darkness."[143] As God increases our knowledge of the depths of our heart, he will "increase in the same proportion the knowledge of himself and the experience of his love."[144] There is no merit to be obtained by taking ourselves off to a desert, or by living in misery and forlornness.[145] This point can hardly be overstated when so many streams of spirituality emphasise that this life is essentially one of pain, suffering and sorrow, and these are to be welcomed and embraced because they are the major means of weaning us from sinful desires and pleasures. Wesley agrees that God will withdraw if we grieve the Spirit by outward or inward sin, either of omission or commission, along with such things as pride, anger, spiritual sloth, foolish desire, or inordinate affection.[146] "But that he ever withdraws himself because he *will*, merely because it is his good pleasure, I absolutely deny." For this is against "the whole tenor of Scripture. It is repugnant to the very nature of God; it is utterly beneath his majesty and wisdom…'to play at *bo-peep* with his creatures'."[147]

Life in the Body

When Wesley reflected on whether wandering thoughts in prayer were a sin or not, he came to the conclusion that while they may be caused by sin, it might simply be the result of the "natural union between the soul and the body."[148] He affirms that the body is now corrupted and presses down the soul and we will need to discern which thoughts are sinful and which are not. We can pray to be delivered from sinful ones but the latter are inherently a part of present bodily life.[149] He tries to explain to Mrs. Savage the difference between sinfulness and helplessness: "The former you need feel no more; the latter you will feel as long as you live. And, indeed, the nearer you draw to God, the more sensible of it you will be. But beware this does not bring you into the least doubt of what God has done for your soul."[150] Wesley was convinced that an "Abundance of deficiencies must remain as long as the soul remains in this house of clay. So

---

[143] For a fuller discussion of Wesley's understanding of "heaviness" in the Christian's life, see below.

[144] *Works* 2, "Heaviness through Manifold Temptations," 231.

[145] *Works* 2, "Heaviness through Manifold Temptations," 232-33.

[146] *Works* 2, "Heaviness through Manifold Temptations," 229. See also *Letters* (Telford) VIII: 138-39.

[147] *Works* 2, "Heaviness through Manifold Temptations," 229-30. See n. 43.

[148] *Works* 2, "Wandering Thoughts," 129.

[149] *Works* 2, "Wandering Thoughts," 130-37. Outler sees this as an important sermon on the limits of perfection, along with "On Sin in Believers" and "The Repentance of Believers."

[150] *Letters* (Telford) V: 330-31.

long the corruptible body will more or less darken and press down the soul. But still your heart may be all love, and love is the fulfilling of our law. Still you may rejoice evermore; you may pray without ceasing and in everything give thanks."[151] Because human life is bodily life

> the animal frame will affect more or less every power of the soul; seeing at present the soul can no more *love* than it can *think*, any otherwise than by the help of bodily organs. If, therefore, we either *think, speak*, or *love* aright, it must be by power from on high. And if our affections or will continue right, it must be by continued a miracle. Have we reason to believe, or have we not, that God will continually sustain the stone in the air?[152]

He told Elizabeth Bennis: "As thinking is the act of an embodied spirit, playing upon a set of material keys, it is not *strange* that the soul can make but ill music when her instrument is out of tune. This is frequently the case with you; and the trouble and anxiety you then feel are a natural effect of the disordered machine, which proportionally disorders the mind."[153] Nevertheless, he rejects the linking of sin with bodily infirmity, because the latter are "involuntary failings" and do not bring guilt. So while they are "deviations from the holy and acceptable and perfect will of God, yet they are not properly sins"; there is no guilt and no separation between the person and God. It is in this context that he affirms:

> Nothing is sin, strictly speaking, but a voluntary transgression of a known law of God. Therefore every voluntary breach of the law of love is sin; and nothing else, if we speak properly. To strain the matter farther is only to make way for Calvinism. There may be ten thousand wandering thoughts and forgetful intervals without any breah of the law of love, though not without transgressing the Adamic law. But Calvinists would fain confound this together. Let love fill your heart, and it is enough![154]

Wesley is deeply convinced that there is no condemnation for things we have no power to help: "There is no guilt, because there is no choice."[155] In what

---

[151] *Letters* (Telford) V: 212-13. See also *Letters* (Telford) V: 6, 56; *Letters* (Telford) VI: 40.

[152] *Letters* (Telford) V: 4. See *Works* 13, "Thoughts upon Necessity," 528-46, for an extended treatment of the nature of the body and its relationship with our spiritual nature.

[153] *Letters* (Telford) V: 284.

[154] *Letters* (Telford) V: 322.

[155] *Works* 1, "The First-fruits of the Spirit," 241. In "Thoughts upon Necessity" mentioned above he specifically examines whether we are genuinely free to make choices in our bodily condition, or if we are impelled by some form of necessity due to our physical existence. A modern analysis of this problem from a Wesleyan perspective can be found in Joel B. Green, *Body, Soul and Human Life: The Nature of Humanity in the Bible* (Milton Keynes: Paternoster, 2008).

follows we will look at a number of things that arise from our present bodily existence and how they can be hindrances in our walk with God.

FAULTY JUDGEMENT

Wesley was sure that perfection in love did not mean perfection in knowledge. An imperfect knowledge of people and events inevitably leads to faulty judgement about them or the situation and this certainly impacts the relationship itself. This can be illustrated from Wesley's own friendship with William Robarts, who had served the Methodist movement for a long time faithfully and effectively. In September 1782 Wesley writes to him and accuses him of being deeply covetous because he will not now help others financially, though he has a business, an estate and no children. Because of this attitude, Wesley says he will break fellowship with him. Robarts replies a few days later and denies the charge; he is no longer able to be as generous in his support because his business is failing. As a consequence, he is now drastically economising and it had nothing to do with him being covetous, God being his witness. William then accuses Wesley of condemning him out of hand, and asks where is Wesley showing any evidence of the love that should think no evil?[156] A few days later Wesley rejects his plea and William now writes a letter to end the contact because of Wesley's lack of charity.[157] Several more letters are exchanged in August of the following year in which Wesley accuses Robarts of pride and of not walking as once he did.[158] Robarts writes an impassioned plea back rejecting Wesley's reading of the situation and saying how he had faithfully served Methodism for 40 years at his own cost, and once more accuses Wesley of a lack of love and justice in condemning him out of hand. Wesley responds within a few days claiming he has certain knowledge of Robarts' case but acknowledges that perhaps his finances were not now as great as they had been.[159] It appears that William's letter finally convinced Wesley of the true plight of his finances and they were reconciled.[160] Over the next few years there are warm and positive letters of encouragement, ending with Wesley urging him to become a preacher (for which he has all the gifts) and to leave his failing business behind.[161] The correspondence shows how a faulty judgement based on one set of evidence almost led to a complete loss of friendship, with both men claiming they were acting in a Christian manner. It illustrates how easy it is to do this and how it can lead to a breakdown in

---

[156] *Letters* (Telford) VII: 140-41. Telford comments that Robarts actually was innocent, as subsequent events were to prove.
[157] *Letters* (Telford) VII: 142-43.
[158] *Letters* (Telford) VII: 185.
[159] *Letters* (Telford) VII: 186-87.
[160] *Letters* (Telford) VII: 188.
[161] *Letters* (Telford) VII: 299. See also *Letters* (Telford) VII: 302, 343; *Letters* (Telford) VIII: 227-28.

relationship. It is a sure test of the quality of our relationship with God and with each other as to how we handle this. Will we seek to maintain the friendship and be willing to forgive and be reconciled, or will we insist that we are correct in our understanding and judgement and so withdraw from the relationship? This is equally true when applied to our judgement of communities and organisations. How many have left a church fellowship convinced that they were right in their understanding and judgement, and everyone else was wrong?

HEAVINESS

Earlier in this chapter we looked at Wesley's rejection of "spiritual darkness" as a necessary component of spiritual progress, but how he allowed for the "heaviness of soul" and the impact this has because we no longer sense God's presence and love. He identifies "heaviness" with experiencing grief and sorrow; it is a strong, settled sorrow that "continues for some time, as a settled temper, rather than a passion—even in them that have living faith in Christ, and the genuine love of God in their hearts." This may impact their affections, their behaviour and their body.[162] Wesley says it may arise from an extended period of temptation as well as from illness and disease (whether brief or extended). It may also arise from nervous disorders, because "faith does not overturn the course of nature: natural causes still produce natural effects."[163] He notes we may experience it from a range of circumstances, such as personal calamity, poverty, or death of a loved one. Wesley is confident that God "would have our affections regulated, not extinguished," and therefore sorrow and grief can exist without sin.[164] What Wesley is describing fits with what we know as depression; this is a normal and natural component of human life, though in some cases it can become a severe and debilitating illness. Wesley does not see depression, whether mild or severe, short term or longer-lasting, as sin or a sign of God's displeasure with us. He reminded Mrs Marston:

> Undoubtedly as long as you are in the body you will come short of what you would be, and you will see more and more of your numberless defects and the imperfection of your best actions and tempers. Yet all this need not hinder your rejoicing evermore and in everything giving thanks. Heaviness you may sometimes feel; but you need never come into darkness.[165]

In another letter to her he rejects the notion that "darkness" is an essential element in our Christian experience. Unless we grieve the Holy Spirit, he will not take away what is given but will add to it until we "come to the measure of the full stature of Christ." She is encouraged to share in the select society not only the joys and comforts of her spiritual journey, but also the sorrows,

---

[162] *Works* 2, "Heaviness through Manifold Temptations," 225. See also 222-223.

[163] *Works* 2, "Heaviness through Manifold Temptations," 227.

[164] *Works* 2, "Heaviness through Manifold Temptations," 228.

[165] *Letters* (Telford) V: 196. See also *Letters* (Telford) V: 198.

weaknesses and temptations. Wesley sees this as very important as a means of knitting the group together.[166] This is an important reminder of the importance of sharing honestly both the ups and the downs in our Christian walk. Note, however, that she is to share this with a small group of her fellow-Christians, not in a large public meeting where it can easily be misunderstood or misjudged.

Wesley was concerned that some Christians would identify these times of depression (or even simply the absence of emotion) as the irrefutable evidence of sin in their life. He urges Damaris Perronet to continue faithfully "in spite of all coldness and wanderings" in prayer. The "sinking of spirits" does not imply "preceding unfaithfulness" and it is probably due to the weakness of her body. She is to keep trusting and focusing on God himself, and not her current feelings.[167] It is vital to keep our focus on God himself and not our experience of God. This is why we live by faith and not by feelings, since they are not an infallible indicator of our spiritual life, either positively or negatively. Sadly, some churches create the impression that Christians are to be endlessly on some kind of spiritual high, and people should only share their victories and positive experiences. In such a setting, it is little wonder that so many never discover the true depths of a life with God. Wesley believed that God does "permit" heaviness as a trial of our faith, with the goal of deepening our spiritual life by increasing our hope of glory, our joy in the Lord, his love and holiness. It will also help purify us from such things as pride and self-will. The Spirit works through all of these things to "Bring us to expect all our strength from, and to seek all our happiness in, God.[168] However, Satan will use all these as his opportunity to undermine our confidence in God and his love.[169] This reinforces why we need close fellowship with wise and mature Christians, to help hold us steady in Christ when we are going through these times.

PAIN AND SUFFERING

As we saw in the second chapter, the consequence of personal and corporate sin in God's perfect creation led to the corruption of every aspect of it, and the evil unleashed has impacted all life from that moment onwards. Disease, disaster and death are now the lot of humanity and will remain so until the return of Christ and the renewal of all things. The loss of our personal relationship with God resulted in human depravity that impacts all of our relationships and would lead to their destruction were it not for God's prevenient grace. It is through grace that the harmful effects of this are minimised for most of us most of the time—though death will come to us all. As we have seen, God cannot

---

[166] *Letters* (Telford) V: 198.
[167] *Letters* (Telford) V: 235. See also *Letters* (Telford) IV: 221; *Letters* (Telford) VI: 241; *Letters* (Telford) VII: 185.
[168] *Works* 2, "Heaviness through Manifold Temptations," 232-33.
[169] *Works* 2, "Heaviness through Manifold Temptations," 229.

arbitrarily overrule this state of affairs without denying the very qualities of love and liberty that characterise our relationship with him and with others. This means that we suffer the consequences of the choices of all those who came before us, those alive now (including ourselves), and we in our turn will contribute to the pain and suffering of the next generation. This aspect of life in the body is possibly the most difficult to reconcile with Wesley's claim that love, holiness and happiness go together. It is obvious to most of us why they would be a challenge to the life of God in the soul, because we expect a God of goodness, love and power to quickly set us free from pain and suffering, as well as grief and sorrow. If he does not, then we question what kind of a God it is that allows these things to continue, and it leads so many to question why we should have any confidence in God's care of his creation and his creatures. We struggle to see how a devastating personal illness or the death of a child could in any way be a demonstration of God's providential care! It is an issue the church has wrestled with from the beginning and it is equally present in the biblical record of both the Old and New Testaments. We are tempted to either embrace some form of fatalism (this was God's will) or believe life is simply a chaotic and random happening beyond even God's power to control. Wesley could not accept the first because of his belief that God is a God of love who takes seriously the reality of human choices and their consequences, nor could he accept the second because of his belief in God's providential governance of his creation. Wesley is certain that human life is not simply a matter of randomness and chaos. In a letter to Mrs. Hall he affirms that "It is not wisdom to impute either our health or any other blessing we enjoy merely to natural causes. It is far better to ascribe all to Him whose kingdom ruleth over all. And whether we have more or less bodily strength is of little concern so we are strong in the Lord and in the power of His might. He gives strength when it is wanted."[170] He equally rejects the notion that everything is predestined by God and that we are simply passive recipients of God's plans and purposes. Exactly how this works remains a mystery and Wesley's attempted explanations of it are no more satisfactory than anyone else's.[171] The critical issue is that of trust in a God who loves us supremely and who has demonstrated the depth of that love by the life, ministry, death and resurrection of Jesus Christ. This is why he can tell Mary Cooke "That all trials are good you cannot always see (at least for the present), but you may always *believe*."[172]

When Ebenezer Blackwell lost his house in a fire, Wesley wrote to him and said:

---

[170] *Letters* (Telford) VI: 223. See also *Letters* (Telford) VI: 28.
[171] He told Peggy Dale that we will not know how God governs his world till after death; see *Letters* (Telford) V: 33.
[172] *Letters* (Telford) VII: 378.

Shall not these things work together for good? Perhaps God was jealous over you, lest your heart should lean to any of the things of earth. He will have you to be all his own; to desire nothing but him; to seek him and love him with your whole heart. And he knows what are the hindrances, and what means will be most effectual toward it. Then let him work according to the counsel of his own will.[173]

In this, as in everything, Wesley believes God has taught them to say that the Lord gives, and the Lord takes away, so blessed be his name (Job 1:21).[174] The reason the fire might be a blessing rather than a curse has to do with his attitude to it—can he see the presence of God in the situation and still maintain his trust in him? Wesley shared with Blackwell from his own experience: "The doctrine of a particular providence is what exceeding few persons understand, at least not practically, so as to apply it to every circumstance of life. This I want—to see God acting in everything, and disposing all for his own glory and his creatures' good."[175] Like the Apostle Paul, Wesley can say: "I have learned by the grace of God in every state to be content. I have in this respect done what I ought and what I could. Now let God do what seemeth Him good. What peace do we find in all circumstances when we can say, 'Not as I will, but as Thou wilt'!"[176] It is this level of trusting commitment that is at the heart of our response to the trials and tests of life, some of which come to us as a result of our own choices, some by the actions of others and others by the environment around us.

While Wesley believes that part of trusting God is accepting what comes our way by his providence, he also says that we are not to seek out such trials and tests. He tells Damaris Perronet that many trials come which are hard physically and spiritually, "and if you chose for yourself, you ought not to choose the situation you are now in If you did, it would be a great hurt to your soul. It would hinder the work of God in you. But you do not choose for yourself; God chooses for you: and He cannot err."[177] He expands on this in a letter to Hannah Ball:

There are two general ways wherein it pleases God to lead His children to perfection—doing and suffering. And let Him take one or the other, we are assured His way is best. If we are led chiefly in the latter way, the less there is of our own choice in it the better. It is when we fly from those sufferings which God chooses for us that we meet with 'spiritual deaths' and 'spiritual martyrdoms,' as

[173] *Works* 26: 311.

[174] *Works* 26: 322.

[175] *Works* 26: 581.

[176] *Letters* (Telford) IV: 21.

[177] *Letters* (Telford) V: 234.

some speak—that is, plainly, God punishes us either by Himself or by the devil for going out of His way.[178]

The notion that God would deliberately send us pain and suffering is hardest of all to accept—what kind of a God is it that would do such a thing to those whom he professes to love? Wesley says to Mrs. Johnston: "The truth is, God allots us health or sickness, ease or pain, just as He sees one or the other is best for us."[179] This same confidence in the goodness of God's provision is seen in a letter to Mrs. Moon: "He that governs all things well for His own glory and for the good of them that love Him sees that it is best for you to be led in a strait and thorny way, and therefore permits it by His adorable providence. And you experimentally find that all these things are for your profit, that you may be a partaker of His holiness."[180] He reminds her that the "light afflictions" she faces now have to be set over against the greater glory to come.[181] Wesley does not pretend that they have no impact on our life and says that these afflictions are experienced as something grievous and not joyous.[182] However, we are to keep the same confidence in God expressed by the Apostle Paul in 2 Corinthians 4:16-18 and it is this assurance that our life is in God's hands that enables us to trust him with the situation, even when it seems so absolutely unjust from our perspective. When Samuel Furly wonders why God does not answer prayer for deliverance, Wesley reminds him that the times of comfort and spiritual blessings are in God's power. God alone truly knows why our prayers are not answered as soon as they are offered, though he thinks that sometimes it is due to a sin of omission (not following the light or using the power we have) and sometimes it is to break our stubborn will and destroy pride in our own understanding: "Certainly you are in the hands of Him that loves you, and that will speedily deliver, if you persevere in waiting for Him and in rejecting all comfort but that which flows from the Spirit of adoption, crying in your heart, Abba Father!"[183] Going through suffering was never to be received passively and he told Hannah Ball to take the recommended medicine even as she continued to pray and trust God: "our point is to improve by everything that occurs—by good or ill success so called, by sickness or health, by ease or pain; and this we can do through Christ strengthening us."[184] It is evident that Wesley himself found that trusting God with all the experiences of life was the only way to live: "It is well that our life and all things pertaining to it are in His hands. He orders all things well; and being assured of this, we need be careful for nothing: it is enough that in all things we may make our requests with

---

[178] *Letters* (Telford) VI: 75-76.

[179] *Letters* (Telford) VI: 315.

[180] *Letters* (Telford) VI: 20. See also *Letters* (Telford) VII: 316.

[181] *Letters* (Telford) VI: 21.

[182] *Letters* (Telford) VI: 27.

[183] *Letters* (Telford) III: 212. See also *Letters* (Telford) VI: 310-11, 337.

[184] Letters (Telford) VI: 27-28. See also *Letters* (Telford) V: 277.

thanksgiving."[185] Without this belief in God's providential care, the trial and tests of life would almost certainly destroy our relationship with him.

DEATH

Life expectancy in 18th Century Britain was still under 40 years of age, due to the very high infant mortality rate.[186] Fatal diseases were rampant and coupled with extreme poverty, poor diet and primitive medical services, most families dealt with death on a very frequent basis. This is a far cry from the situation in most technologically advanced countries today, and when death does come it is so often in the sanitised setting of a hospital or nursing home. One of the hardest things those of us living in such countries struggle to accept is the way Wesley counselled those recently bereaved, encouraging them to see it as a blessing. This seems a callous response to death and serious illness, especially for those who had suffered the death of an infant or young child. He wrote to Adam Clarke soon after the death of his eldest daughter: "But you startle me when you talk of grieving so much for the death of an infant. This was certainly the proof of inordinate affection; and if you love them thus all your children will die. How did Mr. De Renty behave when he supposed his wife to be dying? This is a pattern for a Christian."[187] This "pattern" was explained when he wrote to Hannah Ball: "We may feel, and yet resign like the Marquis De Renty when he apprehended his wife was dying. And this is a proof, not of want of affection, but of such an affection as is well pleasing to God."[188] He expressed a similar conviction when he wrote to his niece Sarah Wesley following the death of her father (his own brother): "God does not expect us to be sticks or stones. We may *grieve* and yet not murmur. It is very possible to *feel* and still *resign*. And this is Christian resignation."[189] In a similar vein Wesley wrote to Arthur Keene when his young daughter was dying: "You have all need of patience while you hear every day that poor little maid bemoaning herself. She is permitted thus to linger in pain, not only for her own sake (seeing the greater her sufferings are here the greater will be her reward); but likewise for your sakes, that your 'wills may be melted down and take the mould divine.'"[190] After she had died, Wesley tells him: "We may see the mercy of God in removing your little one into a better world. It was a mercy for

---

[185] *Letters* (Telford) VI: 310. God's providence is not just associated with trials and test, it is also related to blessings as well. He told Mrs. Middleton: "I am called to work: you are called to suffer. And if both these paths lead to the same parish, it is enough"; see *Letters* (Telford) VII: 317.

[186] David Cutler, Angus Deaton and Adriana Lleras-Muney. "The Determinants Of Mortality," *Journal of Economic Perspectives*, 2006, v20 (3, Summer), 97-120.

[187] *Letters* (Telford) VIII: 253. See the letter to his wife a few days later in which he says again the Lord loves those whom he chastens; *Letters* (Telford) VIII: 255-56.

[188] *Letters* (Telford) VI: 166.

[189] *Letters* (Telford) VIII: 69. See also *Letters* (Telford) VII: 110.

[190] *Letters* (Telford) VIII: 3.

you as well as for her. I was afraid she would have continued in pain long enough to have taken her mother with her. But God does all things well."[191] The death of adults at a young age was no less uncommon. He wrote to Lady Maxwell after learning that her husband had died after only two years of marriage, followed six weeks later by her son and only child. He notes God has "given you affliction upon affliction; He has used every possible means to unhinge your soul from things of earth, that it might fix on Him alone. How far the design of His love has succeeded I could not well judge from a short conversation." The Holy Spirit uses this "heaviness" of grief to convince her of sin, unbelief and want of Christ (which is her greatest need).[192] Robert Carr Brackenbury's wife (aged 21) had died a few days after an accident and Wesley says he will find comfort from God who disposes all things for his glory and the good of those who love him. "I am firmly persuaded the present dispensation, severe as it may appear, will be found in the event a means of greater blessings than any you have yet received."[193]

Similar conclusions are draw from letters to Sarah James, Mrs. Pywell and Mrs. Rose. For all of them, the afflictions are a means to foster their relationship with God and deepen it, as long as they keep trusting and stay resigned to God's will.[194] Wesley told Mrs. Woodhouse of his hope that her own sickness and bodily weakness would be of use to her neighbours, since pain and death remind us riches have no benefit. She is richer than all of them because "you have in heaven a better and a more enduring substance."[195] A similar point is made when writing to his niece Sarah Wesley just after the death of her cousin Thomas Waller at just 30 years of age:

> In taking away your expectation of worldly happiness God has been exceeding gracious to you. It is good for you that you have seen affliction and been disappointed of your hope. The removal of Mr Waller into a better world may be another blessing to you: as is everything which disengages us from transient things and teaches us to live in eternity.[196]

Wesley sees the grief and sorrow that comes from bereavement as a means that God uses to foster a closer relationship with him and to free people for more effective service in the kingdom. Neither of these is likely to encourage people in this day and age to think well of God and to believe he is supremely interested in their happiness. Perhaps here Wesley's 18th Century world and ours are furthest apart, though many other areas of the world without our technology and medical services might not be as surprised by his apparent

---

[191] *Letters* (Telford) VIII: 5.
[192] *Letters* (Telford) IV: 250. See also *Letters* (Telford) VII: 129.
[193] *Letters* (Telford) VII: 112. See also *Letters* (Telford) VIII: 114.
[194] *Letters* (Telford) VI: 124-25, 134, 369. See also *Letters* (Telford) VII: 80-81, 322.
[195] *Letters* (Telford) VI: 251-52.
[196] *Letters* (Telford) VII: 65-66.

insensitivity. It is important to be reminded that behind the apparent insensitivity is a deep Christian conviction that this life is neither all there is, nor is it the best part of human existence. Wesley passionately believed that the richest experiences were to be found beyond our death. After our resurrection we will enter into the fullness of life in a renewed creation and here "our union with our human friends will be more perfect…than it can be while we are encumbered with the house of clay."[197]

SUFFERING AND SPIRITUAL FORMATION

Given the reality of human pain and suffering on a personal and a community scale, Wesley affirms that we are neither to treat suffering as of no moment, nor to be devastated by it.[198] He is confident that suffering is not necessarily the evidence of personal sin. He told Walter Churchey: "You have indeed had a sea of troubles. But I have not yet heard any one say it was your fault; which I wonder at, because it is the way of the world still (as it was in the days of Job) always to construe misfortune into sin."[199] He is equally certain that suffering is not necessary for us to be truly holy: "*we must not imagine that such a degree of suffering is necessary to any degree of holiness* [emphasis mine]. In this God does certainly act as Sovereign; giving what He pleases, and by what means He pleases. I believe the holiest man that ever lived was the Apostle John; yet he seems to have suffered very little."[200] It is similar to the advice he gave Mary Stokes:

> We are sure the means which our blessed Lord uses to conform us to His image are (all circumstances considered) the very best; for He cannot but do all things well: Therefore, whenever it pleases Him to send affliction, then affliction is best. Yet we must not imagine He is tied down to this, or that He cannot give any degree of holiness without it. We have reason to believe from the earliest records that St. Paul suffered a thousand times more than St. John. And yet one can hardly doubt but St. John was as holy as he or any of the Apostles. Therefore stand ready for whatsoever our Lord shall send; but do not require Him to send you affliction. Perhaps He will take another way; He will overpower your whole soul with peace and joy and love; and thereby work in you a fuller conformity to Himself than ever you experienced yet.[201]

The point of it all was to respond in ways that enabled us to deepen our relationship with God: "It little matters whether we escape pain or suffer it, so it be but sanctified. Without some suffering we should scarce remember that we are not proprietors here, but only tenants at will, liable to lose all we have at a

---

[197] *Letters* (Telford) VIII: 56.

[198] *Works* 3, "On Patience," 172.

[199] *Letters* (Telford) VII: 196.

[200] *Letters* (Telford) VII: 101.

[201] *Letters* (Telford) V: 323.

moments warning. Happy it were if we continually retained a lively impression of this on our minds; then should we more earnestly seek that portion which shall never be taken from us."[202] He is aware how prone we are to settle for earthly happiness found in and through God's creation, rather than to embrace lasting happiness in a relationship with our Creator. The suffering and pain we experience here are a reminder to us that life's meaning and purpose cannot be found in any experience divorced from the love of God. That is why he can tell Mary Stokes: "He has delivered you from the vain expectation of finding happiness in the things of earth; and I trust you will be entangled no more in that snare. You know where true joys are to be found."[203] In none of this, does Wesley claim we will find suffering easy to accept: "No chastening is joyous for the present; but it will bring forth peaceable fruit. The Lord gave, and the Lord hath taken away—that He may give you Himself."[204]

In 1782 Wesley wrote to an unnamed gentleman who had just lost someone very close to him. Wesley recounts how almost 50 years earlier in a situation of personal grief, he heard the words of the Lesson for the day, "Son of man, I take from thee the desire of thine eyes with a stroke."[205] Wesley remembers that he was so affected he could not speak,[206] but God soon enabled him to say that his will was good. He then tells to the man:

> I trust He has taught you that great lesson, which reason alone cannot teach. He has always one end, whether in His pleasing or painful dispensations, to wean us from all things here below and to unite us to Himself. You see the present dispensation of His providence in a true light. He is vindicating His right to your whole heart and claiming you for His own. And He can make you large amends for all He has taken away by giving you Himself.[207]

So this "medicine" needs to have its full effect in the person's life, and he is being called to give himself fully up to God. Wesley advises that he select two or three mature Christians for close fellowship and break off friendship with those who do not know God, except for the needs of his business. He encourages him that if he does this he will meet his dear friend again in a little

---

[202] *Letters* (Telford) IV: 185. See also *Letters* (Telford) VII: 253.

[203] *Letters* (Telford) V: 230.

[204] *Letters* (Telford) VII: 202. See also *Letters* (Telford) VIII: 156

[205] The phrase, "Son of man, I take from thee the desire of thine eyes with a stroke," is from Ezek. 24:16 and was part of the Second Lesson used in Evening Prayers. It was the passage that spoke to Wesley himself over the loss of Sophy Hopkey. See *Works* 18: 176 and the diary entries for March 4, 1737 on 479-80. He quoted it again to Thomas Bigg over the loss of marriage to Grace Murray in October 7, 1749; see *Works* 26: 388-89.

[206] *Letters* (Telford) VII: 155.

[207] *Letters* (Telford) VII: 156.

while.[208] For the Christian death is not the end; it opens up a life with God that is to be enjoyed eternally, totally free of grief, pain, sorrow and suffering. Western countries are almost in a state of denial over death, and with technology and modern medicine we do everything to put it off as far as possible. Even aging is rejected with our endless addiction to diets and exercise to keep any signs of advancing years away. It is little wonder we don't relate to Wesley's pastoral advice on this. The reference to Ezekiel 24:16 is used by Wesley in a number of other letters dealing with tragic loss. He wrote to Samuel Bradburn in 1786 soon after the death of his wife, which he took very hard:

> But still, even when we can say, 'It is the Lord,' it is hard to add, 'Let Him do what seemeth Him good.' I remember formerly, when I read these words in the church at Savannah, 'Son of man, behold, I take from thee the desire of thine eyes with a stroke.' I was pierced through as with a sword, and could not utter a word more. But our comfort is, He that made the heart can heal the heart. Your help stands in Him alone. He will command all these things to work together for good.[209]

This comfort cannot come from the circumstances and situations we experience, for many of them are deeply painful, but it can come from a rich, trusting relationship with God, who is able to meet us at the point of our deepest need and enable us to live in the power of his love. He reminds Ellen Gretton that affliction purifies us, and while we are not to despise it, nor are we to count it as an insignificant or accidental thing, "but receive it as a token of His love."[210] If God visits us with adversity, he will send a blessing with it, and it will be for our benefit as a means of weaning us from the world and uniting us more closely to him.[211] If God later changes it for prosperity, this will also be for our good: "It is our wisdom to improve the present state, be it one or the other. With what we will be we have nothing to do. We need take no thought for the morrow."[212] For Wesley, the greatest health of all is "to be filled with the spirit of love and of an healthful mind," and this God will always supply.[213]

---

[208] *Letters* (Telford) VII: 156.

[209] *Letters* (Telford) VII: 314-15. See also *Letters* (Telford) VIII: 116.

[210] *Letters* (Telford) VII: 97.

[211] *Letters* (Telford) VII: 104-105.

[212] *Letters* (Telford) VII: 105. See also *Letters* (Telford) V: 317.

[213] *Letters* (Telford) IV: 256.

Chapter 5

Spiritual Formation:
Helps to Developing the Life of God in the Soul

When we think about spiritual formation we often focus on such things as Bible reading and study, personal prayer, meditation, and various devotional aids and practices. So many of these are focused on the individual's spiritual development and practiced privately. Personal prayer and Bible reading are not just for my benefit but are to be seen as a means of cultivating our relationship with God, preparing us to more effectively love others. Wesley's insistence that we are to love both God and neighbour means that we cannot deepen of our life with God without engagement with other people, and the depth of our life with God is intimately linked to the depth of these relationships. The life of God in the soul is not to be reduced to a focus on "my" welfare; it must always be about "our" welfare, enabling us to demonstrate our love in practical ways. It is this spiral of deepening relationships that is critical to the whole picture of Wesleyan spirituality. In what follows we examine some of the things Wesley recommended to his people for enhancing their life with God, the fellowship of the church and the people of their community.

Means of Grace

Wesley acknowledged that relationships don't develop automatically, they need to be formed and nurtured. This involves an active participation in those activities that will foster a deepening of the bonds between the parties. These 'activities' are the means of grace and they enable the enlarging of our capacity to receive and give love, as well as our inclination to actually do so, through an ongoing relationship with God and then with the neighbour. They must not be substituted for the actual relationship nor become an end in themselves. The 'means' can be categorised as works of piety and this includes such things as prayer, Bible study, small groups, corporate worship, fasting, self-denial, the covenant service, and the Lord's Supper; works of mercy that includes such things as visiting the sick, and doing good to others.[1] They give objectivity to our subjective experiences of God and provide practices which help us to develop a critical self-awareness of our hidden deceptions, mixed motives and

---

[1] For a thorough examination of the Wesleyan means of grace, see Henry H. Knight III, *The Presence of God in the Christian Life: John Wesley and the Means of Grace* (Lanham: Scarecrow Press, 1992).

societal conditioning. The means oppose any static conception of grace as something given to us in the past and therefore we need no longer worry about our current state. Likewise, they correct the notion that by grace we are 'instantly' perfect, apart from and outside a process of growth. Both views tend to stress we need 'only believe,' which sees perfection as absolute sinlessness and fails to take seriously the distinction between voluntary and involuntary sin. All of the means are tied very closely to community support and it is this relational aspect that I want to briefly mention here.

In his sermon "The Means of Grace" (1746) Wesley gives the following definition: "By 'means of grace' I understand outward signs, words, or actions ordained of God, and appointed to this end—to be the ordinary channels whereby he might convey to men preventing, justifying, or sanctifying grace."[2] He emphasises that they are only of value as a "means" to an "end"; without the Spirit of God there is no intrinsic power in them. It is God alone who is the source of all grace: "We know likewise that he is able to give the same grace, though there were no means on the face of the earth. In this sense we may affirm that with regard to God there is no such thing as means, seeing he is equally able to work whatsoever pleaseth him by any or by none at all."[3] This can be pictured in terms of the need for plants to have water if they are to live and flourish. Rain can fall on an area and water all the plants in that location, and in this sense there is no direct involvement of any 'means' at all. Water can also be conveyed to specific plants by a bucket or by a hose, and these are specific 'means' used to carry it from a source to the location. However, neither the bucket nor the hose have any power in themselves to water the plant—they simply carry the water, which is the actual source of refreshment. Wesley is affirming that God can bless his people in all sorts of non-specific ways but he can also bless them through specific means—such as reading the Bible, prayer or acts of service to the neighbour. The Bible is simply a book with words on its pages and it has no power at all to nourish us (like the hose); however, if we read these words open to the grace of God, the Holy Spirit will work in our hearts through the channels provided by these words. It is God alone who changes us and there is no power in the words separated from the Spirit. Wesley reminds his people that both works of piety and works of mercy are "real means of grace" and *both* are essential for spiritual vitality.[4] In a letter to Mrs. Gair he said that "The great danger is that you should forsake the sacred channels of His grace. Only abide in the way. Read, meditate, pray as you *can*, though not as you *would*. Then God will return and abundantly lift up the light of his countenance upon you."[5] He re-emphasises that "outward religion is nothing worth without the religion of the heart; ... external worship is lost

---

[2] *Works* 1, "The Means of Grace," 381.
[3] *Works* 1, "The Means of Grace," 382.
[4] *Works* 3, "On Visiting the Sick," 385.
[5] *Letters* (Telford) VI: 117.

labour without a heart devoted to God; that the outward ordinances of God then profit much when they advance inward holiness, but when they advance it not are unprofitable and void, are lighter than vanity; yea, that when they are used, as it were, *in the place* of this, they are an utter abomination to the Lord."[6] However, it is a "fatal delusion" to think that "outward religion" has no place.[7] For example, ministry to the neighbour requires personal involvement as visiting the sick cannot be done by proxy. Such ministry is essential, not only for the benefit of the neighbour, but also for our own spiritual welfare.[8] He told Mrs. Savage that "By stirring up the gift of God that is in you, you will find a constant increase of inward life. Labour to be more and more active, more and more devoted to Him. Be ready to do and suffer His whole will; then will He 'Sink you to perfection's height, the depth of humble love.'"[9]

Christian Lifestyle

As we have seen, Wesley taught that the life of God in the soul impacts both our being and our doing. The primary help for developing the life of God in the soul is the presence of God's love in the heart: "He whom you fear [God], whom you love, has qualified *you* for promoting his work in a more excellent way. Because you love God you love your brother also. You love not only your friends, but your enemies; not only the friends, but even the enemies of God."[10] It is love alone that enables us to face whatever comes our way personally and in service to others: "what prospect of danger will then be able to fright them from their labour of love! What suffering will they not be ready to undergo to save one soul from everlasting burnings! What continuance of labour, disappointment, pain will vanquish their fixed resolution!"[11] In terms of ministry to others, Wesley writes: "Indeed it is hard for any to persevere in so unpleasing a work unless *love* overpowers both pain and fear. . . . The presence of him whom their soul loveth will then make their labour light."[12] This is true both for those personal disciplines essential for our own spiritual health and witness, and those required for our service for others.

---

[6] *Works* 1, "The Means of Grace," 379. See also 378.

[7] *Works* 1, "The Means of Grace," 380.

[8] *Works* 3, "On Visiting the Sick," 389.

[9] *Letters* (Telford) VI: 58. See also *Letters* (Telford) VII: 302.

[10] *Works* 2, "The Reformation of Manners," 321. See also *Works* 2, "The Reformation of Manners," 315.

[11] *Works* 2, "The Reformation of Manners," 315. See also 316.

[12] *Works* 2, "The Reformation of Manners," 314.

Simplicity (Single Intention)

Wesley has consistently affirmed that God created us "for himself, to know, love, and enjoy him. As the sun is the centre of the solar system, so…we need not scruple to affirm that God is the centre of spirits."[13] However, we are continually surrounded "with persons and things that tend to draw us from our centre." By nature we are easily distracted and we need God's power through faith in Christ to re-centre us and keep us focused.[14] Wesley defines dissipation as "the uncentring the soul from God,"[15] and the cure for it is the faith that works by love and simplicity in all our intentions, with purity in all our affections.[16] In the sermon "The Witness of our own Spirit" (1746) Wesley emphasised the importance of "simplicity" and a "single intention":

> We are then simple of heart when the eye of our mind is singly fixed on God; when in all things we aim at God alone, as our God, our portion, our strength, our happiness, our exceeding reward, our all in time and eternity. This is simplicity: when a steady view, a single intention of promoting his glory, of doing and suffering his blessed will, runs through our whole soul, fills all our heart, and is the constant spring of all our thoughts, desires, and purposes.[17]

This can only ever be done by the power and grace of God operating in our life by the Spirit: "As soon as ever the grace of God (in the former sense, his pardoning love) is manifested to our soul, the grace of God (in the latter sense, the power of his Spirit) takes place therein. And now we can perform, through God, what to man was impossible."[18] Wesley says this comes down to a simple goal: "pursue one thing: happiness in knowing, in loving, in serving God."[19] It was in essence the advice he gave to Thomas Broadbent, who had ample reason to praise God for his blessings on his labours. Wesley was confident that these will increase as long as Broadbent does not entangle himself with the affairs of this life: "If you seek your happiness in God alone, you will never be disappointed: if in anything else, you surely will; for all creatures are broken cisterns. Let your eye be single."[20] Those of us living in rich nations face endless distractions as the world of advertising offers us the latest item that will enrich our life and make everything wonderful. Adverts come to us in an unending stream, assuring us that if we just buy this new product, we will be

---

[13] *Works* 3, "On Dissipation," 117.

[14] *Works* 3, "On Dissipation," 118-19.

[15] *Works* 3, "On Dissipation," 120.

[16] *Works* 3, "On Dissipation," 122. He particularly recommends the writings of à Kempis and Jeremy Taylor, both of whom stress the necessity of a "single eye"; see 122-23.

[17] *Works* 1, "The Witness of Our Own Spirit," 307.

[18] *Works* 1, "The Witness of Our Own Spirit," 309.

[19] *Works* 3, "On Dissipation," 123.

[20] *Letters* (Telford) VIII: 258.

happy and fulfilled, and all our relationships will flourish. Even if we ourselves cannot afford it, we will aspire to possess it one day and this longing easily displaces or distracts us from our life in God. It is little wonder that we need the help of the Holy Spirit to keep focused on God. However, the Holy Spirit can best work in our life and relationships when we are open to acquiring the wisdom and discernment that comes from the knowledge and experience of the people of God.

Knowledge and Wisdom

Given our current technology, what Wesley says about books in this section will apply equally well to all the other forms of accessing knowledge available to us today. Near the end of his life and ministry he wrote to George Holder and told him: "It cannot be that the people should grow in grace unless they give themselves to reading. A reading people will always be a knowing people."[21] What Wesley had in mind is seen in a number of letters to his niece, Sarah Wesley. He affirmed to her that "It is certain the Author of our nature designed that we should not destroy but regulate our desire for knowledge."[22] He cautioned her about reading books that are not helpful to her spiritual life and it was important that she be guided by her father and himself on what to read.[23] He then gives guidance on a suitable program of study and books to read, beginning with the Bible: "All you want to know of Him is contained in one book, the Bible. And all you learn is to be referred to this, either directly or remotely." She is to spend at least an hour a day reading and meditating on the Bible, reading every morning and evening a portion of the Old Testament and the New Testament with the *Explanatory Notes*. Then he gives a long list of works covering a very wide range of subjects from the arts and sciences, as well as religion.[24] This will give Sarah all the knowledge that any reasonable Christian would need, but the focus was to remain on knowing God and Jesus Christ whom he has sent.[25] He warns her against reading "trash" (novels, romances and such), because they will rob her of spiritual health in the same way that eating trash robs people of bodily health.[26] This is a much needed caution for us today in a world of endless distraction through television, cinema, and the internet. These are not wrong in themselves, any more than books were in Wesley's day. It is the content that either helps spiritual health or detracts from it—and to differentiate the valuable from the worthless we often need the help of the Spirit and the wisdom of the community.

---

[21] *Letters* (Telford) VIII: 247.

[22] *Letters* (Telford) VII: 81.

[23] *Letters* (Telford) VII: 78.

[24] *Letters* (Telford) VII: 82-83.

[25] *Letters* (Telford) VII: 83.

[26] *Letters* (Telford) VII: 237.

Wisdom discerns the ways of God in each situation, rather than applying a universal pattern to be followed by all people in all circumstances. In a letter to John Dickins in 1789 Wesley laid out the basic approach to counselling others: "What I nightly wish is that may all keep close to the Bible. Be not wise above what is written. Enjoin nothing that the Bible does not clearly enjoin. Forbid nothing that it does not clearly forbid."[27] For example, Thomas Willis wrote to Wesley in 1744 seeking his advice on keeping the *Rules of the Band Societies*, especially the one about not buying or selling anything at all on the Lord's Day. Willis said that he keeps this rule, except for selling milk on Sunday mornings "which I believe is a work of necessity and mercy," but if he is wrong he will cease. He explains himself by saying that some in the class are milk sellers and they take milk to Bristol every Sunday morning and the new rule is a burden to them. He points out that the national laws allow the sale of the milk, the cows must be milked on Sundays, the children must be fed, and if it is not used it will not keep till Monday. Perhaps surprisingly, Wesley agreed with him.[28] Willis also mentions the rule about being at a word in buying and selling. He says this is fine for shops, but not markets, where goods rise and fall and you cannot tell what the goods will be till arriving at the market itself—neither in buying nor selling. Wesley agrees with this as well.[29] Both of these letters provide a very good example of the critical distinction between the letter and the spirit of the law, and the need of wisdom to discern the best course of action in the circumstances. Wesley also recognised the importance of the person's conscience and their own standing before God. In 1789 he wrote to Mrs. Bowman concerning a dispute between herself and her son over the possession of plant hot houses and flower gardens. Wesley does not think there is any harm in them "because neither of them is forbidden in Scripture, and it is sinful to condemn anything which Scripture does not condemn." He says that to condemn all those who keep flower gardens or hot houses "is a sin against both God and their neighbours; and one of them might say, 'Why am I judged of another man's conscience? To my own Master I stand or fall.'"[30] We shall see some further example of this later in the chapter.

Providence

As we saw in the chapter 3, Wesley is certain that human life is not simply a matter of randomness and chance. In a letter to Mrs. Hall in 1776 he affirms that "It is not wisdom to impute either our health or any other blessing we enjoy merely to natural causes. It is far better to ascribe all to Him whose kingdom ruleth over all. And whether we have more or less bodily strength is of little

---

[27] *Letters* (Telford) VIII: 192.
[28] *Works* 26: 117.
[29] *Works* 26: 117.
[30] *Letters* (Telford) VIII: 125.

concern so we are strong in the Lord and in the power of His might. He gives strength when it is wanted."[31] He equally rejects the notion that everything is predestined by God and that we are simply passive recipients of God's plans and purposes. He maintains a confidence in God's care and provision for us while also fully allowing for our liberty to make choices. Exactly how this works remains a mystery and Wesley's attempted explanations of it are no more satisfactory than anyone else's, but the critical issue is that of trust in a God who loves us supremely. He told Mary Cooke "That all trials are good you cannot always see (at least for the present), but you may always *believe*."[32] If we are confident about God's unwavering love for us, then we will be willing to trust him and the sufficiency of his grace when all the evidence appears to deny this. In a letter to the business man Ebenezer Blackwell (shortly after his house had probably burnt down in a fire), Wesley says he believes God has taught them to say that the Lord gives, and the Lord takes away, so blessed be his name (Job 1:21).

> Shall not these things work together for good? Perhaps God was jealous over you, lest your heart should lean to any of the things of earth. He will have you to be all his own; to desire nothing but him; to seek him and love him with your whole heart. And he knows what are the hindrances, and what means will be most effectual toward it. Then let him work according to the counsel of his own will.[33]

The danger is being identified here is spiritual idolatry—loving what God gives (his business and the benefits it brings in this case) more than God the Giver. As we saw earlier, this is an ever-present temptation for Christians and an essential element of God's pure love for us is his discipline. While this seems to have gone out of fashion in much of Western society, love and discipline go together if we are truly interested in the well-being of the other. In bringing up our children, a failure to discipline usually leaves the child with little self-control and they simply respond to any situation as their mood and self-interest leads them. There is, of course, a vast difference between discipline and punishment; Wesley believed that God disciplines us for our own good but he does not punish us—though we do have to face the consequences of our choices. From a human perspective, the difference between the two may 'appear' miniscule in some circumstances and this is why our understanding of God's nature and commitment to trust him is so vital. The reason the fire might be a blessing rather than a curse has to do with Blackwell's attitude to it—can he see the presence of God in the situation and still maintain his trust in him? Wesley shared with Blackwell from his own experience and reflected that "whatever God calls us to, he will fit us for," with many more making

---

[31] *Letters* (Telford) VI: 223.
[32] *Letters* (Telford) VII: 378.
[33] *Works* 26: 311.

shipwreck of their lives in the calm than in the storm.[34] Wesley shares the challenges he is facing in his own marriage: "What a blessing it is to have these little crosses, that we may try what spirit we are of. We could not live in continual sunshine. It would dry up all the grace of God that is in us."[35] He shares how hard it was to travel with Mrs. Wesley due to her endless complaints about conditions, while none of them ever upset him. He finds it hard to bear with her continually finding fault with God's provisions: "The doctrine of a particular providence is what exceeding few persons understand, at least not practically, so as to apply it to every circumstance of life. This I want—to see God acting in everything, and disposing all for his own glory and his creatures' good."[36] As his marriage deteriorated further, he tells Blackwell: "I have learned by the grace of God in every state to be content. I have in this respect done what I ought and what I could. Now let God do what seemeth Him good. What peace do we find in all circumstances when we can say, 'Not as I will, but as Thou wilt'!"[37]

The matter of trusting God is one thing when we go through difficulties that we regard as due to impersonal circumstances or the ill-will of another person, but it would seem harder to accept the notion that our situation was deliberately given to us by God. Wesley says to Mrs. Johnston: "The truth is, God allots us health or sickness, ease or pain, just as He sees one or the other is best for us."[38] So he can tell Damaris Perronet that many trials come which are hard physically and spiritually "and if you chose for yourself, you ought not to choose the situation you are now in If you did, it would be a great hurt to your soul. It would hinder the work of God in you. But you do not choose for yourself; God chooses for you: and He cannot err." She is called to trust him in the trial and all will be well.[39] This same confidence in the goodness of God's provision is seen in a letter to Mrs. Moon: "He that governs all things well for His own glory and for the good of them that love Him sees that it is best for you to be led in a strait and thorny way, and therefore permits it by His adorable providence. And you experimentally find that all these things are for your profit, that you may be a partaker of His holiness."[40] He reminds her of the "light afflictions" she faces now in comparison to the greater glory to come.[41] This reflects the same confidence expressed by the Apostle Paul in 2 Corinthians 4:16-18. It is this confidence that our life is in God's hands and that because he is loving, merciful and good, we can trust him with the situation

---

[34] *Works* 26: 492.

[35] *Works* 26: 555.

[36] *Works* 26: 581.

[37] *Letters* (Telford) IV: 21.

[38] *Letters* (Telford) VI: 315.

[39] *Letters* (Telford) V: 234.

[40] *Letters* (Telford) VI: 20. See also *Letters* (Telford) VII: 316.

[41] *Letters* (Telford) VI: 21.

even when we cannot explain it. Without this belief in God's providential care, the trial and tests of life would probably destroy our trust. It is evident that Wesley himself found that trusting God with every experience in life was the only way to live: "It is well that our life and all things pertaining to it are in His hands. He orders all things well; and being assured of this, we need be careful for nothing: it is enough that in all things we may make our requests with thanksgiving."[42] We also need to remember that God's providence is not just associated with trials and tests, it is related to blessings as well. He told Mrs. Middleton: "I am called to work: you are called to suffer. And if both these paths lead to the same parish, it is enough."[43]

In a series of letters to Freeborn Garrettson in 1789, Wesley seeks to deal with the relationship of providence and human freedom in decision making. The immediate context was the place of service that Garrettson was to take in his service for God. Wesley thought that it really did not matter where a person served as long as they were fully employed for God and were following God's providence. In an interesting turn of phrase, he says this can appear as "a kind of holy disordered order."[44] In other words, God's providential working in our life is not always open to our discernment—it must be a matter of trust. A related issue has to do with the way that Garrettson uses the word "freedom" in his letters. Wesley says, "This is a word much liable to be abused. If I have plain Scripture or plain reason for doing a thing well. These are my rules, and my only rules. I regard not whether I had freedom or no. This is an unscriptural expression and a very fallacious rule. I wish to be in every point, great and small, a scriptural, rational Christian. . . . . Will you break your word because you do not find freedom to keep it? Is not this enthusiasm?"[45] In a later letter Wesley deals with the leading of the Spirit and how we can avoid using "freedom" as an excuse not to do God's will. We need to obey a clear text of Scripture, and then we can be guided by suggesting reasons for each step we take (Wesley's experience) rather than relying on impressions, as God himself "judges the last to be the least desirable way, as it is often impossible to distinguish dark impressions from divine or even diabolical."[46] In other words, where the teaching of Scripture is clear we cannot use our "freedom" to go against it without thereby committing sin. Where it is not specific (and this covers most of life's daily choices), it is a matter being sensitive to the leading of the Spirit and Wesley thinks this is best discerned by sound reasoning and wisdom. Here the role of the community and experienced Christians is invaluable, as well as the records left to us throughout the history of the church. God's providence is also seen in the provision of ministry opportunities that

---

[42] *Letters* (Telford) VI: 310.

[43] *Letters* (Telford) VII: 317.

[44] *Letters* (Telford) VIII: 112.

[45] *Letters* (Telford) VIII: 112.

[46] *Letters* (Telford) VIII: 154.

otherwise might have been missed. He told Mrs. Johnson that her ministry to the inconsolable parents of a young man who had recently died was clearly providential. The young man's death occurred just as she and her husband were returning to the location and they were immediately able to be with the parents to minister to them.[47]

Self-Denial and Taking Up Your Cross

Wesley had always emphasised the place of Christian liberty in the life with God and neighbour. Certainly, as we have seen, love cannot exist without it. However, the ever-present danger was that liberty would turn into self-indulgence and this was certainly not healthy. In his 1760 sermon "Self-Denial" (based on Lk. 9:23) Wesley deals with this tendency. He notes that the command in Luke to take up your cross daily and follow Jesus is universal in its scope and is "absolutely, indispensably necessary, either to our becoming or continuing his disciples."[48] The need for it flows from the fact that "the will of God is the supreme, unalterable rule for every intelligent creature; ... this is the natural, necessary result of the relation between creatures and their Creator."[49] He defines self-denial as "the denying or refusing to follow our own will in anything" because we are convinced that "that the will of God is the only rule of action to us."[50] This has not been our natural inclination since the Fall due to the total corruption of our nature: "our will, depraved equally with the rest, is wholly bent to indulge our natural corruption." He is adamant that we cannot follow both God's will and our selfish will—it is one or the other. If we follow our own will we simply strengthen its perverseness and increase the corruption of our nature.[51] Self-denial, then, is "to deny ourselves any pleasure which does not spring from, and lead to, God" no matter how pleasant or agreeable it may seem to us.[52] The failure of self-denial is shown by clinging to our favourite sin, by the failure to repent and demonstrate its fruits, spiritual sloth, and not using or neglecting the means of grace in our pursuit of holiness.[53]

In an important section he distinguishes this from taking up your cross, which "is anything contrary to our will, anything displeasing to our nature";[54] on our Christian journey, we need to do both. Taking up our cross is more intense than self-denial, as it is not simply foregoing pleasure but requires actually enduring pain. In doing God's will we may encounter something that is

---

[47] *Letters* (Telford) VII: 253-54.
[48] *Works* 2, "Self-Denial," 238.
[49] *Works* 2, "Self-Denial," 241.
[50] *Works* 2, "Self-Denial," 242.
[51] *Works* 2, "Self-Denial," 242.
[52] *Works* 2, "Self-Denial," 243.
[53] *Works* 2, "Self-Denial," 246-48.
[54] *Works* 2, "Self-Denial," 243.

grievous to experience, contrary to our will and displeasing to our nature; this is what Wesley calls a "cross." He thinks this usually arises with the need to metaphorically pluck out our right eye or cut off our right hand to part us from a foolish desire, inordinate affection, or to separate ourselves from the object of it—and this is always painful.[55] Likewise, for God to heal the sickness of sin, to cure foolish desires or inordinate affections is also painful. He gives the example of the rich young ruler giving away his wealth because of the need to heal his covetousness. We "bear our cross" when we "endure what is laid upon us without our choice, with meekness and resignation" and we "take up our cross" when we "voluntarily suffer what it is in our power to avoid; when we willingly embrace the will of God, though contrary to our own; when we choose what is painful because it is the will of our wise and gracious Creator."[56] While we all experience this reality, yet it is always "my" cross:

> It is prepared of God for him; it is given by God to him, as a token of his love. And if he receives it as such, and (*after using such means to remove the pressure as Christian wisdom directs*) [emphasis mine] lies as clay in the potter's hand, it is disposed and ordered by God for his good, both with regard to the quality of it and in respect to its quantity and degree, its duration and every other circumstance.[57]

It is important to note that it is our choice to embrace the cross and we do so only for love of God and other people, though we are perfectly at liberty to reduce the impact of it. In all of this, God acts as the "physician of our souls" for our profit and participating in his holiness. Wesley uses the example that healing a wound may cause pain due to the removal of the putrefied or unsound tissue in order to preserve the healthy part. This argument was certainly powerful in his day, when anaesthesia was practically unknown; it is a much less convincing argument for those of us with access to efficient forms of pain relief and the expectation that we should never have to suffer. He also uses the illustration of enduring the loss of a limb rather than the loss of the whole body. However,

> It does not imply the disciplining ourselves…, the literally tearing our own flesh: the wearing of haircloth, or iron girdles, or anything else that would impair our bodily health…, but embracing the will of God, though contrary to our own; the choosing wholesome, though bitter, medicines; the freely accepting temporary pain, of whatever kind, and in whatever degree, when it is either essentially or accidentally necessary to eternal pleasure.[58]

---

[55] *Works* 2, "Self-Denial," 243. See n. 17 on Wesley's two great loves: Sophy Hopkey and Grace Murray, 243-44.

[56] *Works* 2, "Self-Denial," 244.

[57] *Works* 2, "Self-Denial," 245. See also *Letters* (Telford) VI: 227.

[58] *Works* 2, "Self-Denial," 245.

Once again, Wesley is clear that there is no spiritual benefit from the types of spirituality that think mortifying the flesh improves the soul.

Taking up your cross could be as simple responding to a request from Wesley to move from a dearly loved preaching circuit to one that is difficult in order to help out another preacher, as was the case with Joseph Sutcliffe.[59] It might be having an uncomfortable conversation with a fellow Christian about some aspect of their life or ministry.[60] It may not even entail any pain or suffering as such. Writing to his brother Charles Wesley in 1788, John told him that though he is presently suffering due to his poor health, God still has things for him to do "provided you now take up your cross (for such it frequently must be) and go out at least an hour in a day."[61] Note that the 'cross' is not the illness itself, but going out each day when he does not feel like it. So it is doing something he could reasonably avoid, it is not condemned by Scripture, it is not suffering as such, but a freely chosen action for the benefit it brings—either to others, or in this case, to his own health. Sometime it was to embrace a major challenge in ministry for the Lord's sake. Wesley wrote to John Fletcher in 1773 about his objections to being the one who would take on the leadership of the Methodist movement when Wesley died because he could not bear the crosses sure to come his way. Wesley responded: "You are not able to bear them now; and they are not now come. Whenever they do come, will He not send them in due number, weight, and measure? And will they not all be for your profit, that you may be a partaker of His holiness?"[62] He made the same point to Mrs. Bradburn who was enjoying the ministry at Birstall because the people were teachable and loving. He told her that "as you have fewer crosses, I expect you will have better health. Yet crosses of one kind or another you must still expect. Otherwise you must go out of the world. But every cross will be proportioned to your strength; and you will always find His grace sufficient for you."[63] All this underscored the need for patience while God did his work in the heart. He defines it as a "a gracious temper wrought in the heart of a believer by the power of the Holy Ghost. It is a disposition to suffer whatever pleases God, in the manner and for the time that pleases him."[64] Wesley believed that "Patience does not imply the not feeling this; it is not apathy or insensibility." Nor is it simply stoicism at one extreme or dejection at the other. We are kept from all these by seeing God, whose nature is love, as the "author" of our suffering so that we can share in his holiness. If we submit to God in the suffering we will experience peace, joy, hope and love.[65] Qualities such as

---

[59] *Letters* (Telford) VIII: 240.

[60] *Letters* (Telford) VI: 218.

[61] *Letters* (Telford) VIII: 41. See also 42.

[62] *Letters* (Telford) VI: 12.

[63] *Letters* (Telford) VII: 198. See also *Letters* (Telford) VIII: 44, 78, 109, 158.

[64] *Works* 3, "On Patience," 171.

[65] *Works* 3, "On Patience," 172.

courage, Christian zeal and good works are also involved, but finally "Is it any less than the 'perfect love of God', constraining us to love every soul of man, 'even as Christ loved us'?" The fruit of this is a constant resignation to God, giving up all we are, have and love as a "holy sacrifice."[66]

Health

In a letter to Mrs Cock in 1790 he says he is sad to learn of her illness but reminds her that the Lord loves whom he chastens. However, this does not mean a passive acceptance of her situation and he encourages her to do all she can to regain her health: "And if you can recover your health, you ought; for health is a great blessing."[67] This was his conviction all through his ministry and can be illustrated in his letters to numerous correspondents. It is an important point on which to be clear; for all his advice to accept the chastening of the Lord and submitting to his will, he very rarely saw poor health as such to be a blessing or a help to spiritual health. He told Robert Carr Brackenbury that "It is undoubtedly our duty to use the most probable means we can for either preserving or restoring our health. But, after all, God does continually assert His own right of saving both souls and bodies. He blesses the medicines, and they take place; He withdraws His influence, and they avail nothing."[68] As he reflected on the situation of a Mrs. Knapp, he concluded that "Your body frequently presses down your spirit by reason of your nervous disorder." He then gives her some very practical advice that may lessen if not remove the disorder that has to do with her sleeping patterns; she ought not to stay up too late, not even for reading or prayer. His reasoning here is tied to the damage she may do to her own health by a misguided notion that God prefers us to ruin our health for spiritual purposes and he uses this little phrase: "do not offer murder for sacrifice."[69] This is a favourite phrase of Wesley's and occurs many times in his writings. In other words, wilfully damaging our own health because we think it will be a sacrifice pleasing to God that will further our effectiveness in ministry, is equivalent to "murder." He wrote in a similar vein to Robert Carr Brackenbury, telling him that preaching regularly will help his health as long as the service finishes within the hour: "The want of observing this has many times hurt you; and we must not offer murder for sacrifice. We are not at liberty to impair our own health in hopes of doing good to others."[70]

---

[66] *Works* 3, "On Patience," 173.

[67] *Letters* (Telford) VIII: 221.

[68] *Letters* (Telford) VII: 209-10.

[69] *Letters* (Telford) VII: 52.

[70] *Letters* (Telford) VII: 90. See also *Letters* (Telford) VII: 240, 313, 380; *Letters* (Telford) VIII: 27, 190.

He told his niece, Sarah Wesley, that she needs to keep her trust in God even when a troublesome sore is healing very slowly.[71] However, trusting God is not the same as a stoical acceptance of the state of our health. Wesley had a lengthy correspondence with Dorothy Furly, and a portion of it dealt with her poor health and its impact on her spiritual life. This could so easily have been a source of her turning away from God. A letter in 1756 sets the tone for the heart of his pastoral advice: "It is a happy thing if we can learn obedience by the things which we suffer."[72] Suffering in and of itself will not automatically promote spiritual life and we have to learn to obey God in all things, because it does not come naturally to us. He assures Dorothy that God will give her health if this is best, with the spiritual and bodily vigour to work for him: "And this strength will either increase or decrease in the same proportion with your sense of His love," which can be lost by sinning, omitting duty, giving way to pride, anger or any other inward sin such as not praying, being lazy or slothful. However, we have no need to lose the sense of God's love any more than it is necessary to sin or omit duty.[73] The critical element here is the quality of our relationship with God, rather than the circumstances in which that relationship is conducted. Later in the year he reminds her that God works in his own way in different persons, so she must not build on the experience of others. Consistent with his advice to others, he points out that "heaviness and darkness" can be due to disease and she is to keep praying faithfully and God will reveal to her if it is sin at the root.[74] He confirms that sickness itself, and even approaching death will not promote spiritual life,[75] and she needs to keep praying for God's healing power. Regarding divine healing, Wesley says: "There is a wonderful mystery in the manner and circumstances of that mighty working whereby He subdues all things to Himself and leaves nothing in the heart but His pure love alone."[76] God is free to respond to our prayers in the time and manner of his choosing, not our demanding.

Spiritual Friendships

Wesley wrote to Frances Godfrey in 1789 encouraging her to keep moving forward in her Christian journey: "From what you have already experienced, you know there is one happiness in the earth below and in heaven above. You know God alone can satisfy your soul either in earth or heaven. Cleave to Him with full purpose of heart. If you seek happiness in anything but Him, you must be disappointed." Yet in the same letter he asks if she is finding satisfaction in

---

[71] *Letters* (Telford) VIII: 229.

[72] *Letters* (Telford) III: 208.

[73] *Letters* (Telford) III: 215.

[74] *Letters* (Telford) III: 230-31.

[75] *Letters* (Telford) IV: 15.

[76] *Letters* (Telford) IV: 55-56.

some of her fellow Christian companions on the journey to heaven and if she does not have any, she must make them *"for none can travel that road alone* [emphasis mine]. Then labour to help each other on that you may be altogether Christians."[77] This affirms what he has consistently taught over the span of his ministry—a healthy Christian life is a life lived not just with God but also with the neighbour. He told Freeborn Garrettson that "It is a very desirable thing that the children of God should communicate their experience to each other; and it is generally most profitable when they can do it face to face."[78] This was from a man with such an extensive correspondence, and it underscores that love can best be expressed and friendships nurtured face-to-face. While letter writing in his day and email, social media and Skype in our day, are all vital ways to express and nurture relationships, they cannot replace our physical presence in the life of the other. It is, as the Bible reminds us, why God could only fully reveal himself to us through the incarnation of Christ.

All our relationships have to be worked at; including those within the Christian fellowship, and this is not always an easy task. The Wesleyan emphasis on the love of God and the love of neighbour made some wonder about the depth of this love and whether it was possible to love others too much. In two letters to Elizabeth Baker in 1788 he responds to her question concerning this and says: "In one sense this cannot be; you cannot have too much benevolence for the whole human race: but in another sense you may; you may grieve too much for the distress of others, even so much as to make you incapable of giving them relief which otherwise you should give them."[79] In the follow-up letter he tells her that you would imagine there could be no harmful consequence of having the deepest concern for the sin and misery of others, but experience shows otherwise. He gives the example of Lucretia Smith, an outstanding example of a Christian, who "reasoned on that question, 'Why does not the God of love make every one as happy as me?' till she lost all her happiness, all her peace, which she never recovered since."[80] We often find it difficult when our friends offer us advice that was not asked for, or we are reproved for something we did or did not do; but it is the depth of love in the relationship that will help us to receive even these things as a blessing.[81] Given our human weaknesses, some of the most mature Christians can still be very hard to get on with and he urged Mrs. Nuttal to join the local Methodist Society, even though they are not all "angels" but "weak, fallible creatures" because they will be helpful to her.[82] One of the great hindrances to forming

---

[77] *Letters* (Telford) VIII: 158. See also *Letters* (Telford) VII: 162; *Letters* (Telford) VIII: 127; *Works* 25: 339.

[78] *Letters* (Telford) VII: 276.

[79] *Letters* (Telford) VIII: 85.

[80] *Letters* (Telford) VIII: 88.

[81] *Letters* (Telford) VI: 166.

[82] *Letters* (Telford) VII: 122.

any new relationship or deepening a casual friendship is prejudice. Wesley explained to Lady Maxwell that while prejudice is common to all, it will not damage a relationship unless it becomes fixed in the mind. This is not changed by increased understanding as it is a matter of the heart; we cannot be prejudiced against any that we love till that love declines. This is why it is so important to share what is in our heart with one another.[83] In a letter to Henry Moore he advised him that the only way he can fix his troubled relationship with Arthur Keene is to "conquer him by love."[84] He gives similar advice to Mrs. Bradburn: "Look kindly on them that have wronged you most. Speak civilly, yea affectionately, to them; they cannot stand it long:... I have set my heart upon you being a happy woman and overcoming all your enemies by love."[85] Given even our best intentions, relationships within the church can fracture. Wesley noted in a letter to Mrs. Brisco that the work in Thirsk was greatly hindered by a misunderstanding between two of the members and this needs to end for the sake of the witness of the Society. He asks her to work at reconciling them for the benefit of all.[86] Wesley was often asked whether his preachers and key leaders should take the step beyond friendship and marry. Wesley was aware that Lady Huntingdon forbade her preachers to marry: "All I can say in that respect is, 'If thou mayst be free, use *it* rather.' I married because I needed a home, in order to recover my health; and I did recover it. But I did not seek happiness thereby, and I did not find. We know this may be found in the knowledge and enjoyment and service of God, whether in a married or single state. But whenever we deny ourselves and take up the cross for His sake, the happier we shall be both here and in eternity."[87] On the other hand, he can write to George Holder: "If you and your wife strengthen each other's hands in God, then you will surely receive a blessing from Him. But (it) is not abundance of money or any creature that can (make) *us* happy without Him."[88]

Practical Advice for Spiritual Formation

Wesley's understanding of Christian perfection raised many practical questions for his Methodist people, and often led to extended personal correspondence to supplement his visits. His extended correspondence with Mrs. Elizabeth Bennis began in August 1763 and many of the early letters were taken up with questions of the witness of the Spirit to heart holiness. He tells her that "you may frequently be in heaviness, and may find your love to God not near so

---

[83] *Letters* (Telford) IV: 317.

[84] *Letters* (Telford) VIII: 63. See also *Letters* (Telford) VIII: 22.

[85] *Letters* (Telford) VII: 307.

[86] *Letters* (Telford) VII: 329.

[87] *Letters* (Telford) VIII: 223.

[88] *Letters* (Telford) VIII: 247.

warm at sometimes as it is at others. Many wanderings likewise, and many deficiencies, are consistent with pure love" but she may continue to claim the abiding witness of the Spirit.[89] Her testimony of this grace remained present over the years and in 1766 Wesley notes that a Methodist preacher has lately denied any witness of sanctification; she has a direct testimony and is urged to share it because "Nothing is a stronger incitement to them that seek after the same blessing.... Indeed, if they are not thirsting after this, it is scarce possible to keep what they have: they can hardly retain any power of faith if they are not panting after holiness."[90] Like many, Elizabeth struggled with the relationship between Christian perfection and human weakness: "A thousand infirmities are consistent even with the highest degree of holiness, which is no other than pure love, an heart devoted to God, one design and one desire. Then whatever is done either in word or deed may be done in the name of the Lord Jesus."[91] In 1767 he reminds her that "The essential part of Christian holiness is giving the heart wholly to God; and certainly we need not lose any degree of that light and love which at first attend this: it is our own infirmity if we do; it is not the will of the Lord concerning us. Your present business is not to reason whether you should call your experience thus or thus, but to go straight to Him that loves you, with all your wants, how great or how many soever they are." This grace is received by simple faith, "Nevertheless you will still be encompassed with numberless infirmities; for you live in an house of clay, and therefore this corruptible body will more or less press down the soul, yet not so as to prevent your rejoicing evermore and having a witness that your hear is all His. You may claim this: it is yours; for Christ is yours."[92]

Ann Foard is another correspondent trying to understand the nature of the experience of pure love in the light of our humanity. In 1764 he recommends reading his own *Thoughts upon Perfection* and *Farther Thoughts* to help her understand the relationship between Christian perfection and human frailty. Ann believes she once tasted of the blessing but has now lost it. Wesley affirms there is no state under heaven from which we might not fall, but if she keeps her desire to be all love, she need not worry about tomorrow.[93] In another letter a few weeks later he reminds her that both justifying and sanctifying faith are the free gift of God, who is not bound by time, so he can sanctify within a day of justifying as well as in 100 years. There are good witnesses to being sanctified within a few days of being justified and he gives the example of 12 year old Sister Hooley who received the blessing within 9 days. He admits that usually there is some time between them but it is not an invariable rule.[94] "All

---

[89] *Letters* (Telford) IV: 221.

[90] *Letters* (Telford) V: 6.

[91] *Letters* (Telford) V: 6.

[92] *Letters* (Telford) V: 56.

[93] *Letters* (Telford) IV: 266. See also *Letters* (Telford) V: 69.

[94] *Letters* (Telford) IV: 268.

who think this must think we are sanctified by works, or (which comes to the same) by sufferings; for otherwise, what is time necessary for? It must be either to do or to suffer. Whereas, if nothing be required but simple faith, a moment is as good as an age."[95] In a particularly insightful comment, he tells her that "we are continually forming general rules from our own particular experience." So Sarah Ryan and Sarah Crosby suppose all must take as long as they did. Concerning her question about "speaking sharply or roughly, or even a seeming want of meekness, with perfection" he says that he is "fearful of condemning whom God has not condemned. What I cannot understand I leave to Him."[96]

Ann's struggles concerning her spiritual experience continue, and in 1766 Wesley writes to her: "I am deeply concerned for your happiness; and a measure of happiness you may enjoy as long as you feel any love in your heart to God, though it be but a small degree. Be thankful for what you have, and in peace and love wait for the whole promise."[97] A few months later he encourages her to keep seeking and not to give up "till God gives you the full enjoyment of the glorious liberty which you then tasted. Do not imagine that this is afar off; or that you must do and suffer a great deal before you attain it— I dare not affirm that. Has not Christ done and suffered enough for you?... Why should you not now be all love? All devoted to Him that loves you?"[98] Ann, like so many others, believed that her spiritual life would progress if she suffered more, and it was this lack of suffering that prevented her from receiving all of God's grace. At the beginning of 1767 he tells her that "the crosses you meet with, as they are not of your own choosing, will surely work together for good." She is to maintain daily private prayer, Scripture reading and meditation on God's word, but it is still a gift of grace and the timing is God's: "Does He not now read your heart, and see if it pants for His pure love? If so, are not all things ready? May you not now find what you never did before? Ask Him that loves you, whose nature and whose Name is love!"[99] After several more months of correspondence Wesley tells her not to be fooled by feelings, always be ready to witness, and to seek the faith to claim God's grace. He tells her that many Calvinists have a deep experience of God's ways but are not profitable for her to hear as it just leads to debates, and this will inevitably lead to her giving up full salvation completely.[100] The end of the year sees him still urging her to grow in grace "every hour," to use all the grace given now and expect "now" all she wants: "This is the secret of heart religion—at the present moment to work and to believe. Here is Christ your

---

[95] *Letters* (Telford) IV: 268-69.
[96] *Letters* (Telford) IV: 269.
[97] *Letters* (Telford) V: 25.
[98] *Letters* (Telford) V: 32.
[99] *Letters* (Telford) V: 37.
[100] *Letters* (Telford) V: 60.

Lord, the lover of your soul. Give yourself up to Him without delay; and, as you can, without reserve."[101]

Peggy Dale is another striving to understand and then live a holy life. In June 1765 he writes: "Certainly you not only need not sin, but you need not doubt anymore. Christ is yours. All is yours. You can give Him all your heart; and will He not freely give you all things? But you can only return what He has given you by continually receiving more."[102] Like many others, Peggy found it difficult to reconcile heart holiness with her daily experience; in particular, she struggled with keeping her thoughts focused when praying. Wesley told her: "Although it is certain the kind of wandering thoughts which you mention are consistent with pure love, yet it is highly desirable to be delivered from them, because (as you observe) they hinder profitable thoughts." He believes God will do this for her, perhaps in a moment but it is more likely to be a gradual work.[103] In the last letter of 1765 he continues to offer encouragement and assures her that temptations do not sully the soul, so "Abide in Him by simple faith this moment! Live, walk in love! The Lord increase it in you a thousand-fold."[104] Early in 1766 he warns her against casting away her confidence in God: "There is a right temper, a sorrow for our little improvements, which exceedingly resembles envy. But the anointing of the Holy One will teach you to distinguish one from the other."[105] Things do not seem to be improving and by April he notes that she has almost lost her confidence in God and is giving up on what he has already done. Wesley urges her to stay "simple before God! And if that thought comes (as it may do a thousand times), '*How* do you *reconcile* this or this with pure love?' do not reason, but look unto Jesus, and tell him earnestly and without delay, 'Thou shalt answer for me, O Lord, my God.'"[106] He says again how much more blessing God has for her, and "It comforts me to think that you are sinking deeper and deeper in this [love], and receiving more and more of Him that loves you." In the meantime, she is not to be weary in visiting the poor and sick.[107]

By March 1767 she had evidently been "purified from sin,"[108] but even the pure in heart have further questions about their spiritual life. In May 1767 she asks him about an experience of "displeasure" (was it a sin or a temptation to sin?) and Wesley tells her: "But if it was, what would it prove? Not that your heart *had not been cleansed*, but that, being off your guard, you suffered a degree of evil to re-enter. Was it so? Then (if it be not done already) the Lord

---

[101] *Letters* (Telford) V: 65.
[102] *Letters* (Telford) IV: 305.
[103] *Letters* (Telford) IV: 307.
[104] *Letters* (Telford) IV: 319.
[105] *Letters* (Telford) IV: 321.
[106] *Letters* (Telford) V: 7. See also *Letters* (Telford) V: 8, concerning a similar incident.
[107] *Letters* (Telford) V: 33.
[108] *Letters* (Telford) V: 45.

cleanse you from it this moment!" He goes on to say: "the more vigorously you follow after Him the clearer will that unction be, without which it is not possible on some occasions to distinguish between temptations and sins."[109] Several months later Wesley writes: "I hope you now again find the inward witness that you are saved from sin. There is danger in being content without it, into which you may easily reason yourself." She is not to settle for less than this, as the clear witness is the privilege of all God's children and she may have it if she keeps close to God.[110] He advises her that "If you cleave to Him with simplicity of heart, certainly you need not feel sin any more," though she will feel temptation, and often strongly; in it all she is to keep her trust in the Lord and cling to him.[111] In the September he reminds her: "You have every outward advantage for holiness which an indulgent Providence can give. And, what is happier still, you have a fixed determination to use all those advantages to the uttermost. Let your eye be steadily fixed on the mark! To be all love! All devoted! To have one desire, one work, one happiness, one Christ reigning alone and filling you with His fullness!"[112] At the beginning of 1768, in spite of her spiritual progress, Peggy is still struggling with the nature of the witness of the Spirit. Wesley tells her that all who are sanctified may claim the witness immediately, but not everyone experiences this, nor is it always retained, and it is not constant. Sometimes this happens because the person neglects prayer or they try to reason it all out and let go of "love's divine simplicity." Wesley thinks this is what has happened to her—she gave way to "evil reasoning."[113] He reminds her in a later note: "Let your faith thus work by love, and it will make you fruitful in every good temper and word and work."[114]

Wesley had many correspondents to whom he became a real spiritual mentor and one of these was Mrs. Sarah Ryan. She was appointed housekeeper at the Kingswood school (established by Wesley), and he agrees it is a very difficult post to hold: "It requires all the omnipotent love of God to preserve you in your present station."[115] Her ability to faithfully serve in this challenging environment is tied to the quality of her spiritual life: "Do you do nothing, great or small, merely to please yourself? Do you feel no touch of any desire or affection but what springs from the pure love of God? Do you speak no words but from a principle of love and under the guidance of His Spirit? O how I long to find you unblameable in all things, and holy as He that hath called you is holy!"[116] He reminds her she may be saved from her sin, but not from the

---

[109] *Letters* (Telford) V: 48.
[110] *Letters* (Telford) V: 50.
[111] *Letters* (Telford) V: 62.
[112] *Letters* (Telford) V: 63.
[113] *Letters* (Telford) V: 78.
[114] *Letters* (Telford) V: 87.
[115] *Letters* (Telford) III: 240.
[116] *Letters* (Telford) III: 241.

possibility of mistake, such as thinking too highly or too lowly of a person. "And hence words or actions may spring which, if not sinful in you, are certainly wrong in themselves, and which will and must appear sinful to those who cannot read your heart. What grievous inconvenience would ensue! How would the good that is in you be evil-spoken of! How would the great gift of God be doubted of, if not disbelieved and denied, for your cause!"[117] In January of 1758, after a time of trial that she had experienced, Wesley wants to know if the experience stirred up resentment or did she desire it were otherwise.[118] Wesley comments that she was clearly troubled (apparently to do with praise or criticism) the evening he met her and conflicting passions could be seen in her face (love, sorrow, desire and a kind of despair), but in it all was she upset or was she "calmly stayed on God"? He wonders if the trial was to deepen her knowledge of herself and of God.[119] A number of years later he writes and tells her that there are many things to commend in her life but he is concerned that she appears to be above human instruction, thinking that she understands sanctification better than anyone else, while undervaluing everyone else's experience; she also monopolizes the affections of all and cuts them off from other friendships. He thinks she is also in danger of "enthusiasm" through an over-reliance on dreams and impressions. He concludes by telling her: "I believe there is no saint upon earth whom God does not teach by man."[120] Wesley urges her to be open to the instruction of God through whatever channels he chooses. In a similar vein he told Mrs. Woodhouse that it was his constant rule to believe everyone honest till they prove otherwise; "But were I to give way to my natural temper, I should believer everyone a knave till I *proved* him honest. And that would turn me into a man-hater and make life itself a burthen. Be as determined as you please to seek happiness in the knowledge and love of God. But in the meantime let your delight be in the saints that are upon earth and such as excel in virtue."[121]

Practical Advice for Ministry

Wesley's own ministry experience and that of many of his people offered numerous examples of hardship when seeking to faithfully serve God in a local community. Sometimes the difficulties came from persecution, but at other times it was simply the demanding nature of the work itself. In terms of ministry to others, Wesley writes: "Indeed it is hard for any to persevere in so unpleasing a work unless *love* overpowers both pain and fear."[122] It is only the

---

[117] *Letters* (Telford) III: 242.
[118] *Letters* (Telford) IV: 4.
[119] *Letters* (Telford) IV: 4.
[120] *Letters* (Telford) V: 17-18.
[121] *Letters* (Telford) VII: 39.
[122] *Works* 2, "The Reformation of Manners," 314.

presence of God and his love in the heart that will "make their labour light."[123]
The only enduring source of motivation and encouragement in ministry comes
from the love of God experienced and then shared with the neighbour whom we
serve.[124] Love produces not only courage and patience, but also humility as we
recognise that it is God alone who enables and equips us for this work.[125] It is
only in this context that Wesley can say of those who serve the community:
"what prospect of danger will then be able to fright them from their labour of
love! What suffering will they not be ready to undergo to save one soul from
everlasting burnings! What continuance of labour, disappointment, pain will
vanquish their fixed resolution!"[126] Wesley was aware that the labours of his
people were not always successful in terms of positive responses. In 1779 he
wrote to Kitty Warren and said how glad he is to see she is being faithful in
ministry. He reminds her that she will experience temptations and sometimes
dejection, especially "when you have laboured long in any instance, and see no
fruit of your labour. But remember! You will be rewarded according to your
labour, not according to your *success*." Pride in our accomplishments is a
constant danger but God can deliver her from them all. He encourages her to set
up a small band with two other women and show by example what it means to
live as a Christian.[127] One of his preachers, Thomas Rankin, was struggling to
continue to minister to a person who had been a habitual drunkard before
becoming a Christian and who has now returned to this state after backsliding.
Wesley says the person will not change till he is desperate and, even then, is not
likely to be changed without relapsing more than once or twice He advises
Rankin to first save him from occasions of sin and then to urge the man not to
cast away hope, [128] because "Nothing but this, despair of conquering, can totally
destroy him. As long as he keeps up the faintest hope he will strive against
sin."[129] It is only the transforming power of God's love working through
Rankin's friendship that can offer the man hope, and without hope he will be
destroyed by despair.

Maintaining discipline in the societies was an important part of the
Methodist vision, but at times it could be taken too far. Even within Wesley's
own circle of friends there were cases where he felt the treatment of some
offences was too harsh. In 1783 he writes to Jasper Winscom and reminds him
of their long-standing friendship and therefore Wesley felt he had the freedom
to tell him his thoughts. Winscom's son had married a good woman, but

---

[123] *Works* 2, "The Reformation of Manners," 314.

[124] *Works* 2, "The Reformation of Manners," 315. See also *Works* 2, "The Reformation
of Manners," 317-320.

[125] *Works* 2, "The Reformation of Manners," 316.

[126] *Works* 2, "The Reformation of Manners," 315. See also 321.

[127] *Letters* (Telford) VI: 353.

[128] *Letters* (Telford) VI: 154.

[129] *Letters* (Telford) VI: 155.

without his father's permission. Winscom had then banished him from the house, and Wesley does not blame for this action. However, some time has now passed since that event and he writes: "I advise you to forgive him. I advise you to lay aside your anger (it is high time), and to receive him again (occasionally) into your house. For you need forgiveness yourself; and if you do not forgive, you cannot be forgiven." In Wesley's view, even if Winscom says he has forgiven him but refuses to let him back in the house, genuine reconciliation has not yet taken place. He points out "what if God should say the same to *you*? Then you had better never to have been born." If he persists in treating his son like this, then the son's patience will be worn out, he will become resentful and perhaps bitter, and finally even hate his father. If this happens, then "your implacable anger will cause your son's damnation."[130] So Wesley urges him to a change of heart and of behaviour. Another difficult case involved one of the preachers, William Shent, who had fallen into sin and been disciplined by expulsion from the Society at Keighley. Wesley wrote and asked them to deal in a Christian way with their preacher, who was now suffering greatly. He listed a series of important events in the life of the Society for which Shent was responsible.[131] He has now been turned out because of his sin and Wesley said none of them actually continue to care for him. While it was right to publically expel him from the Society, "must he also be starved? Must he with his grey hairs and all his children be without a place to lay his head? Can you suffer this?... Where is gratitude? Where is compassion? Where is Christianity? Where is humanity? Where is concern for the cause of God?" So he asks them to put him on his feet once more and do it quickly, and it may even be the saving of him and his family.[132] Sometimes those preachers who left the Methodists over a dispute wanted to return. One such case was that of Edward Thomas, who had now reconciled with Wesley and Methodism after a parting and wanted to be restored to ministry. Wesley said: "I am sincerely glad that you are convinced you went too far, and I love you the better for having the courage to acknowledge it. It is now time that all which is past should be forgot, but it will be best to proceed little by little." So he advises that he first be readmitted to the Society, and then after a time be placed in charge of a class, before finally being restored as a local preacher.[133] Love always looks for ways to be reconciled and to restore to usefulness, but wisdom meant that it had to be done in a way that allowed for the genuineness of the change to be demonstrated over time. Timeliness was also important when someone was seeking to return to ministry after an extended time of illness. He told Peard Dickinson that "As soon as ever Sister Dickinson is able to go abroad let her enter upon her labour of love. In things of this kind particularly delays are

---

[130] *Letters* (Telford) VII: 192.
[131] *Letters* (Telford) VI: 333-34.
[132] *Letters* (Telford) VI: 334.
[133] *Letters* (Telford) VIII: 162.

dangerous. Every good purpose will cool and die away if it is not as soon as possible put in execution. Only let us not undertake too much at a time. Generally one visit will be enough for one day, and that should not last above half an hour, or an hour at farthest."[134]

---

[134] *Letters* (Telford) VIII: 129.

Chapter 6

Forming the Life of God in the Soul:
Some Examples of Wesley's Pastoral Guidance

We have already looked at Wesley's pastoral advice in terms of those things that challenge our developing relationship with God and neighbour, as well as those things that help us. This topical approach has its strengths but it does not allow us to follow the story of any one person to see how Wesley deals with the complexity that inevitably arises as the years unfold. He had a large number of people with whom he corresponded over an extended period of time and in this chapter I have selected five of those as examples of some of the major issues that arise in our lives and how Wesley responded to them. The letters cover such things as our spiritual progress (Mary Bishop), dealing with significant health issues (Ann Bolton), depression (Alexander Knox), the relationship of love and holiness (Philothea Briggs), and how love is nourished and expressed in the relationship with God and neighbour (Miss J. C. March). In every case, we really only have Wesley's letters to them, but it still gives us insight into how his advice and wisdom helped them on their spiritual journey over an extended period and how this can provide help for our own life in Christ.

The Correspondence with Mary Bishop

In this correspondence Wesley deals with a number of issues that troubled Mary over the years from her first letter in 1769.[1] They deal with a range of questions about her spiritual progress, both in terms of those things that help and those things that hinder. Her first question has to do with the timing of God's work in the heart and what is necessary before it can be experienced. Wesley reminds her that age is no restriction to the work of God and not every person can name the time when God worked in their heart, because he may or may not make this known in a significant way.[2] Her danger is to want a certain experience before being convinced that God has fulfilled his promises. She is not to wait to be convinced about this and that before being renewed in love; she is simply to pray now, because "Love is all we want; let this fill our hearts, and it is enough."[3] In particular, she is not to listen to those talking about the "darkness of faith" as an essential experience because faith is always about

---

[1] *Letters* (Telford) V: 153-54.
[2] *Letters* (Telford) V: 162.
[3] *Letters* (Telford) V: 191-92.

light.[4] Wesley tells her: "Sometimes there is a painful conviction of sin preparatory to full sanctification; sometimes a conviction that has far more pleasure than pain, being mixed with joyful expectation." There is always a gradual growth in grace which need not be interrupted from time of justification, and she must not wait for pain or anything else to promote her spiritual life.[5]

Mary suffers from poor health and several of his letters deal with the impact of this on her life with God. In 1772 he told her that "Such a degree of sickness or pain *as does not affect the understanding* [emphasis mine] I have often found to be a great help. It is an admirable help against levity as well as against foolish desires; and nothing more directly tends to teach us that great lesson, to write upon our heart, 'Not as I will, but as Thou wilt.'"[6] Illness often impacts the emotional life and Wesley is concerned to help her understand this:

> The difference between heaviness and darkness of soul (the wilderness state) should never be forgotten. Darkness (unless in the case of bodily disorder) seldom comes upon us but by our own fault. It is not so with respect to heaviness, which may be occasioned by a thousand circumstances, such as frequently neither our wisdom can see nor our power prevent; perhaps, too, it was partly owing to the body.[7]

But whatever kind it was, she can benefit from it if she gains humility, seriousness and resignation.[8] Several years later he gives a very practical recommendation that she gets sea air for her health. He goes on to say: "we have now abundant proof that very 'many are made better *by sickness*'; unless one would rather say '*in sickness*' [emphasis his]. This is one of the grand means which God employs for that purpose. In sickness many are convinced of sin, many converted to God, and still more confirmed in the ways of God and brought onward to perfection."[9] This is an acknowledgement that it is not the sickness itself that promotes spiritual vitality, but our response to God during the sickness. He has already told her severe illness producing such a level of pain as to cloud our understanding is not ever a blessing, but he thinks God intends by this particular sickness to wean her from created things so she can find her all in him. He emphasises that even with the limitations imposed by her condition, she can use her time in reading, meditation, prayer, a little serious conversation and, as strength permits, she can do a little good to others.[10]

---

[4] *Letters* (Telford) V: 209.
[5] *Letters* (Telford) V: 210.
[6] *Letters* (Telford) V: 335.
[7] *Letters* (Telford) VI: 111.
[8] *Letters* (Telford) VI: 111.
[9] *Letters* (Telford) VI: 278-79.
[10] *Letters* (Telford) VI: 279.

Mary also struggles with her temperament (apparently she is reserved) and the difficulties she has to feel and express God's love. Wesley devotes a number of letters to this, not least because it was also an issue in his own spiritual walk. He tells her: "They who feel less, certainly suffer less; but the more we suffer, the more we may improve; the more obedience, the more holiness, we may learn by the things we suffer. So that upon the whole, I do not know if the insensible ones have the advantage over us."[11] In other words, the benefit of a temperament that is less sensitive is outweighed by the motivation that suffering gives to escape from the situation, if at all possible. This is not tied to her illness as such, but to how she feels when faced with various kinds of trials, tests and temptations. In a later note he says that "It is certainly most profitable for us to have a variety of seasons. We could not bear either to be constantly in storms or constantly in a calm; but we are not certain, we cannot judge what proportion of one or the other is best for us."[12] She is called to trust in God's provision and to acknowledge that he does all things well.

In 1774 he deals specifically with Mary's reserve and retirement, and her concern about the spiritual impact of mixing with other people. Wesley tells her that relationships may be either helpful or hurtful to our walk with God, and it is our attitude to them that makes the difference. To avoid damaging our spiritual life we must keep a single eye, a steady design, and seek to please others only for their edification; this cannot be done without God's grace and enablement. Mary must conquer her natural reserve and the only way to do this is by going out more and being with people she does not know, or of whom she knows nothing good, or even good people who trifle away their time or indulge in empty conversation.[13] In other words, she will not experience change if all she does is remain with her close friends or stays on her own. Her preference for solitude has implications for potential future marriage and Wesley writes that remaining single has many advantages but it requires a call from God to live that way: "I think none ought to make any vows concerning it, because, although we know what we are and what we can do *now*, yet we do not know what we *shall* be."[14] In other words, she is not to discount the possibilities of grace and how God may work in her life. That is why he says: "Suppose you have more faith and more love (as I would fain think you have), you certainly ought to go out more. Otherwise your faith will insensibly die away. It is by works only that it can be made perfect. And the more the love of solitude is indulged the more it will increase."[15] He notes this is a common temptation, and many have fled to the "desert" as a result; it is what he and Charles did at Oxford. He has learned since is to flee to the Bible, where he learned to do

---

[11] *Letters* (Telford) V: 252.

[12] *Letters* (Telford) VI: 43.

[13] *Letters* (Telford) VI: 127.

[14] *Letters* (Telford) VI: 139.

[15] *Letters* (Telford) VI: 127-28.

good to all as time and opportunity afford. He affirms to her that we can do this without endangering our own soul as long as we focus on "simplicity," which is defined as the grace that casts off all unnecessary reflections on itself.[16] This advice is restated in another letter where he explains that to be able to help those in need is an excellent fruit of "self-denial," as is speaking the truth to those who will not hear it. This will be difficult for one of her temperament but it is "use that brings perfectness." Wesley shares that he labours with the same "infirmity" and has found only one way to conquer: "Take up your cross; when occasion offers, break through: speak, though it is pain and grief unto you."[17] He assures Mary that it will get easier with practice, but failure to do so will stunt her own spiritual life and usefulness in ministry. Apparently she does work at this and in 1781 he writes to encourage her to develop a school for children, but its focus must be to "make Christians" and not simply "genteel" women.[18] In several more letters he gives instruction on the running of the school and the importance of being an example herself.[19]

The Correspondence with Ann Bolton

The extended correspondence with Ann Bolton shows how Wesley dealt with a person who is going through significant health issues, and in what way this relates to the issues of suffering and providence. The early letters in 1771 express his concern about her physical health and the potential impact it has on her life, though he is confident it will not cause her to neglect her Christian walk.[20] Wesley assures Ann of God's continuing help in her situation: "He gives you health as a token for good; He can trust you with it while you give Him your heart. And O stand fast in the glorious liberty wherewith He has made you free! You are not called to desire suffering. Innocent nature is averse from pain; only, as soon as His will appears, yours is to sink down before it."[21] He is consistent in maintaining that suffering in itself is not desirable and it is perfectly acceptable to seek to avoid or minimise it. However, if it still comes our way, we are to submit to God's will as being our greatest good—more than wealth, honour, pleasure and whatever else this world can give.[22] The key test, as always, is whether we truly love God more than the circumstances and situations of life, whether positive or negative. This focus on love and trust is made clear in the next letter where he tells her that the present sufferings will

---

[16] *Letters* (Telford) VI: 128.

[17] *Letters* (Telford) VI: 138-39.

[18] *Letters* (Telford) VII: 62-63.

[19] *Letters* (Telford) VII: 74.

[20] *Letters* (Telford) V: 238-39.

[21] *Letters* (Telford) V: 240.

[22] *Letters* (Telford) V: 240.

lead to purification rather than destruction if she trusts Christ.[23] Notice that it is only if she trusts the Lord; it has no automatic benefit. This is reemphasised a little later when he tells her that she should continue to trust God in the trial: "He is purging away all your dross, that you may be a vessel meet for the Master's use. Happy are they that do His will, and happier still they that suffer it. But whatever you suffer, cast not away that confidence which hath great recompense of reward. In order to keep it, do not reason, but simply look up to Him that loves you."[24] Ann apparently does this and Wesley is glad to note that her health is better and her love has not grown cold as it is this love that will keep her in the midst of temptation to doubt God's providential care.[25] Like others experiencing protracted suffering, Ann had been attracted to the Roman Catholic "Mystic writers" who refer to "self-emptiness, self-inanition, self-annihilation" and the like. Wesley affirms that we need to avoid pride, "yet I cannot approve of recommending humanity by the use of these expressions. My first objection to them is that they are unscriptural." They are also dangerous since they lead to devaluing the gifts of God and make this somehow meritorious: "to imagine we honour Him by undervaluing what He has done.... [so] Acknowledge all His work while you render Him all His glory."[26] He returns to this a little later when he warns against the dangers of "refining upon religion" and seeking something more than "plain, simple love producing lowliness, meekness, and resignation."[27] In a follow-up letter he reminds her of the excesses of George Bell and others who valued extraordinary gifts over love and so were beguiled by Satan.[28] He worries in case she has been taken in by their claims: "Faith and hope are glorious gifts, and so is every ray of eternity let into the soul. But still these are but means; the end of all, and the greatest of all, is love."[29]

Several years later the correspondence returns to her health and he advises her to get "an electric machine" for her health because "You are no more at liberty to throw away your health than to throw away your life."[30] While there is nothing more profitable than the presence of God and attending his inward voice, yet there is a danger even in this: "you may insensibly slide into Quietism, may become less zealous of good works; on the other hand, that you may slide into Stoicism, may suffer loss as to the love of your neighbour, particularly as to that tender affection towards your friends, which does not

---

[23] *Letters* (Telford) V: 256.

[24] *Letters* (Telford) V: 258.

[25] *Letters* (Telford) V: 275.

[26] *Letters* (Telford) V: 313. See also *Letters* (Telford) V: 342.

[27] *Letters* (Telford) V: 347-48.

[28] *Letters* (Telford) V: 349.

[29] *Letters* (Telford) V: 349.

[30] *Letters* (Telford) VI: 97. Later he will encourage her to get plenty of outdoor exercise (especially horse riding) and to watch her diet. See *Letters* (Telford) VI: 202, 219.

weaken but strengthen the soul." [31]   He is concerned she has already suffered some loss by not answering friends' letters.[32] Ann's protracted ill-health continues to impact her spiritual life, particularly in the areas of her mental and emotional states. Wesley writes:

> Your state of mind for some time has been that which the Papists very improperly term a state of Desertion; where in they suppose God deserts or forsakes the soul only for His own will and pleasure! But this is absolutely impossible: I deny that such a state ever existed under the sun. As I observed before, the trouble you feel is in the very root and ground of it, a natural effect of disordered liver, of the corruptible body pressing down the soul.[33]

A little later he tells her: "Undoubtedly Satan, who well understands the manner how the mind is influenced by the body, can, by means of those parts in the animal machine which are more immediately subservient to thinking, raise a thousand perceptions and emotions in the mind, so far as God is pleased to permit."[34] Given the limited understanding of human physiology in Wesley's day, this is a very sound insight and one we do well to remember. Sin is not attached to biology, only to the conscious activity of the person. The distinction between wilful sin and involuntary sin has been dealt with earlier and this is a good example of why it is an important difference when counselling Christians. We may not always be able to distinguish them, but God certainly can and will only hold us finally accountable for the former. Wesley thinks she gave Satan the advantage by reasoning with him over this rather than simply trusting God. As with Mary Bishop, she undoubtedly needs more thankfulness and simplicity in her life. Therefore, she is not to doubt Christ's salvation but must hold fast what God has already given.[35] Given her long battle with poor health, Wesley is concerned about her theological explanation for it and in May 1779 he writes:

> There is little danger of imputing too much to the good providence of God. It is deeply concerned in everything great and small that pertains to the children of God. It disposes all things strongly and sweetly that befall them, perhaps through their own mistake, for their profit, that they may be the more largely partakers of His holiness. He superintends all you do and all you suffer.[36]

---

[31] *Letters* (Telford) VI: 115.

[32] *Letters* (Telford) VI: 116.

[33] *Letters* (Telford) VI: 261.

[34] *Letters* (Telford) VI: 281.

[35] *Letters* (Telford) VI: 281. This has been a problem for Ann, who it seems has tended to try to reason her way through the trials and tests she has faced; see *Letters* (Telford) V: 124, 151, 213, 215-16.

[36] *Letters* (Telford) VI: 345.

Furthermore, whatever we don't choose for ourselves, God chooses for us.[37] In other words, God will not overrule our liberty but he will act for our benefit in all those circumstances in which we find ourselves that are not the product of our own deliberate choice. She evidently comes to a place of peace about this and Wesley illustrates his confidence in God's providence by sharing with her some words of De Renty and an unnamed woman sufferer: "'I was in such distress as was ready to tear my soul and body asunder; and yet at that very time I was as happy as I could be out of heaven.' I do not wonder, therefore, that all the trials you feel do not interrupt the peace of God."[38] There is a clear distinction between the outward reality (the distress) and the inward reality (being happy and at peace). The inner life can remain calm while the outward is ravaged by turbulence and this is possible only by God's grace. Early in the following year he urges her not to despise the chastening of the Lord, but continue to trust God, be patient, and watch against "unprofitable reasonings." He affirms again that the suffering is intended for her spiritual benefit, but that does not mean she should refuse treatments that could ameliorate it.[39] It is not long before he can record how glad he is to hear that "God has delivered you from that torturing pain and that He has established your soul in His pure love and given you the abiding witness of it."[40] Wesley reminds her that

> It is a great step toward Christian resignation to be thoroughly convinced of that great truth that there is no such thing as chance in the world; that fortune is only another name for Providence, only it is covered Providence. Any event the cause of which does not *appear* we commonly say 'comes by chance.' Oh no: it is guided by an unerring hand; it is the result of infinite wisdom and goodness. Such are all the afflictive circumstances that have followed you in a constant succession almost from your childhood. He that made the Captain of your salvation perfect through sufferings has called *you* to walk in the same path, and for the same end—namely, that you may 'learn obedience' (more full, inward obedience, a more perfect conformity to His death) 'by the things you suffer.'[41]

He encourages her to spend time with friends, as a means to confirm her health and refresh her spirit and he reminds her of the future in God in heaven, with no more sorrow or suffering.[42]

Apparently her health was not the only source of her suffering and in 1781 Wesley records how he is sorry to learn of further heavy trials she is facing. Since she now has generally good health, he wonders if it has to do with the

---

[37] *Letters* (Telford) VI: 345.

[38] *Letters* (Telford) VI: 373-74.

[39] *Letters* (Telford) VI: 382.

[40] *Letters* (Telford) VII: 24.

[41] *Letters* (Telford) VII: 45-46.

[42] *Letters* (Telford) VII: 46.

burden of caring for her brother?[43] He is sure that she does not murmur or fret about the situation, "But you cannot avoid grieving (unless when the power of the Highest overshadows you in an extraordinary manner). And even this will shake the tenement of clay."[44] Ann may well be suffering more than necessary because she is keeping these things to herself.[45] He urges her to find a friend who can be her support and she ought to ask God for such a one.[46] It seems that a marriage proposal was also in the offing and that would have provided her with a close friend, but it came to nothing and so adds to her pain. Wesley shares how his own young sister was deceived by a marriage proposal but, by keeping her heart open to God and sharing with John, she gained a complete victory over the hurt. This will be true for Ann as well and then she will be able to use her own experience to help other young people.[47] Her fellow-Christians need to be warned not to think that if they were deceived in a marriage proposal, they were equally deceived over their life in Christ. He emphasises that "While you help others, God will help you"; so she is not to bury the talent God has given to her.[48]

In March 1785 Wesley returns again to the subject of divine providence because she is in danger of two extremes: making too much or too little of God's chastening. "This you do whenever you look at any circumstance without seeing the hand of God in it." She is apt to link two things that don't belong together and draw the wrong conclusions as a result.[49] Once again he urges her to find a close friend in whom to confide because Wesley himself is at too much of a distance to make his letters alone truly effective.[50] This is advice that he shares with many of his correspondents, because face-to-face relationships are an essential part of spiritual formation. While God can, and does, provide grace for those who experience a solitary life through no choice of their own, it is not the norm. All non-physical forms of communication have their place but they cannot substitute for actual physical presence. In 1786 he writes to her about the blessing that will come our way when Christ returns: "that reward will undoubtedly be proportioned, first to our inward holiness our likeness to God, secondly to our works, and thirdly to our sufferings; therefore for whatever you suffer in time, you will be an unspeakable gainer in eternity."[51] Note the order here: it is our relationship with God that is primary (whatever the actual circumstances of life), then our ministry to the 'neighbour'

---

[43] *Letters* (Telford) VII: 49-50.
[44] *Letters* (Telford) VII: 83.
[45] *Letters* (Telford) VII: 133-34.
[46] *Letters* (Telford) VII: 223-24.
[47] *Letters* (Telford) VII: 233.
[48] *Letters* (Telford) VII: 233.
[49] *Letters* (Telford) VII: 263.
[50] *Letters* (Telford) VII: 278.
[51] *Letters* (Telford) VII: 358. See also *Letters* (Telford) VIII: 251.

and then finally our personal suffering. So while suffering comes to all of us as an inescapable element of our present reality, it is not essential for spiritual formation. In 1787 he affirms: "He [God] chastens you long for *your profit*, that you may be a partaker of His holiness. He chastens you also for your *profit* that you may be more holy and consequently, more happy. But His ways are in the deep waters and His footsteps are not known"[52] We cannot comprehend God's ways when we go through trial and we may never understand the reason this side of death; only afterwards will we know and see God has done all things well. "If you had not seen trouble in the years that are past, you would not have been what you are now" and this is because she has learned obedience by her suffering.[53] At the beginning of 1789 Wesley reiterates that God is teaching her to trust him further than she can see him. While we all experience the same salvation, "there is great variety in the manner wherein God is pleased to lead them. Some of them are called to act much for God, some to rejoice much, some to suffer much. All of these shall receive their crown. Bur when the Son of Man shall come in His glory, the brightest crown will be given to sufferers."[54] In the context of his earlier letters, this is only true for those who continue to trust God in the midst of the suffering, not merely because they have suffered. Later in the year Ann's sister dies and Wesley says it is well she has learned to say that the Lord gives, he takes away and blessed be the name.

> But why does our Lord inflict this upon us? Not merely for His pleasure, but that we may be partakes of His holiness. It is true one grand means of grace is doing the will of our Lord. But suffering it is usually a quicker means and sinks us deeper into the abyss of love. It hath pleased God to lead you in the way of suffering from your youth up until now. For the present this is not joyous, but grievous; nevertheless it has yielded peaceable fruit.... Cleave to Him still with full purpose of heart.[55]

In 1790 he reflects again that she is in the school of God and that the Lord loves those he chastens. Sometimes the chastening comes because of our own choices and he tells her: "From the time you omitted meeting your class or band you grieved the Holy Spirit of God, and he gave a commission to Satan to buffet you; nor will that commission ever be revoked till you begin to meet again." Her ministry has been a great blessing to many and he urges her to re-engage it again without delay. Even if she cannot speak a word, is sick or well, whether she feels she can or not, she is just to go: "Break through! Take up your cross. I say again, do the first works; and God will restore your first love!"[56] It seems

---

[52] *Letters* (Telford) VIII: 9.

[53] *Letters* (Telford) VIII: 40. See also *Letters* (Telford) VIII: 84, 117.

[54] *Letters* (Telford) VIII: 110.

[55] *Letters* (Telford) VIII: 157-58. See also *Letters* (Telford) VIII: 190-91.

[56] *Letters* (Telford) VIII: 246.

she takes up his advice, for in 1791 he expresses his gladness that her health is better.[57]

The Correspondence with Philothea Briggs

The focus of this correspondence is on love and holiness in relationship to the inner life of the person. Philothea is troubled by her strong feelings and the thoughts and suggestions arising in her mind which cause her to doubt the work of God in her soul. In each of these areas she faces strong temptation and longs to know how to distinguish human infirmities from actual sins. In 1771 Wesley writes to her and assures her that temptations are a normal part of Christian experience and not evidence of God's absence from the heart: "all temptations will work together for good; all are for your profit that you may be partaker of His holiness. You may always have an evidence both of God's love to you and of yours to Him. And at some times the former may be more clear, at other times the latter. It is enough if, in one case or the other, you simply stay your soul upon Him."[58] To rely on feelings is always to become fretful and open to the temptation to doubt God. It is not the 'feeling' of love that is critical, but the continued trust in God's love based on his actions in the saving work of Christ. There is always the danger of even a Christian mistaking Satan's voice or their imagination for God's voice. Wesley tells her that "you can distinguish one from the other, not by any written rule, but only by *the unction of the Holy One*. This only teaches *Christian prudence*, consistent with simplicity and godly sincerity."[59] It seems that she normally has very strong feelings and this also makes her susceptible to doubting God's work in her life.[60]

> Truth and falsehood, and so right and wrong tempers, are often divided by an almost imperceptible line. It is the more difficult to distinguish right and wrong tempers or passions, because in several instances the same motion of blood and animal spirits will attend both one and the other. Therefore in many cases we cannot distinguish them but by the unction of the Holy One. In the case you mention all self-complacency or self-approbation is not pride. Certainly there may be self-approbation which is not sin, though it must occasion a degree of pleasure.... And this joy is neither better nor worse for being accompanied with a natural motion of the blood and spirits. Equally natural and innocent is the joy which we receive from being approved of those we love. But in all these instances there is need of the utmost care, lest we slide from innocent joy or self-

---

[57] *Letters* (Telford) VIII: 254.

[58] *Letters* (Telford) V: 240.

[59] *Letters* (Telford) V: 241.

[60] *Letters* (Telford) V: 253-54.

approbation into that which is not innocent, into pride (thinking of ourselves more highly than we ought to think), or vanity, a desire of praise.[61]

Once more, we can see how Wesley separates those experiences that arise from our human constitution and those that arise from our deliberate choice. God does not intend to turn us into creatures that are devoid of emotion as the evidence of our holiness. He created us with a rich emotional life and experiencing pleasure and joy is normal. Wesley admits that these good feelings can easily slide into sinful ones and it is only the work of the Holy Spirit that can alert us to the danger and help us to avoid it. That means that while others may have opinions about how we express our feelings, they cannot actually know if the behaviour is sinful or not. It is our own attitude that is critical; do we submit our concerns to the ministry of the Spirit and the advice of mature Christians, or do we not.

Philothea is also worried about the "thoughts and suggestions" that pass through her mind. Wesley tells her that these are just as a person of lively imagination may expect because Satan delights to attack us where we are weak:

> But these and a thousand clouds passing over your mind prove nothing as to the state of your heart: see that this be devoted to Him, and it is enough... However, then, your imagination may be affected, you will have the testimony of a good conscience toward God. Not but that you may plead that promise, 'The power of God shall keep your hearts and minds through Christ Jesus.' As the former word takes in all your passions, so does the latter all the workings of your reason and imagination.[62]

The vital distinction lies in the source of the thoughts and whether we do or do not give assent to them and dwell on them; this will inevitably lead us into actual sin. Wesley tells her that "If useless words or thoughts spring from evil tempers, they are properly evil, otherwise not; but still they are contrary to the Adamic Law: yet not to the law of love; therefore there is no condemnation for them, but they are a matter of humiliation before God. So are those (seemingly) unbelieving thoughts; although they are not your own, and you may boldly say, 'Go, go, thou unclean spirit; thou shalt answer for these, and not I.'"[63] He reminds her that there are times of nearer access to God and we need to make good use of them, focusing on what is most important: "'Walk in love, as Christ also loved us and gave Himself for us.' All is contained in humble, gentle, patient love. Is not this, so to speak, a divine contrivance to assist the narrowness of our minds, the scantiness of our understanding? Every right temper, and then all right words and actions, naturally branch out of love. In

---

[61] *Letters* (Telford) V: 266.
[62] *Letters* (Telford) V: 273.
[63] *Letters* (Telford) V: 313.

effect, therefore, you want nothing but this—to be filled with the faith that worketh by love."[64]

In 1772 Philothea is still struggling with her affections being too impetuous and uneven and she seems to think that an experience of Christian perfection would make everything calm. Wesley assures her that "nature yields to healing grace,"[65] and this can further improve as she perseveres in her life with God: "All that is amiable, holy and happy! Already He that loves you gives you a taste of what He has prepared for you. Let patience have its perfect work, and you shall be perfect and entire, lacking nothing. See that you make the best of life!"[66] Wesley tells her that to set perfection too high will drive it out of the world, so she is to remain firm in what she has and not lose it by a false humility.[67] However, her temperament continues to trouble her and she wonders if a higher degree of suffering would change it? Wesley writes:

> You shall have exactly as much pain and as much disappointment as will be most for your profit, and just sufficient to
> > Keep you dead to all below,
> > Only Christ resolved to know.
> Never make it a matter of reasoning that you have not either a larger or smaller share of suffering. You shall have exactly what is best both as to kind, degree, and time. Oh what a blessing it is to be in His hand who 'doeth all things well'![68]

He reminds her that spiritual growth is not always clear and perceptible, but when she is sensing nothing it does not follow that God's work in the soul has ceased, "especially while your desire is unto Him, and while you choose Him for your portion. He does not leave you to yourself, though it may seem so to your apprehension."[69] He reminds her again that it is generally easy to distinguish temptation and sin, but sometimes it is not: "Voluntary humility, calling every defect a sin, is not well-pleasing to God. Sin, properly speaking, is neither more nor less than 'a voluntary transgression of a known law of God.'"[70] Philothea is not easily assured by his advice and her cheerful disposition continues to distress her, especially when compared to the seriousness of some other mature Christians. Wesley assures her that she does not need to be "as serious" as Miss March or Nancy Bolton. God is happy with her cheerful disposition and he will give her more or less reproach just as he chooses, so she is to leave it all in his hands who orders everything well.[71] Even

---

[64] *Letters* (Telford) V: 299.
[65] *Letters* (Telford) V: 315.
[66] *Letters* (Telford) V: 316.
[67] *Letters* (Telford) V: 317-18.
[68] *Letters* (Telford) V: 323-24.
[69] *Letters* (Telford) V: 331.
[70] *Letters* (Telford) V: 341.
[71] *Letters* (Telford) V: 348.

this does not bring her peace and in 1773 he returns again to the difficulties she continues to have with her feelings. This time it has to do with her feelings for other people. He comments that his own mother felt as she does: "She did not *feel* for others near so much as my father did; but she *did* ten times more than he did."[72] Later he will write: "Grace in one sense will make all things new. And I have sometimes known this done to such a degree that there has been no trace of the natural temper remaining. But generally the innocent natural temper does remain, only refined, softened, and cast into the mould of love."[73] This was a difficult truth for Philothea to accept, as it is for so many who think that only a placid emotional state is evidence of heart holiness.

The Correspondence with Alexander Knox

This extended correspondence is with a young man who apparently suffers some form of epilepsy and is very prone to depression. It gives us insight into Wesley's counsel to one dealing with both a long-term illness and its impact on his emotional and spiritual life. In the first letter in 1776 Wesley sees the illness in a positive light because Knox has been greatly blessed in his family life, his friendships and his own nature. This means that he could easily be induced to find his happiness in the admiration of others. Wesley tells him: "Your illness will continue just so long as is necessary to suppress the fire of youth, to keep you dead to the world, and to prevent you seeking happiness where it never was nor ever can be found. Considered in this view, it is a great blessing and a proof of God's watchful care over you."[74] He thinks that a brief illness could not have saved him from pride through teaching him meekness, lowliness of heart "and to seek all your happiness in God."[75] Wesley believes that the illness is partly natural and partly the gift of God to balance the petulance of youth and foolish desires, but he assures him: "Is not health at hand, both for soul and body!"[76] This is another example of Wesley's understanding of God's providential care; Alexander did not choose to put himself in the situation where he would inevitably contract the illness but God can work a blessing from it. However, that does not mean that he has to passively accept it (even though it is of spiritual benefit), and Wesley gives him advice on an appropriate treatment "for your almost continual depression of spirits, which is a bodily as well as spiritual malady."[77] Early in the following year Wesley notes his disorder is getting less and there is good reason to hope it will eventually be removed: "it is certainly the design of Him that loves you to heal both body and soul; and

---

[72] *Letters* (Telford) VI: 18.
[73] *Letters* (Telford) VI: 45.
[74] *Letters* (Telford) VI: 204.
[75] *Letters* (Telford) VI: 205.
[76] *Letters* (Telford) VI: 219-220.
[77] *Letters* (Telford) VI: 212.

possibly He delays the healing of the former that the cure of the latter may keep pace with it."[78] In Wesley's opinion, God does not want him to lose what he has suffered, as it will be for his spiritual benefit.[79] This delay in healing is obviously concerning to Alexander and Wesley gives an assurance that God neither forgets nor despises him: "But He frequently delays giving bodily health till He heals soul and body together. Perhaps this is His design concerning *you*."[80] Wesley is puzzled as to why he has not gone salt water bathing as he advised, affirming that there is to be no passive acceptance of the situation.[81] His real concern over Alexander's spiritual state is that he is still a "servant of God" but not yet "a son of God."[82] He must wait patiently for God to complete the work and not despair because Wesley has "little doubt of seeing [him] an healthy as well as an happy man."[83]

It becomes apparent that it is Alexander's emotional state that causes Wesley as much concern as his physical well-being. At the beginning of the following year (1778), Wesley thinks that the health of his body and mind would improve if he would just live for today and not fret about tomorrow.[84] It is evident that he is having trouble trusting God and is experiencing lengthy bouts of depression because of his situation (this is noted in a number of Wesley's letters from this period).[85] Wesley says he has for too long despised the "small" things God has done for him; he is still too lukewarm and must stir up the gift of God and be thankful for what God has done (apparently a small improvement in his health). Alexander clearly worries that this small measure of healing will be taken away from him and Wesley affirms that he has no right to expect his improved health to continue.[86] He agrees that

> you cannot claim it from God's justice; you do not merit it at His hands. But is this the measure whereby He deals with His poor creatures? Does He give us no more blessings than we deserve? Does he treat us in all things according to His justice? Not so; but mercy rejoices over judgement! Therefore expect from Him, not what you deserve, but what you want—health of soul and health of body: ask, and you shall receive; seek, and you shall find; not for your worthiness, but because 'worthy is the Lamb.'[87]

---

[78] *Letters* (Telford) VI: 259.
[79] *Letters* (Telford) VI: 259-60.
[80] *Letters* (Telford) VI: 269.
[81] *Letters* (Telford) VI: 269.
[82] *Letters* (Telford) VI: 272-73.
[83] *Letters* (Telford) VI: 273.
[84] *Letters* (Telford) VI: 307-308.
[85] *Letters* (Telford) VI: 309, 314, 315.
[86] *Letters* (Telford) VI: 317.
[87] *Letters* (Telford) VI: 318.

This is a strong reminder that God's mercy and grace are the source of everything we enjoy in life and we never arrive at a place where we can earn those blessings. The problem is a lack of trust in God's love and goodness towards us. If we see him as one who is fickle or who takes delight in making our life difficult, then we will live in fear that anything God gives he can capriciously take away—and this seems to be Alexander's worry. Wesley has often pointed out (on the basis of Scripture) that God is love, and his love in our hearts casts out the fear he will act in an arbitrary manner towards us; the presence of fear demonstrates we do not yet know the fullness of his love. Shortly after this Wesley is sorry to learn the fits have returned and he shares an account of one who was instructed to think only of God's mercies in Christ and how it changed his despondency. Wesley thinks this intentional focus might be good for Alexander and encourages him to try, while continuing to ride as often as he can.[88] His continual advice on medicines and exercise are part of his conviction that being healed by means is as much an answer to prayer as if the cure was directly given. Alexander is to give himself totally to the Great Physician for the healing of both soul and body, for both inward and outward health. Wesley is sure that his bodily disorder affects his mind and thinks this is more a matter of diet than medicine for a cure.[89]

In 1779 Wesley affirms again that God was merciful to him with this affliction because it humbled him and showed what was in his heart. God is still working in his life and there is hope of a cure.[90] At the end of the year, after receiving a long account of Knox's disorder, Wesley again observes:

> It is undeniable (1) That you have a bodily complaint. Your nerves are greatly disordered; and although it is only now and then that this rises so high as to occasion a fit, yet it has a constant influence upon you so as to cause a dejection of spirits. This dejection is no more imputed to you as a sin than the flowing of the blood in your veins.[91]

He remains convinced that those things that impact our temperament and emotional life arising from biological causes are not sin, therefore, their expression cannot be sin as long since there is no wilful concurrence with them. In the same letter Wesley notes that he still has little faith (trust) and this is another source of his uneasiness. The next observation he makes is: "You want to have the love of God fully shed abroad in your heart: you have only now and then a little touch of thankfulness, a small spark of that divine fire; and hence anger, or at least fretfulness and peevishness, more or less, will naturally arise." In Wesley's opinion the main cause of his despondency are the temptations of Satan, who injects thoughts into his mind and then accuses him for them. He

---

[88] *Letters* (Telford) VI: 320.

[89] *Letters* (Telford) VI: 327-28.

[90] *Letters* (Telford) VI: 350-51.

[91] *Letters* (Telford) VI: 364.

urges Alexander to remember that God is on his side; he cares for him, keeps him and helps him with his infirmities, purifying him and readying him for the blessing which is at hand.[92]

At the beginning of 1780 Wesley thinks it worthwhile trying the mineral water as it is very likely God will make it a means of lessening, if not removing, his bodily disorder. Once more he urges him to not simply give into the depression, but to be out in the fresh air and exercising; "you have no reason to expect the spirit of an healthful mind unless you use the means that God has ordained." Wesley thinks that attendance at chapel, where he can hear the gospel, would be greatly beneficial and he is to trust God with the outing as he is not likely to be more uncomfortable there than he is at home.[93] Pragmatically, if it does not work as planned, then having two fits is less evil than losing 50 precious opportunities of attending chapel to hear the preacher. He urges him to break through the fear, which is a mere snare of the devil, because God is ready to save.[94] Wesley's blunt pastoral advice must have strained the relationship because at the end of the year Wesley affirms he remains his friend and it is a deeper friendship now than when it began. He repeats his conviction that it is Alexander's body that presses down his soul, and if God heals the body the mind will be far easier. Though the trial has been protracted, he does not despair of seeing him a happy man and full of peace and joy in believing.[95] He comments how Knox is very good at finding arguments against himself, and if he puts his mind to it he will never run out of them and therefore will not find the place of victory that God longs to grant. Wesley agrees with him that God will not give faith to the double-minded, but he can take away the double-mindedness first and then give faith, and he can do that "today." It will take a "miracle," but why should he not expect one, for God always upholds his word. God knows him in his faults, but will always respond to his cry for help; he must not keep "reasoning" over the situation.[96] In 1785 Wesley gives him his mature thoughts on his situation. Knox does not go to church or preaching house in case he has a fit and falls down and disturbs everyone.[97] Wesley says this is not good; he cannot be sure that he will have a fit and having a fit once every month is less of an evil than shutting himself up. He is only harming his health the more by not getting out and having exercise in the fresh air. "And you hurt your soul by neglecting the ordinances of God, which you have no authority to do unless you were sick in bed." He is to go out today and trust God for the outcome. In an insightful comment he adds: "if your

---

[92] *Letters* (Telford) VI: 364.

[93] *Letters* (Telford) VI: 377.

[94] Letters (Telford) VI: 378.

[95] Letters (Telford) VII: 39-40.

[96] Letters (Telford) VII: 44.

[97] *Letters* (Telford) VII: 272.

mother hinders you, she will kill you with kindness."[98] In the next letter Wesley gladly notes that he is getting out and about a bit each day and soon he can return to public worship, for without this he will forego God's blessing.[99]

The Correspondence with Miss J. C. March

This is perhaps the most extended pastoral correspondence that engaged Wesley, and it covers some 37 letters from 1760 to 1777. They are almost entirely focused on entering into and maintaining a relationship of "pure love" with God and neighbour. In the first letter written in March 1760 he tells her that the works of God to uncover the heart need not make us miserable; it can be consistent with peace and joy in the Holy Spirit. No matter how deeply convinced of sin she is, she must not let go her confidence in God. His closing prayer is for the God who loves her to fill her heart with his pure love.[100] This will not happen automatically and she is to make use of all the means of grace available to her, of which "Prayer is certainly the grand means of drawing near to God; and all others are helpful to us only so far as they are mixed with or prepare us for this." While the comfort of prayer can be lost by wandering thoughts, the benefits cannot; she is not to fight this but ask God for help and she "may undoubtedly remain in peace and joy until...perfected in love." That is why it is important she not get involved in disputes with those who reject Methodist teaching but must simply say she believes otherwise.[101] Wesley encourages her to testify to her present experience of God while learning to see him in all things and trust him.[102] He gives an assurance that all who are born of God and those who are sanctified experience this in an instant, yet they undoubtedly grow gradually before and after it (this is not surprising if holiness is essentially relational), but it need not be a long time between the two. He then goes on to say: "Much less is there any necessity for much suffering: *God can do his work by pleasure as well by pain* [emphasis mine]." We need to expect God to do his work now "without waiting till we have either done or suffered more."[103] This reiterates his advice to other correspondents and emphasises the centrality of faith itself, not the circumstances in which faith is exercised. If we believe we need to do or suffer a certain amount before God can act, it becomes salvation by works rather than grace.

Towards the end of the year he assures her that conviction for sin is not the same as condemnation: "You are condemned for nothing, if you love God and

---

[98] *Letters* (Telford) VII: 273.
[99] *Letters* (Telford) VII: 279-80.
[100] *Letters* (Telford) IV: 85-86.
[101] *Letters* (Telford) IV: 90.
[102] *Letters* (Telford) IV: 91.
[103] *Letters* (Telford) IV: 100.

continue to give Him your whole heart."[104] This keeps the focus on the relationship of love rather than the level of performance achieved. She apparently begins to follow his advice and at the end of the year he writes: "Go on; you shall have all you seek, because God is love…. Certainly peace and joy in believing are the grand means of holiness; therefore love and value them as such." The law of works is now superseded by that of love because Christ died for us and we are not condemned for coming short of perfect performance because of his intercession. "I believe it is impossible not to come short of it, through the unavoidable littleness of our understanding. Yet the blood of the covenant is upon us, and therefore there is no condemnation." He closes by reminding her that "the law of love is exactly marked out in the 13th of the [First of] Corinthians. Let faith fill your heart with love to Him, and all mankind; then follow this loving faith to the best of your understanding; meantime crying out continually, 'Jesus is all in all to me.'"[105] The relationship with God does not progress as fast as she had hoped and this leads her to believe she will never receive the blessing because it has not been received yet. She is also troubled by those who claim the experience but don't live up to it and subsequently say it does not exist. In these circumstances Wesley tells her it is very important that she keep close to the "rule" (Scripture) and her "guide" (Holy Spirit).[106]

At some point in 1761 Miss March seems to have experienced the pure love of God but now faces new challenges as she seeks to remain in this relationship. Wesley assures her of God's witness to both her sins being forgiven and being saved from sin, but they are frequently intermittent and not necessarily linked to any specific failure on her part.[107] His letters now contain a number of specific questions on her spiritual state and he urges her to continue to grow in grace: "believe more, love more: you cannot love enough. Beware of sins of omission."[108] At the end of 1762 he encourages her to keep close to other Methodists because fellowship is important for spiritual health.[109] In the following year he is concerned about her understanding of Christian Perfection, as she seems to be reasoning herself out of the experience: "This much is certain: they that love God with all their heart and all men as themselves are scripturally perfect";[110] this has to be true or else God mocks us with his promises. However, we have this treasure in an earthen vessel "which presses down the immortal spirit," so that all our thoughts, words and actions are imperfect and come short of the standard that would apply if we had a

---

[104] *Letters* (Telford) IV: 109.
[105] *Letters* (Telford) IV: 124.
[106] *Letters* (Telford) IV: 157.
[107] *Letters* (Telford) IV: 170.
[108] *Letters* (Telford) IV: 181.
[109] *Letters* (Telford) IV: 190.
[110] *Letters* (Telford) IV: 208.

perfect body. That is why we always need the merits of Christ's death.[111] At some point after this Miss March loses the experience and in 1764 he writes to her: "I cannot doubt a moment but you were saved from sin. Your every act, word, thought, was love, whatever it be now. You was in a measure a living witness of the perfection I believe and preach—the only perfection of which we are capable while we remain in the body. To carry perfection higher is to sap the foundation of it and destroy it from the face of the earth."[112] He is concerned that in "aiming at a perfection which we cannot have till hereafter, you should cast away that which now belongs to the children of God. This is love filling the heart. Surely it did fill yours, and it may do now, by simple faith." He urges her to talk with those who would build her up and not tear her down, while doing away with false humility and giving no place to evil reasoning.[113] Wesley is concerned that her unwillingness to share honestly with the band members is harming her spiritual life. He notes that entering a "wilderness state" after "deliverance from sin" has happened to others and the most likely cause of her present spiritual state is "evil reasoning" that leads her to cast away her confidence in God by doubting both faith and grace.[114] This will now become a recurrent theme in his letters to her and it illustrates what happens when we depart from simple faith and try to reason our way through the trials and tests of life. This is seen in August 1765 when Wesley expresses concern that she may have moved from the simplicity of the gospel and he warns her again of the dangers of reason and false humility.[115] Going through trials is not unusual and it "does not prove there is sin in your heart or that you are not a sacrifice to love." It is very important that she hold fast what is attained and expect full communion "this moment." Wesley thinks "reasoning" or some inward or outward omission is still the problem.[116] The struggles continue and towards the end of 1765 he shares with her that about 20 people in Bristol testify to being saved from sin—they always love, pray, rejoice, give thanks and have the witness of the Spirit. If they lose this it is easy to think they never had it. Wesley notes that 400 in London had the same experience and he is not sure if it is restored suddenly, by many steps, or in an instant.[117] More worryingly,

> You seem to think pain, yea much pain, must go before an entire cure. In Sarah
> Ryan it did, and in a very few others. But it need not: pain is no more salutary
> than pleasure. Saving grace is essentially such, saving pain but accidently. When
> God saves us by pain rather than pleasure, I can resolve it only into His justice or

[111] *Letters* (Telford) IV: 208. See also *Letters* (Telford) IV: 212-13, 215-16.
[112] *Letters* (Telford) IV: 251.
[113] *Letters* (Telford) IV: 251.
[114] *Letters* (Telford) IV: 270.
[115] *Letters* (Telford) IV: 310.
[116] *Letters* (Telford) IV: 310-11.
[117] *Letters* (Telford) IV: 313.

sovereign will. To use the grace we have, and now to expect all we want, is the grand secret. He whom you love will teach you this continually.[118]

This is the same advice he had given her earlier, but she seems to have been heavily influenced by the experience of Sarah Ryan and has convinced herself that this must become her experience.

In 1768 the correspondence turns to matters that have to do with her relationships in the Society. She is apparently being commended for her life and ministry and he cautions her that "Without any sin we may be in a sense pleased with the approbation of those we esteem and love. But here we have need of much prayer, lest this should degenerate into pride or vanity." A genuine knowledge of ourselves through the work of the Spirit is true humility and without this we cannot be free from vanity and pride.[119] Later in the same year Wesley tells her that since she does not have many outward trials, "it is highly needful you should have some inward ones; although they need not be either many or long. If you will walk closely with God, He is able to give any degree of holiness, either by pleasure or pain."[120] The sense of "rest" given to her during her recent sickness need not be lost, no matter what name it is called. He tells her that Mary Thornton had experienced the pure love of God and the testing is not a sign it is lost—so don't let others reason her out of it. He records his surprise that several who are filled with love don't desire to die and be with the Lord; he wonders if God only gives this near the time of death and perhaps in many it would not be of much use—"First let them learn how to live."[121]

The relationship between a heart filled with love and feelings was one that clearly troubled Miss March, as it did for so many others. Wesley writes that it is easy

> to imagine that no degree of sorrow could be found in an heart that rejoices evermore; that no right temper could be wanting, much less any degree of wrong temper subsist, in a soul that is filled with love. And yet I am in doubt whether there be any soul clothed with flesh and blood which enjoys every right temper and in which is no degree of any wrong one, suppose of ill-judged zeal, or more or less affection for some person than that person really deserves.[122]

This is because of the weakness of understanding which results from the "soul's union with a corruptible body." He goes on to say that "There is so close a connexion between right judgement and right tempers as well as right practice, that the latter cannot easily subsist without the former. Some wrong temper, at least in a small degree, almost necessarily follows from wrong

---

[118] *Letters* (Telford) IV: 313-14.

[119] *Letters* (Telford) V: 82.

[120] *Letters* (Telford) V: 95.

[121] *Letters* (Telford) V: 148.

[122] *Letters* (Telford) V: 192.

judgement." Wesley thinks this is what is meant by people saying sin remains while the body remains.[123] In an important letter he tells her that using the grace given is the best way to receive more, and by using the faith she has it will increase. Her sense of wants and weaknesses with trials and temptations do no real hurt, though they bring heaviness for a time and decrease joy in the Lord. She must not focus on this, even though we may generally link our spiritual state with our feelings. He reminds her that we cannot measure our state spiritually by our joy alone, as this is the most variable of our sensations and often depends on our bodily well-being. It is better to take love joy, peace, meekness and gentleness *together* with resignation for a guide.[124] Then he tries to clarify for her the difference between her frame of mind and state of her soul. He is not sure there is a real difference, but perhaps the former is "a single, transient sensation" whereas the latter is "a more complicated and lasting sensation." He notes that some use frame to refer to "fleeting passions" and state to refer to "rooted tempers," but he is not convinced by it.[125] He also advises her to "deal very closely" with those in her care, because "Advices and admonitions given at a distance will do little harm or good."[126]

In early 1771 he can record how glad he is that she has finally broken through these "evil reasonings" which stopped her enjoying what God gives freely. "Always remember the essence of Christian holiness is simplicity and purity; one design, one desire—entire devotion to God. But this admits of a thousand degrees and variations, and certainly it will be proved by a thousand temptations; but in all these things you shall be more than conqueror."[127] She is always to be aware of the danger of pride, especially because she has so many outward advantages. "Happy are you if you use these for that single end, to be outwardly and inwardly devoted to God, and that more entirely than you could be in different circumstances."[128] In other words, her wealth and position are not in themselves a hindrance to her spiritual life; it is her attitude that makes the difference. In the next letter he reminds her that "The dealings of God with man are infinitely varied, and cannot be confined to any general rule; both in justification and sanctification. He often acts in a manner we cannot account for."[129] This leads him to respond to one of her comments: "yet it is sure you are a transgressor still—namely, of the perfect, Adamic law. But though it be true all sin is a transgression of this law, yet it is by no means true on the other hand (though we have so often taken it for granted) that all transgressions of this law are sins: no, not at all—only voluntary transgressions of it; none else

---

[123] *Letters* (Telford) V: 192.
[124] *Letters* (Telford) V: 200.
[125] *Letters* (Telford) V: 200.
[126] *Letters* (Telford) V: 201.
[127] *Letters* (Telford) V: 238.
[128] *Letters* (Telford) V: 238.
[129] *Letters* (Telford) V: 255.

are sins against the gospel law."[130] She is still concerned about the relationship of her feelings to the experience of pure love: "Those reasonings concerning the measure of holiness (a curious, not useful question) are inconsistent with pure love, but they tend to damp it; and were you to pursue them far would lead you into unbelief."[131]

> What you feel is certainly a degree of anger, but not of sinful anger. There ought to be in us (as there was in our Lord) not barely a perception in the understanding that this or that is evil, but also an emotion of the mind, a sensation or passion suitable thereto. This anger at sin, accompanied with love and compassion to the sinner, is so far from being itself a sin, that it is rather a duty. St. Paul's word is, 'not easily provoked' to any paroxysm of anger: neither are you; nevertheless, I suppose there is in you, when you feel a proper anger at sin, an hurrying motion of the blood and spirits, which is an imperfection, and will be done away.[132]

Wesley follows this up with another letter dealing with the place of our emotions, telling her that there are "various kinds and various degrees of communion with God" and we can't confine it to one only. He reminds her that we can pray even when the heart is "dry" and God can work even in this state. Above all, she is to "go on until all your heart is love."[133] The next letter continues the same pastoral concern:

> As long as we dwell in an house of clay it is liable to affect the mind; sometimes by dulling or darkening the understanding, and sometimes more directly by damping and depressing the soul and sinking it into distress and heaviness. In this state doubt or fear of one kind or another will naturally arise. And the prince of this world, who well knows whereof we are made, will not fail to improve the occasion, in order to disturb, though he cannot pollute, the heart which God hath cleansed from all unrighteousness.[134]

Wesley advises her to be careful in ministering to Philothea Briggs who has many defects in her "natural temper" and much grace will be needed for her to be "altogether a Christian." He says that grace will not shine in her as it would in others and Miss March is to encourage what is of God and tenderly reprove what is of nature.[135] He goes on to say that in 1st Corinthians 13 "you have the height and depth of genuine perfection; and it is observable St. Paul speaks all along of the love of our neighbour, flowing indeed from the love of God. Mr. De Renty is an excellent pattern of this. But many things in his fellowship with God will not be explained till the Holy Spirit explains them by writing them on

---

[130] *Letters* (Telford) V: 255.

[131] *Letters* (Telford) V: 256.

[132] *Letters* (Telford) V: 256.

[133] *Letters* (Telford) V: 261-62.

[134] *Letters* (Telford) V: 267.

[135] *Letters* (Telford) V: 267.

your heart." The "darkness" that clouds her understanding Wesley thinks is due
to the work of Satan, so she must look to God and the cloud will go.[136] In the
next letter he tells her that "In order to be all devoted to the Lord, even those
who are renewed in love still need the unction of the Holy One, to teach them
in all circumstances the most excellent way, and to enable them so to watch and
pray that they may continually walk therein."[137] In 1772 she is still wrestling
with the relationship of faith and doubt. Wesley tells her that unbelief is either a
total or partial absence of faith; all believers experience the latter unless filled
with faith and the Holy Spirit, but even they can pray for its increase. "Entire
resignation implies entire love. Give Him your will, and you give Him your
heart."[138]

Three years later (1774) Wesley writes that she is a living witness to two
great truths: "There cannot be a lasting, steady enjoyment of pure love without
the direct testimony of the Spirit concerning it." The other is setting the
experience of Christian perfection too high. He reminds her that the heart may
experience things you would think incompatible and some of the "tempers and
sensations of those especially that are renewed in love" might appear to be
inconsistent with others. If we try to "reason" it out we get more and more
confused. That is why it is important to trust God when you cannot account for
all the circumstances.[139] The next letter also has to do with feelings: "The
praying much for those we love is doubtless the fruit of affection, but such an
affection is well pleasing to God and is wrought in us by His own Spirit.
Therefore it is certain the intercession that flows from that affection is
according to the will of God."[140] He clarifies for her that "Friendship is one
species of love; and is, in its proper sense, a disinterested reciprocal love
between two persons." Wesley does not think this is possible for the "wicked";
that is, those openly profane, empty of justice, mercy, and truth. He believes
they can have only the "shadow" of genuine friendship, but not the
"substance." On the other hand, Jews and heathens who fear God and do
righteousness can, because the properties of Christian friendship are those of 1
Corinthians 13 in which love produces every good word and work.[141]
Presumably his grounds for this are because they are walking in the light of
God's prevenient grace, whereas "wicked" reject the light they have received.
Miss March's next query relates to her poor relationship with several local
preachers because of her prejudice. He replies: "If one grain of prejudice be in
my mind, I can receive no profit from the preacher. Neither in this case can I
form a right judgement of anything a person says or does. And yet it is possible

---

[136] *Letters* (Telford) V: 268.
[137] *Letters* (Telford) V: 270-71.
[138] *Letters* (Telford) V: 326.
[139] *Letters* (Telford) VI: 88.
[140] *Letters* (Telford) VI: 91.
[141] *Letters* (Telford) VI: 92.

this prejudice may be innocent, as springing from the unavoidable weakness of human understanding."[142] Notice here the link between what we understand about people and our subsequent response. Prejudice in itself is not inherently sinful; it only becomes so when we wilfully persist in it by rejecting further knowledge.[143]

Miss March still struggles with understanding how friendship and love relate, so late in the year he shares his personal experience at Oxford as a means of helping her. He was not willing to quickly form a friendship or keep it going unless he could receive or do some good by it. Other people judged this as evidence of pride, which he denied. He admits that he looks at people's experience in order to estimate their general character, which is a factor in his decision. It seems that both she and his brother look at length of experience while he does not: "I measure the depth and breadth of it. Does it sink deep in humble, gentle love? Does it extend wide in all inward and outward holiness?" He says that Miss Johnson is deep in grace and lives like an angel, yet there are some things in her character he does not admire and he puts this down to "human frailty." He confesses that he once thought stoicism admirable, but not any longer: "I now see a Stoic and a Christian are different characters; and at some times I have been a good deal disgusted at Miss Johnson's apathy. When God restores our friends to us, we ought to rejoice; it is a defect if we do not." We ought to improve our "temper" as much as we can,[144] and this can't be done except by extensive reading, thinking and Christian conversation. It is not sufficient to just read the Bible and we must read widely if we are going to reason well.[145] Towards the end of the year Wesley returns to the subject of how she judges by length of experience and comments: "God is tied down to no rules" and he can do a great work in a little time.[146]

In the same letter he mentions the great calmness and meekness in Betty Johnson but he wants to see still more softness and tenderness: "I want more of human mingled with the divine." This is true even for Miss March herself because some "warmth" is not "sinful anger" and perhaps she would be culpable to be without it. He says again that he desires "no apathy in religion; a Christian is very far from a Stoic." However, in every case, the last appeal is to our own conscience, even though this is "far from being an infallible guide, as every wrong temper tends to bribe and blind the judge."[147] Early in 1775 he declares again that Miss Johnson is too near apathy, and is close to being all intellect and no passion. "It is true by this means we might avoid much pain, but we should also lose much happiness. Therefore this is a state which I cannot

---

[142] *Letters* (Telford) VI: 113.

[143] *Letters* (Telford) VI: 113.

[144] *Letters* (Telford) VI: 129.

[145] *Letters* (Telford) VI: 130.

[146] *Letters* (Telford) VI: 132.

[147] *Letters* (Telford) VI: 133. See also 132.

desire. Rather give me the pleasure and pain too."[148] That leads him to ponder who treads the middle path equally remote from both extremes? He says Jane Cooper was one like this with "the due mixture of intellect and passion" and Miss March should aim to be like her.[149] This does not appear to happen and in mid-year he refers to her continuing "reserve" and wants her to write more freely: "Am not I concerned in everything which concerns you? Which either lessens or increases your happiness? I want you to be as happy and (in order thereto) as holy as an angel, that you may do the will of God on earth as angels do in heaven."[150]

> I am less careful about your increase in knowledge any farther than it tends to love. There is a danger of your laying more stress on this than sound reason requires. Otherwise you would reap much profit from sermons, which do not improve your knowledge—which do not apply to the understanding so directly as to the heart. I feel more want of heat than light. I value light; but it is nothing compared to love. Aim at this, my dear friend, in all public exercises, and then you will seldom be disappointed. Then you will not stop on the threshold of perfection…, but will press on to the mark, to the prize of the high calling of God in Christ Jesus, till you experimentally know all that love of God which passeth all (speculative) knowledge.[151]

Wesley does not see holiness and stoicism going together in a positive light. Many of us remember the creedal confession that God is "without body, parts, or passions" and is "immutable"; we then link the use of passion and immutability in the creed with human emotions, and draw the conclusion that we too are to be passionless.[152] Wesley certainly thought this earlier in his ministry but he came to see that God has created us with a rich emotional life and we don't bring glory to him by either denying its existence or letting it run wild.

In the same letter he agrees that restoring health and living longer are invaluable blessings, but they can be improved to the glory of God. In order to do this she must go and see the poor and sick in their own hovels. This was clearly something Miss March did not want to do personally. He urges her to put off the gentlewoman and "Take up your cross" and follow the example of Jesus.[153] Wesley returns to this topic in the following year (1776) and notes that

---

[148] *Letters* (Telford) VI: 139.

[149] *Letters* (Telford) VI: 140.

[150] *Letters* (Telford) VI: 153.

[151] *Letters* (Telford) VI: 153.

[152] The actual words are found in "The Westminster Confession" but are commonly mentioned in a wide range of theology texts.

[153] *Letters* (Telford) VI: 153.

some of the poor have exquisite taste and sentiment while very many of the rich have none, but that is not important.[154]

> I want you to converse more, abundantly more, with the poorest of people, who, if they have not taste, have souls, which you may forward in their way to heaven. And they have (many of them) faith and love of God in a larger measure than any persons I know. Creep in among these in spite of dirt and an hundred disgusting circumstances, and thus put off the gentlewoman. Do not confine your conversation to genteel and elegant people. I should like this as well as you do; but I cannot discover a precedent for it in the life of our Lord or any of His Apostles. My dear friend, let you and I walk as He walked.[155]

Wesley reflects on the advice of Mr. De Renty, that we may want only to convert worlds but find ourselves cutting timber or carrying bricks and mortar. If this is done in obedience to God, it is more profitable for our soul than the other. A well-instructed Christian is never hindered by any person or thing, for whatever hinders their good works gives a fresh opportunity of submitting their will to God and this makes it more pleasing to God and profitable to their own soul than anything else they could do.[156] In his next letter he goes on to say:

> What I advise you to is, not to contract a friendship or even acquaintance with poor, inelegant, uneducated persons, but frequently, nay constantly, to visit the poor, the widow, the sick, the fatherless in their affliction; and this, although they should have nothing to recommend them but that they are bought with the blood of Christ. It is true this is not pleasing to flesh and blood. There are a thousand circumstances usually attending it which shock the delicacy of our nature, or rather of our education. But yet the blessing which follows this labour of love will more than balance the cross.[157]

He emphasises that the more we realise our obligations to God, the happier we will be, since his yoke is easy and burden light.[158] Wesley powerfully reminds us that love is not simply a warm, fuzzy, feeling and there are times when anything but positive emotions will accompany our service for Christ. While feelings are an essential part of our humanity, they are not to be the master of our lives—that is to be Christ alone. A genuine love for Christ and the neighbour means that we decide whether we will or will not engage in the service God has for us and our emotions may or may not be in harmony with that decision. The Gospel accounts tell us that Christ went to the cross because he loved us, not because he was looking forward to a pleasant experience! The

---

[154] *Letters* (Telford) VI: 206.

[155] *Letters* (Telford) VI: 206-207.

[156] *Letters* (Telford) VI: 207.

[157] *Letters* (Telford) VI: 208-209.

[158] *Letters* (Telford) VI: 209.

account in the garden of Gethsemane shows how deeply distressing it was on a human level but he went through with it for love's sake alone.

In the first letter from 1777 he revisits his concern over the dangers of covetousness for one in her position, and how important it was to save all she could in order to be able to give all she can.[159] He had already cautioned her about keeping her expenses below her income and said that "It is impossible to lay down any general rules, as to 'saving all we can' and 'giving all we can.' In this, it seems, we must needs be directed from time to time by the unction of the Holy One."[160] This is something Wesley has often said before and it reminds us that Christianity cannot ever be reduced to rules and regulations without destroying its very nature as a living relationship with God and neighbour. He tells her that "General rules are easily laid down. But it is not possible to apply them accurately in particular cases without the anointing of the Holy One; this alone, abiding with us, can teach us of all things." For example, the general rule is not to murder "Which plainly forbids everything that tends to impair health, and implies that we use every probable means of preserving or restoring it." But when we come to apply it to particular instances, only the Holy Spirit can teach us what is truly acceptable to God.[161] The last letter that we have from her in Telford's collection was written in December 1777. It seems that she must have written to him about how much he was alone and not involved in engaging the poor because of his lifestyle, apparently seeking to excuse her own attitude. Wesley shares how busy his life is with travel, and how many hours of each day are therefore spent alone, "Yet I find time to visit the sick and the poor; and I must do it, if I believe the Bible, if I believe these are the marks whereby the Shepherd of Israel will know and judge His sheep at the great day; therefore, when there is time and opportunity for it, who can doubt but this is a matter of absolute duty." He shares how at Oxford he lived like a hermit because he doubted any busy person could be saved or retain the Christian spirit amidst the noise and bustle of the world, but God has since taught him otherwise.[162] His letter closes with his deep concern for her: "I am sorry you should be content with lower degrees of usefulness and holiness than you are called to."[163]

---

[159] *Letters* (Telford) VI: 263.
[160] *Letters* (Telford) VI: 207. He had also written to her about the danger of indulging in expensive clothing; see *Letters* (Telford) VI: 209.
[161] *Letters* (Telford) VI: 263.
[162] *Letters* (Telford) VI: 292.
[163] *Letters* (Telford) VI: 293.

Chapter 7

Conclusion

From his earliest days at Oxford until the end of his life, John Wesley believed that the essential nature of God is love, and the nature of this love is demonstrated supremely in the life, death and resurrection of Jesus Christ. We were created in love and for love from the very beginning, placing relationships at the very centre of our existence. Scripture makes it clear that the love of God was poured into our hearts in the original creative act and it is this quality of love that we are to return to God and share with the neighbour. It is in this context that we can best understand Wesley's frequent use of the term "pure love" to describe the nature of our relationship with God. It is associated with the terms "single" and "simple" to give us the picture of a love that is focused on God as the one whom we desire, enjoy, serve and worship above everyone and everything else. All other desires and motives flow from this love, and it is intended to be the only spring from which every thought, word and deed arises. In Genesis chapter 2 we learn that the original solitary 'human' could not fully experience and express this love and relationship just with God alone, nor with any other creature he had made, so God made another like it and human flourishing began. We were not created to live a self-contained existence or to be in permanent seclusion from others of our own kind; a freely-chosen life of perpetual isolation from other humans is to be diminished as a person. God's grace is certainly sufficient for those who are isolated through no choice of their own—but even they 'relate' to others in their imagination and memory. The creation account also implies that healthy relationships involve both men and women (marriage is only one form of this), and freely-chosen, permanent, exclusively single-sex communities are unhealthy.

Wesley consistently claims that "liberty" is an essential element of such a love—it must be freely given, freely received and freely returned. Such a quality of love cannot, by its very nature, be implanted in us as some sort of automatic response, nor can it be coerced. In such free, loving relationships, we are like God in character (holy) and fulfill our creational purpose (happy). It is this understanding of the intimate intertwining of love and liberty that sets the stage for understanding the events in the Garden of Eden in the first three chapters of the Book of Genesis. All human relationships are inherently dynamic because God's gift of love is capable of infinite growth in the human heart. Our God-given liberty is then expressed by our freedom to either enrich or diminish any of our relationships. God gave the first human couple a simple test of their love and trust: in the midst of myriad good choices, don't make this one bad choice. There was no compulsion either way. The tempter suggested that God's motives were underhanded and they freely chose to believe that thought, doubting both God's motives and intentions. Having freely made a disastrous choice, they then had to live with the consequences, both for themselves and the rest of creation. The wrong choice in the Garden of Eden was simply the first domino to topple, impacting all the others in a very long and complex pattern. The damage to the fellowship with God resulted in the impairment of every other relationship and unleashed a trail of corruption and destruction that will continue till the return of Christ. God, out of love alone, acted to rescue the relationship immediately, but the consequences will be felt till the new creation is established in its fullness. Wesley was confident that a God of love would not merely patch-up the original creation but would renew it in ways that made it better than it was before. This was the basis of his confidence that we would not ultimately lose because of that wilful refusal to continue to trust God.

Given the immense privileges of our first estate, Wesley believed that the consequences of the wrong choice made meant that humanity had forfeited the ability to return to God simply by our own will. We have become inherently self-centred, selfish, and self-willed (the essence of sin), and we no longer believe that a relationship with God is our greatest blessing and happiness. We now prefer to seek happiness on our own terms. Because we have no 'natural' interest in restoring the bond with our Creator, any reconciliation has to be initiated by God himself. Wesley said that the offer of salvation in Christ must be faithful to the original creation and that means God cannot coerce the relationship. He saw the answer to the dilemma in prevenient grace, through the direct work of the Holy Spirit in every human heart. This grace enabled every person to respond positively or negatively to God's invitation to be reconciled. If we chose to be open to the invitation, then more grace would be received to enable it; if we did not, then even the grace we had would be slowly forfeited. Wesley believed that very few would ever entirely reject God's grace, but not everyone would be open to a renewed relationship and so the grace would not be effectual for salvation. In this way we remain responsible for our own eternal destiny and God can justly deal with us as such. The offer of salvation in Christ is to fully restore the fellowship with God and neighbour now, but the renewal of our bodies and the rest of the creation will await the day of Christ's return. This fully grace-restored relationship of pure love is all that Wesley means by "Christian perfection" and he believed this was compatible with limited understanding, faulty judgement, defective responses and actions. These latter realities are inseparable from the nature of the body and life in community this side of resurrection, and are not properly sin because they are not deliberate choices. The provisions of the atonement would graciously cover these shortcomings if the person acknowledged them and sought God's help to deal with them. It is against this background that Wesley gave his pastoral advice regarding the life of God in the soul.

A Life of Love

Wesley consistently anchored the Christian life in God's love poured into our hearts by the Holy Spirit, from the initial overtures of prevenient grace through to the experience of pure love and the new possibilities of an unending depth and richness to our bond with God and neighbour. Wesley uses the image of the root (love) and the branches (relationships) to emphasise that you can't have one without the other, with the latter being grounded in former. He is convinced that God's love is fixed towards us and is utterly dependable, no matter our situation. In Wesley's memorable picture, God does not play hide and seek with us. As we allow God's love to fill the heart, our selfish, self-centred and self-willed inclinations are healed and restored to their right orientation, first toward God, then the neighbour and the rest of creation. By seeking to please God in all things, serving him with our total devotion, and enjoying his presence above all others we discover that this actually enables us to be fulfilled as human beings—to be happy. It enables and empowers every other relationship to flourish and lets us enjoy all that God has created without guilt, shame or regret. Such a relationship is perfectly compatible with the limitations of our current bodily existence in its weaknesses and infirmities. Divine love is dynamic and creative, meaning it cannot ever be satisfied with the status quo; there are always new aspects of the relationship to explore and greater depths to experience. Love is constitutionally missional and sharing its richness with only a select few is to betray its nature. Because the love of God is inviting, embracing, enfolding and hospitable, these qualities will be evident in our lives to the degree that we walk in harmony with him by the power of the Spirit. The 'neighbour' is not limited to those we like or from whom we receive benefit; it embraces every human being on the planet and is active in seeking ways to serve them. These relationships must be genuine and not simply a means to manipulate others into becoming Christians. The neighbour is to be embraced and offered hospitality simply because they are people created in God's image and for whom Christ died. Since God reaches out to all, we can do no less. Christian people and Christian communities must not become closed, self-satisfied circles that are inwardly focused on their own piety and spirituality. We must always actively seek to invite others to be a part of God's community, no matter who they are or what background they come from. A life of love can never be reduced to rules and regulations that deal only with outward behaviour and practices. They may be helpful in identifying problematic behaviour and character issues, but they cannot fix them—that belongs to love alone. Wesley says that doctrine, conduct and worship practices are always servants of love, and love will always be manifested in these elements, but they cannot replace it. This means we can love God and neighbour while believing, behaving, and worshipping in different ways. This quality of life is portrayed for us in the life of Christ and is pictured in the Sermon on the Mount. Wesley believed that such a life was possible for every Christian by God's grace.

A Life of Holiness

Wesley can say very simply that to love as God loves is to be holy as God is holy, because to wholeheartedly love God and neighbour is to fulfil all the commandments. Encountering the love of God is inherently transformative, and as we embark on a relationship with him we will be increasingly changed into the likeness of Christ. This is the process of sanctification, leading to a moment when God's love entirely fills the heart and expelling all that is contrary to love—the moment of entire sanctification. Such an experience is still not an end point because our capacity to receive and give love is limitless, as is our capability to express that love in words and actions. This will continue beyond death, into the fullness of eternal life with God and his people in the new creation. Heart holiness is not primarily about separation from the 'sinful' but a positive engagement with God and the neighbour from a heart of pure love. It is fundamentally about a change of perspective, and this is seen in the life of Wesley himself. His experience at the Aldersgate Street meeting in 1738 was not from a wicked sinner to a new Christian, but a transformation of his already-existing relationship with God, centred in a new understanding of Jesus Christ and his service as a ministry of loving grace that was always accepting and inclusive, not rejecting and exclusive. Holiness is not a matter of correct belief, correct conduct or correct worship, as these are defined by us; it is about divine love transforming us at an ever-deepening level and living this out in practice, under the guidance of the Holy Spirit. This is where Susanna's advice to John is so insightful and helpful: sin is whatever weakens or damages our relationship with God, rather than an exhaustive list of do's and don'ts. That means for some people an action or behaviour can be 'sinful' while for others it is not. This is why Wesley emphasised the place of personal and community wisdom in seeking to determine how we can best promote loving relationships as well as eliminating or minimising the kind of things that damage them. It is tied to increasing self-knowledge as we allow the Holy Spirit to uncover those areas in our life where we are not presently aware of their harmful impact. This self-knowledge comes through reading Scripture, helpful literature, prayerful reflection, public worship and deep Christian fellowship. Because love is always seeking the welfare and happiness of the other, it cannot be unconcerned or unmoved by destructive ways of living. Pure love and wilfully destructive behaviours are incompatible, and so holiness does have to do with choices, lifestyles and consequences. Divine love and divine judgement are not incompatible; there is a righteous anger that is the loving response to wilful evil and the devastation it brings. Wesley strongly believed that there are consequences for our wilful wrong choices in both time and eternity; and this includes the reality of eternal separation from God.

A Life of Happiness

The interplay of love, holiness and happiness is clearly seen in God's original creation and we have no real difficulty imagining it will be so again in the new creation experienced after the day of resurrection. The struggle is to believe this could possibly be true in our present state of existence. In a damaged creation, pain, suffering, grief and death are inevitable and we cannot be delivered from them by our best science and technology. If happiness requires the elimination of these, then none can be happy in this life. Some schools of thought see pain and suffering as beneficial experiences because they will wean us from our sinful attachments to the sinful pleasures of life. Some deny their reality for the true child of God, because God wants us all to be healthy, wealthy and prosperous; these are God's gift to anyone who truly lives by faith. Wesley is adamant that a God of love would not and does not delight in the suffering of his creatures. There was no pain or suffering in the original creation and neither will there be in the restored creation. Pain and suffering are not essential elements of our human condition and are never regarded as being good in and of themselves, though God may work in and through them for our ultimate benefit. Happiness is essentially a quality of life that flows from a loving, healthy relationship with God and the neighbour, and not from any other experience or circumstance. To properly relate to God and neighbour is to be happy in the Biblical sense, and it is not tied to health, wealth or prosperity. You can be happy in a relationship of love even when experiencing pain, suffering and grief. This is the paradox that lies at the very heart of Christianity: the weak are strong, the poor are rich, and those who give up their life will gain it. It is the evidence of our spiritual idolatry if we believe we can be truly fulfilled by using things for our own selfish ends, or by any pleasures, possessions, and experiences divorced from the love of God. To know, love and obey God is to be genuinely happy and from this right relationship flows the right exercise of all our faculties and abilities. To believe that Christianity is essentially negative and restrictive is to misunderstand it. God desires that we enjoy and find pleasure in the goodness of his creation both now and subsequently in heaven, when the whole of creation is renewed. Only then, with a resurrected body like that of Christ's, will we experience perfect harmony between the spiritual and physical dimensions of our bodily existence.

Forming the Life of God in the Soul

Looking at what we have said so far, it is clear that spiritual formation in the Wesleyan framework is fundamentally relational. There are personal and private spiritual exercises that are essential, but they cannot replace interaction with the neighbour. We need solitude at times to focus on our relationship with God and there are times when this may even be an extended practice, but

Christianity is not about being a hermit—it is always about being involved in a physical community, because love cannot truly flourish without it.

Being Open and Receptive to the Transformational Power of God's Love

Experiencing the life of God in the soul has to begin by being open to the possibility that a relationship with God is both desirable and possible. Some people know nothing but a positive relationship with God, because from their earliest memory they walked trustingly in the grace God gave them through the Spirit, never losing their fellowship with God. It might not always have been an easy or smooth path, but God was their trustworthy friend and companion from the beginning. Most of us reject the grace God gives at some point in our growing-up years and so we know the reality of human sinfulness, even if not the depths of evil and wickedness. We are deeply attached to spiritual idolatry, believing that happiness can genuinely be found in the pleasures offered by the creation rather than the Creator, and we will not change, or even seriously consider the possibility of change, unless we are dissatisfied with our present experience. This dissatisfaction can arise positively or negatively: from the offer of something potentially more desirable, satisfying, pleasurable, or beneficial that will increase our happiness; or the desire to avoid or remove guilt, shame, suffering, pain or grief. At either of these points we can become consciously aware of the work of the Spirit in our life, and may be open to considering how empty and meaningless life has become. The Holy Spirit faithfully makes us aware of God's loving presence, and the invitation to open up our life to the possibility of change. The initial commitment to be open to the possibilities of divine love must be followed by a willingness to actually receive the work of the Holy Spirit in the heart. You can be open to the possibility of change and never make a decision to embrace it. This is where our freedom to choose is critical; we must make the decision to move from considering God's offer to actually receiving it. Prevenient grace will enable us to be open and receptive to God's love, but the decision to trust and respond is always ours, as are the consequences of our choices. Being open and receptive to the possibility of transformation is not limited to our first conscious contact with God. It is equally true for every step of our journey with him. All of this can be done by the direct work of the Spirit in our heart, or by the use of various means of grace. Of these, the life of the Christian 'neighbour' can often have the greatest impact. This is why it is so important that we live out the love of God in our heart by offering a genuine friendship to others that is not tied to an agenda of them becoming a Christian. Sadly, in so many cases, we break the relationship if there is no response and move on to the next potential convert, leaving the person wondering just how genuine our love and friendship ever was. This is also why we need to be involved in the life of the church community and open to the practices modelled or recommended by them for enriching our life with God. Our personal devotional life is very important, but the greatest transformation comes through the challenges we face in developing God-honouring relationships. If we do not remain open to the possibilities of a deeper relationship, then we will be tempted to settle for our current experience. We may even doubt that a deeper relationship is possible this side of death, and so be content to live with sin and defeat.

Trusting the God of Love

If our relationship with God is to flourish then we must come to the place of trusting him. The struggle to trust God is exacerbated if we have a distorted picture of who he is and what his attitude towards us will be. It is hard to trust God with your life if your picture of him is shaped by some isolated passage in the Old Testament that portray a God of wrath constantly seeking to punish us or make our lives miserable. It is equally difficult if we see God as the Divine Sovereign who rules by inflexible decrees and laws, totally unresponsive to our circumstances; or a God who lives in 'heaven' and is untouched and untouchable by human pain and suffering. Sometimes we think God can be controlled by our prayers, spiritual practices and personal sacrifices; we are then disappointed when it does not work out as we expect. These difficulties are compounded by the voice of the Tempter, who really has not changed the message from Genesis 3, casting doubt on the motivation that lies behind God's words and their truthfulness/dependability. In a world filled with suffering and pain, when our own experiences can be negative and when it seems that those who worship other gods (or deny all gods) flourish, it is very easy to doubt. Yet without trust, no relationship can survive let alone thrive. God's governance of his creation respects our freedom, and neither fatalism nor chaos is an authentically Christian answer to the trials and tests of life or the problem of evil. Ultimately it remains a mystery—and we either trust God and his providential dealings with us, or we do not. The first steps in the relationship with God, from our perspective, are always risky ones. To commit to another person is to be open to being hurt by them if they later reject us, harm us or fail us. This is why Wesley continuously draws our attention (as have Christians from every century) to the reality of God's love shown in the incarnation, ministry and, above all, death and resurrection of Christ as the basis for our trust. This provides the initial 'evidence' and it underscores how much the Christian community must give faithful and repeated witness to it. As trials and tests come, the doubts and fears will re-emerge, and we will need to continuously affirm our trust and venture onwards with Christ. This is why Christian friends and their witness is so important. The depth of our relationship with God is largely determined by the depth of our relationship with others in the Christian church. Wesley constantly warns against trying to reason our way through to an understanding of why things happen as they do, and how God governs his creation. If our trust in the Governor of all creation is secure, then we don't need to understand the mechanism to find peace. Our security is in the relationship, not the circumstance or outcome. When faced with suffering, illness, death, bereavement, or persecution it is particularly difficult to trust God, especially if they continue for extended periods or for a life time. Wesley says we can pray for deliverance and take every right step to heal, minimise or remove the trial, personally or for others; he does not see apathy or stoicism as Christian virtues. Therefore we are actively to seek healing and comfort using all the resources available to us, remembering that God works through means and process just as much as he does directly and instantly. Because love, trust and relationships are interlinked and interdependent, the depth of love and trust determines the depth and strength of relationship. Strong, healthy friendships can survive and even flourish in the midst of great hardship. They also suffer through our weaknesses, faults and failings. Once more, a good relationship can survive all manner of problems if they are caused unintentionally. Our limited understanding and faulty judgement will result in wrong thoughts, words and actions, but love will always seek for reconciliation. In all these things we need to allow God's grace to work in our life in his way and in his timing. As our loving Great Physician, we need to trust him with the process of our 'cure.'

Obedience Flowing from God's Love

It is very easy to say you love humanity in the abstract, or even to say you love someone who is at a distance; the real test is what happens when you meet face-to-face. We can 'love' the poor and dispossessed overseas quite easily, but what happens when we meet them on the street or at our local church? We can easily talk about 'loving' those who hold different opinions about doctrine, conduct or worship practices, as long as they attend a different church; what happens when they become members of our church? Very few Christians admit to racial, cultural or lifestyle prejudice and it is only when we are confronted by the physical presence of the 'other' that we become aware of all the negative feelings they stir up and expose. Sometimes it is much easier to allow the church rules and regulations to replace love and friendship. All our talk about love and relationships is meaningless in the end unless we actually put into concrete practice the full implications of the love of God in our hearts. We need to be open to forming new relationships and deepening existing ones. Our struggles to do this because of prejudice, misunderstanding, and faulty judgement are used by the Spirit to uncover the true state of our heart and just how passionate we really are about loving God and neighbour. Obedience flows from love of God in the heart by the Spirit, and it is not tied to a feeling of love (or any other emotion); we are to obey even if no positive feelings motivate or accompany the decision. This is where self-denial and taking up the cross are so important. There will be many occasions when we don't 'feel' like helping another, or when we don't emotionally connect with a person, but we are still to feed the hungry, give water to the thirsty, clothe the naked, visit the sick and imprisoned—for love's sake alone. The call is always to trust the God of our experience rather than our experience of God. This is especially true for those of us who have the types of personality and temperament that tradition-ally have not been associated with being 'holy.' Too often we have identified placidity as the ideal temperament, though some overvalue excitability and high emotion. We need to realise there is no 'Christlike' personality or temperament, but only varied human temperaments that can be expressed in godly or ungodly ways. We need to trust God with our personality and temperament, allowing the Holy Spirit to refine and mould us in ways that will enhance our flourishing. Depression is not a sign that God has abandoned us, any more than euphoria is a sign of his presence.

If we are to have strong, healthy relationships that glorify God and form us into his likeness, we will need to embrace God's grace, wisdom, discernment, and guidance. We must be receptive to the work of the Holy Spirit through the Body of Christ and the wider community. Particular cases and particular practices will always need the help of the Spirit, both personally and communally. We discern this best by looking to Scripture and the public, long-time interpretation, application and demonstration of its message. Above all, Wesley said, we must realise that no Scripture passage or teaching of the church can ever overturn the truth that God is love or his desire for us all to live in love with him and our neighbour. There is nothing to be gained, but everything to be lost, by permanently fleeing to a desert rather than being engaged in society. We need to receive God's 'work' into our lives directly, as well as through circumstances and situations. However, nothing ultimately substitutes for close friendships, especially those that occur face-to-face. Contact by phone, internet, email, text, and video are all wonderful helps, but none are substitutes for physical presence. Wesley told Miss March that she had to get personally involved with the poor in their hovels, no matter how difficult it was to her sensibilities; she couldn't do it by prayer, by giving money or paying for another to go on her behalf. Our modern electronic communication removes us from the sights, sounds, and smells of the 'poor' and their location, nor can you reach out to touch the other as a physical sign of love, acceptance and support. You can't fully love another from a 'distance'—the incarnation is the most profound evidence for that.

We need to reinvigorate our works of mercy in personal and community practice, for the sake of love alone. It is by a physical, shared relationship, walking and talking together, sharing experiences and meals together, and serving together that enables God to work in ways and at depths that will not happen otherwise. This means that we must be actively involved in reaching out to new people, genuinely offering them hospitality and cultivating the relationship without the hidden agenda of seeking to make them Christian. It means that within the church we must be committed to all who form part of the community and actively seek ways to nourish the relationship by serving them in love. It is precisely the struggles to enter, maintain and develop a variety of relationships that enables the Holy Spirit to work the deepest levels of transformation. The life of God in the soul is essentially pure love filling our heart, expelling all that is contrary to God's nature. This love is fully and freely returned in an ever-deepening fellowship that fully participates in the life of the Triune God. Such a love equally embraces and shares in the life of the neighbour as an essential companion on the journey. It is God's love expressed in these relationships that forms us into the very image of Christ, so that we are consequently both holy and happy in fulfilling our God-given purpose, in spite of the current limitations of our bodily existence.

BIBLIOGRAPHY

Primary Sources

Wesley, John. *The Works of John Wesley*. 14 vols., 3rd ed., ed. Thomas Jackson. London: Wesleyan Methodist Book Room, 1872. Reprint, Kansas City: Beacon Hill Press of Kansas City, 1979.

— *The Journal of the Rev. John Wesley*. 9 vols., ed. Nehemiah Curnock. London: Epworth Press, 1909-16.

— *The Letters of the Rev. John Wesley*. 8 vols., ed. John Telford. London: Epworth Press, 1931.

— *John Wesley*. ed. Albert C. Outler. A Library of Protestant Thought. New York: Oxford University Press, 1964.

— *The Bicentennial Edition of the Works of John Wesley*. 35 vols. projected, ed.-in-Chief, Frank Baker. Nashville: Abingdon Press, 1984-. vols. 7, 11, 25, and 26 of this edition originally appeared as the *Oxford Edition of the Works of John Wesley*. [Oxford: Clarendon, 1975-1983].

— *Explanatory Notes Upon the New Testament*. London: Wesleyan Methodist Book Room, n.d.

Secondary Sources

Baker, Frank. "Practical Divinity-John Wesley's Doctrinal Agenda for Methodism." *Wesleyan Theological Journal* 22, no. 1 (Spring, 1987): 7-15.

Bassett, Paul M., and William M. Greathouse. *Exploring Christian Holiness: The Historical Development*. Vol. 2 Exploring Christian Holiness. Kansas City: Beacon Hill Press of Kansas City, 1985.

Blevins, Dean G. "The Means of Grace: Toward a Wesleyan Praxis of Spiritual Formation." *Wesleyan Theological Journal* 32, no. 1 (Spring, 1997): 69-84.

Borgen, Ole E. *John Wesley on the Sacraments: A Definitive Study of John Wesley's Theology of Worship*. Nashville: Abingdon Press, 1972. Reprint, Grand Rapids: Zondervan, 1985.

— "No End without the Means: John Wesley and the Sacraments." *Asbury Theological Journal* 46, no. 1 (1991): 63-85.

Bray, Gerald. *God is Love: A Biblical and Systematic Theology*. Wheaton: Crossway, 2012.

Brendlinger, Irv A. "Transformative Dimensions within Wesley's Understanding of Christian Perfection." *Asbury Theological Journal* 59, no. 1 & 2 (Spring-Fall, 2004): 117-26.

Bryant, Barry E. "John Wesley's Doctrine of Sin." PhD thesis, King's College, University of London, 1992.

Butler, David. *Methodists and Papists: John Wesley and the Catholic Church in the Eighteenth Century*. London: Darton, Longman and Todd, 1995.

Callen, Barry L. *Discerning the Divine: God in Christian Theology*. Louisville: Westminster John Knox Press, 2004.

Campbell, Ted A. *Methodist Doctrine: The Essentials*. Nashville: Abingdon Press, 1999.

— "The Shape of Wesleyan Thought: The Question of John Wesley's 'Essential' Christian Doctrines." *Asbury Theological Journal* 59:1 & 2 (Spring/Fall 2004): 27-48.

Chapman, David M. *In Search of the Catholic Spirit: Methodists and Roman Catholics in Dialogue*. Peterborough: Epworth Press, 2004.

Charry, Ellen T. *God and the Art of Happiness*. Grand Rapids: Wm. B. Eerdmans, 2010.

Chartier, Gary. *The Analogy of Love: Divine and Human Love at the Center of Christian Theology*. Exeter: Imprint Academic, 2007.

Chilcote, Paul W., ed. *The Wesleyan Tradition: A Paradigm for Renewal*. Nashville: Abingdon Press, 2002.

Cho, John Chongnahm. "Adam's Fall and God's Grace: John Wesley's Theological Anthropology." *Evangelical Review of Theology* 10, no. 3 (1986): 202-13.

Christensen, Michael J. "Theosis and Sanctification: John Wesley's Reformulation of a Patristic Doctrine." *Wesleyan Theological Journal* 31, no. 2 (Fall, 1996): 71-94.

Clapper, Gregory S. *John Wesley on Religious Affections: His Views on Experience and Emotion and Their Role in the Christian Life and Theology*. Metuchen: Scarecrow Press, 1989.

— *The Renewal of the Heart is the Mission of the Church: Wesley's Heart Religion in the Twenty-First Century*. Eugene: Wipf & Stock, 2010.

Cobb, Jr., John B. *Grace & Responsibility: A Wesleyan Theology for Today*. Nashville: Abingdon Press, 1995.

Coleson, Joseph. *'Ezer Cenegdo: A Power like Him, Facing Him as Equal*. 3rd ed. Grantham: Wesleyan/Holiness Women Clergy, 1996.

Collins, Kenneth J. *A Faithful Witness: John Wesley's Homiletical Theology*. Wilmore: Wesley Heritage Press, 1993.

— "The Soteriological Orientation of John Wesley's Ministry to the Poor." *Asbury Theological Journal* 50, no. 1 (1995): 75-91.

— *The Scripture Way of Salvation: The Heart of John Wesley's Theology*. Nashville: Abingdon Press, 1997.

— "A Reconfiguration of Power: The Basic Trajectory in John Wesley's Practical Theology." *Wesleyan Theological Journal* 33, no. 1 (Spring, 1998): 164-84.

— *A Real Christian: The Life of John Wesley*. Nashville: Abingdon Press, 1999.

— *John Wesley: A Theological Journey*. Nashville: Abingdon Press, 2003.

— "The Promise of John Wesley's Theology for the 21st Century: A Dialogical Exchange." *Asbury Theological Journal* 59, no. 1 & 2 (Spring-Fall, 2004): 171-80.

— *The Theology of John Wesley: Holy Love and the Shape of Grace*. Nashville: Abingdon Press, 2007.

Colón-Emeric, Edgardo A. *Wesley, Aquinas and Christian Perfection: An Ecumenical Dialogue*. Waco: Baylor University Press, 2009.

Coppedge, Allan. *John Wesley in Theological Debate*. Wilmore: Wesley Heritage Press, 1987.

Cox, Leo George. *John Wesley's Concept of Perfection*. Kansas City: Beacon Hill Press of Kansas City, 1964.

Crofford, J. Gregory. *Streams of Mercy: Prevenient Grace in the Theology of John and Charles Wesley*. Lexington: Emeth Press, 2010.

Crutcher, Timothy J. *The Crucible of Life: The Role of Experience in John Wesley's Theological Method*. Lexington: Emeth Press, 2010.

Cubie, David L. "Wesley's Theology of Love." *Wesleyan TheologicalJournal* 20, no. 1 (Spring, 1985): 122-54.

Cushman, Robert E. *John Wesley's Experimental Divinity: Studies in Methodist Doctrinal Standards.* Nashville: Abingdon Press, 1989.

Cutler, David, Angus Deaton and Adriana Lleras-Muney. "The Determinants of Mortality." *Journal of Economic Perspectives* 20, no. 3 (Summer, 2006): 97-120.

Dunning, H. Ray. *Reflecting the Divine Image: Christian Ethics in Wesleyan Perspective.* Downers Grove: InterVarsity Press, 2003.

— "The Spirituality of 'Scriptural Holiness'." *Epworth Review* 30, no. 2 (2003): 51-57.

Edgar, Brian. *God is Friendship: A Theology of Spirituality, Community, and Society.* Wilmore: Seedbed, 2013.

English, John C. "References to St. Augustine in the Works of John Wesley." *Asbury Theological Journal* 600, no. 2 (Fall, 2005): 5-24.

Frost, Francis. "The Three Loves: A Theology of the Wesley Brothers." *Epworth Review* 24, no. 3 (1997): 86-116.

Greathouse, William M. *John Wesley's Theology of Christian Perfection* Occasional Paper No. 4 of the Wesley Fellowship. Ilkeston: The Wesley Fellowship, 1989.

Green, Joel B. *Body, Soul and Human Life: The Nature of Humanity in the Bible.* Milton Keynes: Paternoster, 2008.

Gunter, W. Stephen. *The Limits of 'Love Divine': John Wesley's Response to Antinomianism and Enthusiasm.* Nashville: Kingswood Books, 1989.

Gunter, W. Stephen, Scott J. Jones, Ted A. Campbell, Rebekah L. Miles, and Randy L. Maddox, *Wesley and the Quadrilateral: Renewing the Conversation.* Nashville: Abingdon Press, 1997.

Harper, Steve. "John Wesley: Spiritual Guide." *Wesleyan Theological Journal* 20, no. 2 (Fall, 1985): 91-96.

— "Wesley's Sermons as Spiritual Formation Documents." *Methodist History* 26, no. 3 (1988): 131-38.

Headley, Anthony J. *Getting It Right: Christian Perfection and Wesley's Purposeful List.* Lexington: Emeth Press, 2013.

Heitzenrater, Richard P. *The Elusive Mr. Wesley.* 2nd ed. Nashville: Abingdon Press, 2003.

— *Wesley and the People Called Methodists.* 2nd ed. Nashville: Abingdon Press, 1995.

Henderson, D. Michael. *John Wesley's Class Meeting: A Model for Making Disciples.* Nappanee: Evangel Publishing House, 1997.

Jeanrond, Werner G. *A Theology of Love.* London: T&T Clark, 2010.

Jennings, Theodore W. "John Wesley *against* Aldersgate." *Quarterly Review* 8, no. 3 (1988): 3-22.

— "The Meaning of Discipleship in Wesley and the New Testament." *Quarterly Review* 13, no. 1 (1993): 3-20.

Johnson, W. Stanley. "Christian Perfection as Love for God." *Wesleyan Theological Journal* 18, no. 1 (Spring, 1983): 50-60.

Jones, Scott J. *John Wesley's Conception and Use of Scripture.* Nashville: Kingswood Books, 1995.

Knight III, Henry H. *The Presence of God in the Christian Life: John Wesley and the Means of Grace.* Lanham: Scarecrow Press, 1992.

Lancaster, Sarah Heaner. *The Pursuit of Happiness: Blessing and Fulfillment in Christian Faith.* Eugene: Wipf & Stock, 2011.

Langford, Thomas A. *Practical Divinity: Theology in the Wesleyan Tradition.* Rev. ed. Nashville: Abingdon Press, 1998.

Leclerc, Diane. *Discovering Christian Holiness: The Heart of Wesleyan-Holiness Theology.* Kansas City: Beacon Hill Press of Kansas City, 2010.

Lindström, Harald. *Wesley and Sanctification: A Study in the Doctrine of Salvation.* Wilmore: Francis Asbury Press, 1980. Reprint, New York: Abingdon Press, 1946.

Lowery, Kevin Twain. *Salvaging Wesley's Agenda: A New Paradigm for Wesleyan Virtue Ethics.* Eugene: Pickwick Publications, 2008.

Loyer, Kenneth M. *God's Love through the Spirit: The Holy Spirit in Thomas Aquinas and John Wesley.* Washington: Catholic University Press of America, 2014.

Mack, Phyllis. *Heart Religion in the British Enlightenment: Gender and Emotion in Early Methodism.* Cambridge: Cambridge University Press, 2008.

Maddox, Randy L. "John Wesley: Practical Theologian?" *Wesleyan Theological Journal* 23, no. 1-2 (Spring-Fall, 1988): 122-47.

— "Wesleyan Resources for a Contemporary Theology of the Poor." *Asbury Theological Journal* 49, no. 1 (1994): 35-47.

— *Responsible Grace: John Wesley's Practical Theology.* Nashville: Kingswood Books, 1994.

— "Reconnecting the Means to the End: A Wesleyan Prescription for the Holiness Movement." *Wesleyan Theological Journal* 33, no. 2 (Fall, 1998): 29-66.

Maddox, Randy L., ed. *Aldersgate Reconsidered.* Nashville: Abingdon Press, 1990.

McEwan, David B. *Wesley as a Pastoral Theologian: Theological Methodology in John Wesley's Doctrine of Christian Perfection.* Milton Keynes: Paternoster, 2011.

McGonigle, Herbert Boyd. *Sufficient Saving Grace: John Wesley's Evangelical Arminianism.* Carlisle: Paternoster Press, 2001.

Miles, Rebekah L. "'The Arts of Holy Living': Holiness and the Means of Grace." *Quarterly Review* 25, no. 2 (Summer, 2005): 141-57.

Noble, T. A. *Holy Trinity: Holy People: The Historic Doctrine of Christian Perfecting.* Eugene: Cascade Books, 2013.

Oden, Thomas C. *John Wesley's Teachings.* 4 vols. Grand Rapids: Zondervan, 2012-14.

Oord, Thomas Jay. *The Nature of Love: A Theology.* St. Louis: Chalice Press, 2010.

Pasquarello, Michael. *John Wesley: A Preaching Life.* Nashville: Abingdon, 2010.

Peckham, Colin N. *John Wesley's Understanding of Human Infirmities.* Ilkeston: The Wesley Fellowship, 1997.

Rack, Henry D. *Reasonable Enthusiast: John Wesley and the Rise of Methodism.* 3rd rev. ed. Peterborough: Epworth Press, 2014.

Rivers, Isabel. *Reason, Grace, and Sentiment: A Study of the Language of Religion and Ethics in England 1660-1780.* Vol. 1, *Whichcote to Wesley.* Cambridge: Cambridge University Press, 1991.

Rogers, Charles A. "The Concept of Prevenient Grace in the Theology of John Wesley." PhD thesis, Duke University, 1967.

Runyon, Theodore H. *The New Creation: John Wesley's Theology Today.* Nashville: Abingdon Press, 1998.

Sanders, Fred. *Wesley on the Christian Life: The Heart Renewed in Love.* Wheaton: Crossway, 2013.

Schlimm, Mathew R. "The Puzzle of Perfection: Growth in John Wesley's Doctrine of Perfection." *Wesleyan Theological Journal* 38, no. 2 (Fall, 2003): 124-42.

Smith, James K. A. *Desiring the Kingdom: Worship, Worldview, and Cultural Formation*. Grand Rapids: Baker Academic, 2009.

Steele, Richard B. (ed.). *"Heart Religion" in the Methodist Tradition and Related Movements*. Lanham: Scarecrow Press, 2001.

Thomas, Howe Octavius. "John Wesley's Understanding of Theological Distinction between 'Essentials' and 'Opinions'." *Methodist History* 33, no. 3 (1995): 139-48.

Thorsen, Donald A. *The Wesleyan Quadrilateral: Scripture, Tradition, Reason & Experience as a Model of Evangelical Theology*. Grand Rapids: Francis Asbury Press, 1990.

Tracy, Wesley D. "John Wesley, Spiritual Director: Spiritual Guidance in John Wesley's Letters." *Wesleyan Theological Journal* 23, no. 1 & 2 (Spring-Fall, 1988): 148-62.

Turner, John Munsey. *John Wesley: The Evangelical Revival and the Rise of Methodism in England*. London: Epworth Press, 2002.

Tuttle Jr., Robert G. *Mysticism in the Wesleyan Tradition*. Grand Rapids: Zondervan, 1989.

Watson, David Lowes. *The Early Methodist Class Meeting: Its Origins and Significance*. Nashville: Discipleship Resources, 1985.

Wood, A. Skevington. *Love Excluding Sin: Wesley's Doctrine of Sanctification* Wesley Fellowship Occasional Paper #1. Derbys, England: Moorley's Bookshop, 1986.

Wynkoop, Mildred Bangs. *A Theology of Love: The Dynamic of Wesleyanism*. Kansas City: Beacon Hill Press of Kansas City, 1972.

Yrigoyen, Jr., Charles. *John Wesley: Holiness of Heart and Life*. Nashville: Abingdon Press, 1996.

INDEX

ND - #0104 - 270225 - C0 - 229/152/10 - PB - 9781842278000 - Gloss Lamination